THE HISTORY OF NATIONS

Italy

Tara Koellhoffer, *Book Editor*

Daniel Leone, *President*
Bonnie Szumski, *Publisher*
Scott Barbour, *Managing Editor*

GREENHAVEN
PRESS®

THOMSON
™
GALE

San Diego • Detroit • New York • San Francisco • Cleveland
New Haven, Conn. • Waterville, Maine • London • Munich

LIBRARY OF CONGRESS CATALOGING-IN-PUBLICATION DATA

Italy / Tara Koellhoffer, book editor.
    p. cm. — (History of nations)
  Includes bibliographical references and index.
  ISBN 0-7377-1197-3 (pbk. : alk. paper) — ISBN 0-7377-1198-1 (lib. : alk. paper)
    1. Italy—History. I. Koellhoffer, Tara. II. Series: History of nations (Greenhaven
  Press)
  DG467 .I9 2003
  945—dc21
                                                                        2002035428

Printed in the United States of America

Contents

peninsula, religion played a major role in the everyday lives of the people. Many cities developed traditions that centered on beliefs in the powers of their own patron saints.

Chapter 3: The Italian Renaissance

Chapter 4: Italy in Transition: The Seventeenth and Eighteenth Centuries

Chapter 5: From Unification to Fascism

than a united nation. In the mid–1800s, a strong movement for unification, known as risorgimento, was begun by several famous leaders, including Cavour and Garibaldi.

Despite Mussolini's belief that the alliance would benefit his nation, over time, he realized that Hitler's plans did not include Italy as an equal partner.

Chapter 6: Italy's Modern Challenges

FOREWORD

I n 1841, the journalist Charles MacKay remarked, "In read-
ing the history of nations, we find that, like individuals, they
have their whims and peculiarities, their seasons of excitement and recklessness." At the time of MacKay's observation,
many of the nations explored in the Greenhaven Press History
of Nations series did not yet exist in their current form. Nonetheless, whether it is old or young, every nation is similar to an
individual, with its own distinct characteristics and unique story.

The History of Nations series is dedicated to exploring these
stories. Each anthology traces the development of one of the
world's nations from its earliest days, when it was perhaps no
more than a promise on a piece of paper or an idea in the mind
of some revolutionary, through to its status in the world today.
Topics discussed include the pivotal political events and power
struggles that shaped the country as well as important social and
cultural movements. Often, certain dramatic themes and events
recur, such as the rise and fall of empires, the flowering and decay of cultures, or the heroism and treachery of leaders. As well,
in the history of most countries war, oppression, revolution, and
deep social change feature prominently. Nonetheless, the details
of such events vary greatly, as does their impact on the nation
concerned. For example, England's "Glorious Revolution" of
1688 was a peaceful transfer of power that set the stage for the
emergence of democratic institutions in that nation. On the
other hand, in China, the overthrow of dynastic rule in 1912 led
to years of chaos, civil war, and the eventual emergence of a
Communist regime that used violence as a tool to root out opposition and quell popular protest. Readers of the Greenhaven
Press History of Nations series will learn about the common
challenges nations face and the different paths they take in response to such crises. However a nation's story may have developed, the series strives to present a clear and unbiased view of the
country at hand.

The structure of each volume in the series is designed to help
students deepen their understanding of the events, movements,

and persons that define nations. First, a thematic introduction provides critical background material and helps orient the reader. The chapters themselves are designed to provide an accessible and engaging approach to the study of the history of that nation involved and are arranged either thematically or chronologically, as appropriate. The selections include both primary documents, which convey something of the flavor of the time and place concerned, and secondary material, which includes the wisdom of hindsight and scholarship. Finally, each book closes with a detailed chronology, a comprehensive bibliography of suggestions for further research, and a thorough index.

The countries explored within the series are as old as China and as young as Canada, as distinct in character as Spain and India, as large as Russia, and as compact as Japan. Some are based on ethnic nationalism, the belief in an ethnic group as a distinct people sharing a common destiny, whereas others emphasize civic nationalism, in which what defines citizenship is not ethnicity but commitment to a shared constitution and its values. As human societies become increasingly globalized, knowledge of other nations and of the diversity of their cultures, characteristics, and histories becomes ever more important. This series responds to the challenge by furnishing students with a solid and engaging introduction to the history of the world's nations.

INTRODUCTION

T he nation of Italy did not exist as a political entity until 1860. For centuries the Italian peninsula was an assortment of kingdoms and cities, many of which frequently waged war against one another. Despite this lack of unity, Italy has long been viewed as a cultural if not a political unit, and as the birthplace of new ideas has had a long history of influence on events and cultures around the world. Indeed, Italy has been at the forefront of advances in civilization, in politics and religion as well as philosophy and art, for centuries.

From the breakup of the Roman Empire in 476 through the eighteenth and even nineteenth centuries, Italy's diverse traditional kingdoms and city-states had an atmosphere of independence in which cultural innovation flourished and eventually spread to other parts of the world. As an enduring symbol of the lost power of ancient Rome, Italy is often considered a reliable authority on matters of culture, with good reason. As historian George Holmes puts it:

> Of all European countries Italy has been the one with the richest and most varied cultural life, the result of the fact that there have been so many separate centers of art and thought, independent enough to preserve their own individuality. There are, of course, other reasons for the particular importance of Italy in the cultural history of Europe: the long ancient history of civilized life from the Etruscans and the Greek settlers onwards, the legacy of Rome to the medieval world. It is impossible to imagine Italy without the backing of layer upon layer of ancient culture, which makes it quite different from other parts of Western Europe and gave Italian society an extra sophistication.[1]

Italy's long tradition of expansion and innovation precedes the Roman Empire. Italian political systems in particular have been emulated by lawmakers throughout modern history.

11

Ancient Rome and Popular Government

In the early fifth century B.C., a republic, centered in Rome, was established as various kings of the Italian peninsula were forced out of power and the city-state of Rome gradually dominated rival cities and tribes. Ancient Romans created a sophisticated society based on the concept of popular participation in government. Although it was certainly not a society of complete equality (ancient Romans kept slaves and gave women no political power), the Roman Republic was one of the first civilizations to allow its citizens, including those from lower social classes, to take an active role in political affairs.

The Roman system was republican, not democratic, as many people mistakenly believe. Citizens did not vote directly on issues that affected them. Rather, the government was run by military consuls and a Senate of elected officials who represented the Roman people. Politics, oratory, engineering, and architecture flourished during the Republic, but ultimately internal power struggles led to civil war, and in 27 B.C. the Republic was replaced by an empire ruled by one man alone. Even so, the political concept that the Republic had embraced—that a popular government should include all citizens—has since been idealized and imitated by many nations, most notably the United States. Despite its demise, the Roman Republic has remained a symbol of good government and superior cultural achievement.

The Holy Roman Empire

After the fall of the Republic, Rome was led by a series of emperors who controlled a vast territory that stretched from western Europe to Asia and Africa. Among the later emperors was Constantine I, who proclaimed Christianity the official Roman religion in A.D. 312. Gradually, Constantine brought his entire empire—sometimes by force—under the sway of the Christian faith, and the Roman government became tightly tied to the Christian church centered in Rome. Supreme authority in the church was held by the pope, whose authority over all the Christian people of the world helped link Italians both to each other and to neighboring Christian states. Because the pope played such an integral role in the Christian faith, the safety of both the pope himself and his religious center at Rome was a matter of great importance to all Christians. In 773, Charlemagne, the king of the Franks (a people from what is now France), helped protect

Pope Hadrian I from the invading Germanic Lombards. Grateful for the assistance, in 800, the pope crowned Charlemagne as the secular emperor of Rome. This act established the earliest version of what would become the Holy Roman Empire.

During the Middle Ages, the Christian kings and queens of Europe acknowledged Rome as both a political and religious center and, at least in theory, the pope as the ultimate authority. Even so, medieval leaders often came into conflict with the pope. Particularly in Italy, the battle for supremacy was severe. Because the various city-states of the Italian peninsula were politically disorganized, the pope in Rome was the only authority all Italians recognized. This centralization of power made it particularly difficult for local political leaders to govern as they wished. Despite this problem, the leaders of states, who had military backing that the pope did not, usually prevailed when they opposed the pope. To support their spiritual leader, in the 1100s several political and religious groups formed a league to fight the increasing power of Holy Roman Emperor Frederick Barbarossa. The league was successful in this instance, but struggles between the popes and the emperors continued.

Despite the frequent disagreements within the Holy Roman Empire, Italy had once again established a unique governmental system. Instead of one nation led by a supreme leader or even group of leaders, the Empire was a widespread set of countries united by faith, not by politics. In essence, the Holy Roman Empire was a government that left the management of religious matters to the pope, while the leaders of the various nations of the Empire handled their own domestic political affairs. So long as the spheres of religion and politics remained separate, and secular and religious interests did not threaten one another, the system was effective and relatively stable. The separation of religion and political issues was an interesting development, particularly because in many countries, both in Europe and around the world, a nation's monarch was often regarded as its spiritual leader as well. Although, ultimately, the political side of the equation within the Empire would assert its dominance, relegating the pope to a more minor role in the governance of people's lives, the Empire's experiment with dual authority was a novel one that hinted at what other nations would more coherently develop later: the concept of the separation of church and state. This idea, which proved a failure in Italy's Holy Roman Empire, has become a fundamental principle of many democratic governments, including that of the United States.

Perhaps the best-known period in Italy's history is the Renaissance. Beginning in the 1300s and lasting until the early 1600s, the Renaissance was a time of "rebirth," when artists, politicians, and philosophers looked for inspiration to the classical works of ancient Greece and ancient Rome. Among the concepts rediscovered in this new research was the power of popular rule, like that in practice during the golden ages of ancient Greece and Rome. Inspired by these classical examples, popular participation in government was a recurring theme in Italian politics of the Renaissance era.

Among the clearest demonstrations of the power of the democratic impulse is Florence's uprising against the ruling Medici family in 1494. Tired of being led by a succession of privileged leaders who held their positions solely by inheritance, the people ousted the Medicis and forced them into exile. In their place, the Florentines established a people's council headed by an elected official. This was a rare historical example of a group of ordinary citizens—not rival politicians or military leaders—proving that it was possible to assert their will and to radically change the way their government worked. The Medicis were eventually restored to power by the pope, but this unusual application of the democratic impulse in Florence became a common occurrence in decades to come.

The turbulent world of Italian Renaissance politics was also affected by the writings of a controversial statesman named Niccolò Machiavelli (1469–1527). In his most famous work, *The Prince*, Machiavelli offers a brutally realistic portrayal of the current state of politics along with practical, if sometimes cynical, advice on how leaders might rule most effectively. Ever since *The Prince* first appeared in 1513, Machiavelli has continued to exert a powerful influence on politicians and even business leaders who adhere to his philosophy that the end, or goal, justifies the means, even if the means seem unjust or violent.

Fascism: The Downside of Italy's Political Contributions

Although some would characterize Machiavelli's influence as a negative contribution, another aspect of Italy's history is more notorious: the development of fascism. Emerging as a counter to the growing appeal of communism in the late nineteenth century, fascism is an ideology that demands that the interests of the individual be subjugated to the needs of the state. Enforcing this authoritarian government requires a strong leader who holds all political power and who is prepared to squash all opposition by any means, including violence and violation of individual rights.

Italy bears the dubious distinction of being the birthplace of the man who created a fascist rule of law, Benito Mussolini. Mussolini actually coined the term *fascism* for the name of his Fasci di Combattimento, or Fascist Party, in 1919. From that time until his execution by Italian partisans in 1945, he established a brutal totalitarian state in which people were forced by law and induced by propaganda to do whatever was considered best for the nation. As Mussolini rose to ultimate power, eliminated all other political parties and was idealized as the perfect leader, *Il Duce*.

Mussolini used his power to begin to fulfill some of his ambitions for Italy, including the creation of a new empire that would include not only parts of Europe but territory in Africa as well. To help him in his drive for more power, Mussolini turned to Adolf Hitler, the totalitarian dictator of Germany. Under Hitler's influence, Mussolini's authoritarian ideal of government took on a decidedly racist and anti-Semitic tone.

Despite the ultimate demise of the Fascist Party and its founder, the ideas of authoritarian rule combined with virulent racism have not gone away. Even today, small groups of extremists in Italy and elsewhere continue to operate, and sometimes turn to violence in an attempt to broadcast their views. Italy's period of fascist rule had extremely negative consequences for its citizens and the rest of the world.

Italy as a Center of Religion and Philosophy

After Christianity was first introduced to the Roman Empire by Constantine I, Rome became a religious center. Although Constantine at first sought to encourage converts by demonstrating the benefits of his newfound faith, he eventually used pressure and at times actual force to bring the people of Rome's domain under the banner of Christianity. Thanks to his efforts, Christianity spread from Italy to become the dominant religion in the Western world.

As the church grew in importance throughout Europe and the

rest of the world, Italy, where the pope and the higher officials of the church make their home, became the place to which people looked for religious and cultural guidance. Even the powerful rulers of foreign nations turned to Italy when they needed advice on matters of faith. Before he split with the church to form the Church of England, or Anglican church, England's King Henry VIII (1491–1547), one of history's strongest leaders, deferred to the pope in religious matters and asked Rome for advice on how to proceed with personal and political issues. The church in Rome continued as the Catholic Church after the Protestant Reformation, and even today, Italy—and particularly Rome—remains a significant symbol and a source of spiritual guidance for millions of Catholics around the world.

As Europe's foremost religious center, Italy also played a major role in the development of other philosophies. In fact, even before the advent of Christianity, ancient Italian philosophers formed a discipline and body of work that remains a model of scholarly study today.

Ancient Rome and Cicero

Perhaps the most famous philosopher from the Italian peninsula is Marcus Tullius Cicero (106–43 B.C.), who is often considered the finest orator and one of the most talented statesmen of the Roman Republic. Although Cicero also wrote poetry and works about the principles of art, his most memorable writings were philosophical. Writing in the form of dialogues, Cicero depicted an argument between the Epicureans and the Stoics, the two major schools of philosophical thought of the day. Stoics believed that a good life comes from having knowledge, and that experiencing all aspects of living, including both pleasure and pain, is necessary to finding true happiness. Stoics became highly involved in politics as they sought to create a brotherhood of all people, based on their own ideas about life and the achievement of wisdom. Epicureans, on the other hand, believed that the pursuit of intellectual pleasure was the only path to the ideal life, and they did their best to avoid entanglements—particularly in politics—so that they would not have attachments that might distract them from their attempts to make life worthwhile. For the Epicureans, the meaning of life was concentrated on every individual's pursuit of happiness, through learning and finding a way to conquer fears of death and the unknown. The interests of society in general came second to this important quest.

As a proponent of Stoic philosophy, Cicero did his best to demonstrate that people should try to live in harmony with nature and each other. Ultimately, he was murdered on the orders of the three leaders of Rome—Marc Antony, Octavian (later Augustus Caesar), and Marcus Lepidus—for his active opposition to the increasingly imperialistic Roman government. However, his writings continued to be read and studied. Today, his work remains among the most widely used classical texts in the study of language as well as philosophy. Cicero's writings are especially useful for those learning Latin. Because he did not think the Latin spoken in his day was elegant enough to express his thoughts well, Cicero added words and significantly refined the language to make it more aesthetically pleasing as well as expressive. In so doing, he created a new style that was adopted by the writers who followed him. Because of the strength of his convincing philosophical arguments and his contributions to language and literature, Cicero was a major influence on the people of many nations, both in his own day and beyond.

Humanism

Although the ancient Romans may be the Italian philosophers studied most often in schools today, Italy may actually be best known for a later philosophy that originated there in the fourteenth century, humanism. This school of thought holds that human beings are at the center of the universe and that despite Christian concepts of original sin and human weakness, people are capable of achieving perfection during life, not just after they die and ascend to heaven. Through reason and determination, humanists argued, people can find happiness. Humanism was the driving force behind the Renaissance, and since that time, its conception of human existence and the ability to improve oneself has profoundly influenced secular thinkers.

One of the earliest humanists was Petrarch (1304–1374). Raised in Florence, Petrarch received a copy of Cicero's writings from his father. The beauty, clarity, and unquestionable logic of Cicero's arguments helped inspire Petrarch to develop a new way of thinking and to search for truth within his own life and worldview. As he grew up and became a writer himself, Petrarch began to inject into his works elements of individuality, an early sign of his eventual development of humanistic thought. As historian Jacques Barzun explains:

> [Petrarch] fashioned [one of his writings] into a shapely quasi narrative work, a kind of allusive autobiography. This was new. And it was also an expression of his intense interest in himself: "I am unlike anybody I know." He declared that art is an individual matter, not something within the reach of all professionals. "Everyone should write in his own style.". . . Introspection followed by self-portraiture is linked in Petrarch with another novelty, the express desire for eternal fame.[2]

Petrarch's unusual sense of self-consciousness and his wish to be recognized for his own contributions challenged a long tradition in which individuality was sacrificed in favor of an emphasis on the general good. At the time humanism was first introduced, many people were astonished by its presumptuousness and claimed that the humanists sought to eliminate religion to create a world based solely on human reason. Although some modern humanists may, in fact, renounce the concept of God, Renaissance humanists for the most part remained devoutly religious.

Most humanists argued that because the Bible stated that God had created people in his own image, it was only natural that humans should be the most important life forms in the world, and that it was no sin to attempt to make themselves as perfect as possible during their time on earth. Petrarch, in particular, worked hard to try to reconcile his own ideas of human development on earth with his seemingly contradictory belief in the type of self-denial practiced by the religious orders of the day.

Over time, the belief in the power of the individual has expanded far beyond Petrarch's early theories. Petrarch's humanism had a profound impact on the development of Western thought, in which individuality was considered as important as, if not more important than, the needs of the state. This stood in marked contrast to most Eastern philosophies of government, which tended to view the needs of the general good as more pressing than those of the individual. Over time, in most Western nations, the power of individuality and the worth of every human being have come to be viewed as almost a self-evident truth. Especially in democratic societies such as the United States, the idea that each person's life has immeasurable value, a lesson learned from the humanists and their philosophical mentor Petrarch, is a foundational belief.

The Enlightenment

The Enlightenment, which is also known as the Age of Reason, spanned the years between the mid-seventeenth century and the early nineteenth century. During this period, a new breed of philosophers insisted that the world could be best understood through science and reason. These intellectuals demanded that people abandon the traditional, superstitious views that had so often led to religious intolerance and violence in the past. Although the Enlightenment's most recognizable participants were French and English philosophers, such as Voltaire (1694–1778), Jean-Jacques Rousseau (1712–1778), and John Locke (1634–1704), natives of the Italian peninsula also made notable contributions.

Unlike most other Enlightenment thinkers, Italy's philosophers focused most of their debate not on the common condition of all humanity but on the issues that concerned the Italian peninsula alone. From those considerations, some philosophers did branch out to search for universal truths, but for the most part, Italy itself was the main topic of contemplation.

During this period, Italy was under foreign political domination. It was not yet a united nation, and control of its various kingdoms changed hands from one European power to another. Despite this lack of political autonomy, Italy's removal from the larger world of international intrigue and war helped its artists and philosophers focus their efforts on the creation of innovative works. Philosophers discussed the best ways to make Italy more modern and more capable of participation in European affairs. As historian Stuart Woolf explains:

> Whatever the differences among the intellectuals, what united them was their sense of what they saw as the appalling backwardness of the Italian states compared to the progress of Europe (by which they meant western Europe). Superstition and privilege, as much as Italy's past, were seen everywhere as blocking reform.[3]

These intellectuals, who included Pompeo Neri and Francesco Maria Gianni, did make significant progress toward the development of social ideals and in bringing Italians into the age of modern ideas.

Probably the best-known Italian figure of the Enlightenment was a philosopher whose works discussed not traditional topics such as the formation of society or the place of human beings in the universe, but rather, crime and punishment. His name was Cesare Beccaria (1738–1794) and he lived in Milan. Historian J.M. Roberts demonstrates Beccaria's influence on his own and future generations: "The Italian Enlightenment would be assured of a remembrance even if it had thrown up only Beccaria, the author of a book which founded penal reform and the criticism of penology and gave currency to [made part of the intellectual vocabulary] one of the great slogans of history, 'the greatest happiness of the greatest number.'"[4] In 1764, Beccaria published a celebrated treatise on criminal law in which he argued that punishment should aim to discourage other people from committing the same crimes. It should not, as had often been argued up to that point, seek to take revenge on the criminal for his or her actions. This proposition was an astounding innovation. Rarely had people considered whether criminals should have rights—if only the right to fair treatment—before Beccaria made his convincing arguments.

Beccaria's work had a far-reaching impact. Governments of

the Western world instituted reforms in their criminal law and prison systems to more closely align punishment of convicted criminals with the nature and degree of their offense, rather than assigning all convicts a fixed sentence of death, torture, or imprisonment, regardless of the crime, as had often been the case in the past. Although penal systems remained brutal by modern standards for many years to come, Beccaria had begun a process that would eventually help create a more impartial system of justice. Some of his ideas—the right to be considered innocent until proven guilty and the right to a fair trial—have become fundamental principles in the judicial systems of many countries, such as the United States, today.

Italy's Greatest Contribution: Art

Although Italy has certainly made its mark in many fields, it is for the enduring tradition of artistic excellence that Italians may be best recognized. From ancient Rome to the modern day, Italy has been a daring pioneer, leading the way toward the creation of new artistic styles.

Ancient Rome is widely known for the exquisite sculpture its artists produced. Although most Roman sculptures were copies of older Greek works, Roman artists added an unprecedented dimension of reality to their portrayal of the human body that was a major influence on later artists. One of the best-known sculptures of ancient Rome depicts Augustus Caesar, in full armor, after his defeat of Marc Antony in 27 B.C. Although the features of his handsome and determined face are remarkably lifelike, more attention is paid to the detail of his breastplate and clothing than to the structure of his body. This focus on objects rather than human beings would change over time, thanks to Italian artists. A great deal more effort would be devoted to perfecting the musculature and position of the human body than to depicting symbolic displays of the objects in a work of art.

It is likely that no period in the history of art could possibly exceed the contributions of the Italian Renaissance, arguably the most admired period in art history in Italy or any other country. Renaissance artists made one significant change that made their works almost completely different from anything that had come before. Thanks to the prevalence of humanist thought, Renaissance artists were inspired to depict the human body as a perfect form, one that should be appreciated for its beauty and functionality rather than covered in shame and considered sinful.

Painter and sculptor Michelangelo Buonarroti (1475–1564) made human beings a focal point of his works. His most famous sculpture, the *David*, is an exquisitely beautiful male nude. In this work and many others, ordinary people (as opposed to religious figures such as God, saints, and angels) were presented as perfect physical specimens. This new style was intended to illustrate the humanist argument that human beings themselves were at the heart of the universe and were capable of approaching, if not actually achieving, perfection.

Among Michelangelo's rivals and inspirations was Leonardo da Vinci (1452–1519). One of the most inventive artists of the Renaissance, Leonardo was also one of the leading scientists of his day. Using techniques he developed through his study of cadavers as well as living models in various types of motion, Leonardo helped begin a movement toward an extremely realistic depiction of the human body. At the same time, he experimented with new techniques of shading and color, creating hauntingly beautiful landscapes and portraits, including the *Mona Lisa* and *The Last Supper*, still considered masterpieces of art.

The enormous respect and admiration for Italian Renaissance painters and sculptors created a legacy for the nation that has remained strong even to the modern day. Throughout history, people from all over the world have found inspiration and instruction in Italian art. This trend has continued even as the types of popular art changed over time. Italy has kept pace and remained a center for groundbreaking styles. Although traditional forms of art, such as painting and sculpture, have continued to grow and evolve in Italy as elsewhere, other Italian creations have also come to be considered art.

Most notably, during the twentieth century Italy became known as a center of a new type of art—fashion design. Once appreciated primarily for function, clothing has become a form of expression akin to any work on canvas. Historians Peter D'Epiro and Mary Desmond Pinkowish describe the extensive Italian contribution to this distinct art:

> So many shelves of books and sheaves of magazine pages are dedicated to the artistic achievements and commercial successes of Italian fashion, that no more than a selection can be mentioned here: Capucci and his geometric coats, Cavalli's rhinestone jeans, Laura Bi-

agiotti and her cushy cashmeres, Krizia's lighthearted designs, Fendi's furs, the outlandish knitwear of Missoni, Prada's sophisticated mix of fabrics, and the architectural shapes of Gianfranco Ferré. And how exquisitely Italy's trove of jewelers, who trace their craft back to Ghiberti and Cellini, can enhance a fine dress or jacket with a brooch or a pair of earrings.[5]

Italy remains a leading source of unique, bold themes for art in all its forms.

Influential Italy

Thanks to its many contributions to world culture, Italy has been held in great respect for ages. The negative developments for which Italy is known—most notably, fascism—are far outweighed by the many benefits Italy has brought to civilization. In part, this almost unfailingly positive view of Italy stems from the fact that Italy has proven itself to be a nation that is willing to take the risks necessary to make the kind of innovations that will become extremely useful to people all over the world. As D'Epiro and Pinkowish explain, Italy has always made its cultural advances with a unique style:

> Functionality and beauty are the very essence of Italian civilization. From the beginning, Italian genius has tended to be practical, down-to-earth, and concerned with getting things done, but it has also emphasized form, harmony, and radiance. A Roman aqueduct is not only durably functional but also lovely in its curves and proportions. . . . The greatest achievements of the people who brought us the Renaissance have occurred mainly in the useful pursuits of life—law, political philosophy, business practices, anatomy and other applied sciences, exploration—and those that enhance life's beauty and pleasure.[6]

Notes

1. George Holmes, ed., *The Oxford History of Italy*. New York: Oxford University Press, 1997, pp. vi–vii.

2. Jacques Barzun, *From Dawn to Decadence: 500 Years of Western Cultural Life*. New York: HarperCollins, 2000, pp. 49, 50.

3. Stuart Woolf, "Italy 1600–1796," *The Oxford History of Italy*, ed.

George Holmes. New York: Oxford University Press, 1997, pp. 135–37.

4. J.M. Roberts, *The Penguin History of the World,* 3rd ed. New York: Penguin Books, 1995, p. 665.

5. Peter D'Epiro and Mary Desmond Pinkowish, *Sprezzatura: 50 Ways Italian Genius Shaped the World.* New York: Anchor Books, 2001, p. 362.

6. D'Epiro and Pinkowish, preface to *Sprezzatura,* n.p.

THE HISTORY OF NATIONS
Chapter 1

Ancient Italy and the Roman Empire

Early Italy and the Founding of Rome

Italy has a long and colorful history, and its people have been responsible for some of the greatest cultural achievements and most respected political ideals of all time. Despite Italy's many contributions to the world, however, historians can verify little about the nation's ancient origins. Even the settlement of the city of Rome, which went on to become the center of the most powerful empire on earth, is shrouded in mystery. Because there is no written record left by the ancient settlers of Italy, historians use legends to learn about the people and the society in which they lived.

Author Dorothy Mills was head of the history department at Brearley School in New York and wrote about Rome and other ancient cultures, including the Greeks. In this selection, Mills uses what limited knowledge historians have accumulated about ancient Italy to explain how the peninsula was most likely settled. She discusses how the widely varying cultural influences of different settlers, including the Etruscans, Latins, and Greeks, blended together to create the highly successful city of Rome. Mills also recounts the legend of the brothers Remus and Romulus, who were supposedly rescued by a she-wolf before they went on to build a great city, which Romulus, as its founder, named after himself.

In very ancient times Italy was inhabited by a number of different peoples, about whom very little is known. It is thought that in those far-away, misty days when the peoples of the world were wandering in search of homes, certain tribes crossed the Alps and came down into Italy. They must have found some of the prehistoric inhabitants in possession of the land, and they probably fought them and overcame them, slaying many and then mingling with the rest and occupying the land. These first settlers are now looked upon as the original inhabitants of Italy.

Dorothy Mills, *The Book of the Ancient Romans: An Introduction to the History and Civilization of Rome from the Traditional Date of the Founding of the City to Its Fall in 476 A.D.* New York: G.P. Putnam's Sons, 1927. Copyright © 1927 by Dorothy Mills. Reproduced by permission.

Some of these tribes settled north of the Tiber [River] and then spread over Central Italy, the Umbrians in the districts near the Adriatic [Sea] and the Sabines in the mountains of the interior. All the hill-tribes in Central Italy were considered as descended from the Sabines who sent out numbers of colonists to neighbouring districts. At one time, when the Sabines had been engaged in a long war with the Umbrians, they made a vow that they would consecrate to the gods all the products of that spring, called by them the Sacred Spring. All the children born during that season were consecrated to Mars [the god of war], and when they had grown to manhood they were sent forth, with a bull as their leader, to seek new homes wherever the gods willed. The bull lay down to rest in a certain village, whereupon the Sabine youths drove out the inhabitants and, after sacrificing the bull to Mars, established themselves in that place. These colonists became known as Samnites.

The Latins Arrive

To the banks of the Tiber came another tribe, the Latins, who gave to the region where they settled the name of Latium. This was a fertile land, and the Latins soon grew more prosperous than the tribes in the more hilly interior. At first, like all early peoples, they consisted of a number of separate tribes, but Latium was a district much exposed to attack from hostile neighbours, and the Latins soon found that for mutual protection and defence it was necessary to form some kind of organization. So it came about that thirty communities joined together and formed the Latin League. As some centre was necessary for such a league, a place where a common assembly could be held, where justice could be dispensed and where there might be a common sanctuary, Alba Longa [in central Italy] was made the chief town and head of the League. Very little is known about the early history of the Latin League, but it is important because the joining together of a number of communities with one common centre which belonged to them all, was the beginning of that sense of national unity which was to become a characteristic of the Roman people.

These were the early Italian peoples who lived in Italy, but as early, probably, as from the eleventh century B.C. onwards, other peoples appeared, two of which left an abiding mark on the early civilization of Italy. These were the Etruscans and the Greeks.

Arrival of the Etruscans

The Etruscans settled in the coast region north of Rome and there they developed a civilization of their own.... Their settlements were made in very early times, some of them at least as early as 1000 B.C., but it was towards the end of the seventh century B.C. that they were at the height of their power. Very much still remains to be learnt about the Etruscans, when they came into Italy and whence they came, for their writing has not yet been fully deciphered, but Roman writers have left some account of what they knew about them. They were ruled by a king who wore a crown and a purple robe and who sat on an ivory throne, and they had a code of laws which gave them rules for the conduct of daily life in the community and for different ways of interpreting the will of the gods. They were specially skilled in the art of augury, the art which interpreted signs in nature as outward expressions of the will of the gods, and they believed that special meanings were attached to such phenomena as thunder and lightning and the flight of birds.

Etruscan Influences

The Latins were much influenced by the Etruscans and learnt many things from them. The Etruscans may themselves have been influenced by the early Greeks, especially in their architecture, painting and sculpture. They were richer, more prosperous and more skilful than their neighbours and were a people of great importance in early Italy. They were a commercial people, but they do not seem to have had an adventurous spirit ... and they waited for trade to come to them rather than sail out on to uncharted seas in search of it. Etruscan influence can be seen in the early art and architecture of the Latins, in some of their amusements, such as gladiatorial shows, and in their religious beliefs. A great many Etruscan tombs have been found, and from the care with which the dead were buried and the articles which were buried with them, the Etruscans evidently believed in a future life.

Greek Influences on Italy

Greater than the Etruscan influence on the early peoples of Italy was that of the Greeks. Colonists from Greece had settled in the South of Italy and as far North as the Bay of Naples, and they gave the name of Magna Graecia to this whole region. The Greek cities were active in trade, powerful, wealthy and luxurious. One of the most important was Tarentum, a city which had an excellent harbour, and which was one of the most prosperous trading ports in the South of Italy. Tarentum was noted for its fine wool and purple dye. . . .

These were the peoples who in historic times first inhabited Italy. In time one city, very small and unimportant at the beginning of her history, was to rise from their midst, destined to conquer them all, to unite them and to rule them. Where Greece had failed, Rome was to succeed, for having first united the peoples not only of Italy but of the then known world, she was to give them a real sense of national unity. . . .

The Legend of Remus and Romulus

According to the most ancient tradition, Aeneas [a soldier and son of the goddess Venus], after the fall of Troy, fled from the burning city accompanied by his father and his little son, Ascanius, together with a few faithful followers. After many adventures he reached the coast of Italy, where, so good omens assured him, should be his home and the land over which his descendants should rule. The King of Latium came out to drive back the strangers, but he was defeated by Aeneas, who then made peace with him and after a time wedded his daughter, Lavinia. After the death of the King, Aeneas ruled in his place, until he was slain in battle fighting against the Etruscans. Ascanius then became King, and finding the city in which his father had lived too small for the increasing population, he founded Alba Longa and made it his chief city.

The descendants of Aeneas ruled in Alba Longa for three hundred years. At the end of this time the rightful King was Numitor, but he was dethroned by his brother Amulius, who, fearing lest Rhea Silvia, the daughter of Numitor, should have sons who might grow up and claim the kingdom, caused her to be made a priestess of the goddess Vesta. Amulius thought that all was well and that his brother would never be strong enough to regain his kingdom, when news was brought to him that Rhea Silvia had twin sons of great beauty, whose father was none other than the god Mars. "But neither gods nor men sheltered her or her babes from the King's cruelty; the priestess was thrown into prison, and the boys were ordered to be thrown into the river."

Now it happened that just at this time, the Tiber had overflowed its banks and the servant who had been charged to drown the infants, left them in the shallow water on the bank, thinking that it would be deep enough to drown them. But the river went down and the infants were left on dry ground at the foot of a fig-tree. Here, tradition tells us,

> a thirsty she-wolf from the surrounding hills, attracted by the crying of the children, came to them, and nursed them, and was so gentle towards them that the king's flock-master found her licking the boys with her tongue. According to the story this man's name was Faustulus. He took the children to his hut and gave them to his wife to bring up.

Faustulus knew who these boys were, and he brought them up well, and, it is said, actually

> with the knowledge and secret assistance of Numitor. They went to school and were well instructed in letters and other accomplishments befitting their birth. And they were called Romulus and Remus. As they grew up they proved brave and manly and of undaunted courage. But Romulus seemed rather to act by counsel, and to show the sagacity of a statesman, and in all his dealings with their neighbours, whether relating to feeding of flocks or to hunting, gave the idea of being born rather to rule than to obey. . . .

When Romulus and Remus had reached manhood, they learned who they were, and how Amulius had taken the throne which belonged of right to their grandfather. A plot was formed, Amulius was slain, and Numitor replaced on the throne. But Romulus and Remus had been so long accustomed to take the lead amongst their companions, that they were not content

> to dwell in Alba without governing there, nor would they take the government into their own hands during the life of their grandfather. Having therefore delivered the dominion up into his hands and paid their mother befitting honour, they resolved to live by themselves, and build a city in the same place where they were in their infancy brought up.

They began to build, but the brothers could not agree as to

which should be the founder of the city or who was to give his name to it and rule it. So they decided to consult the guardian gods . . . and in this way to settle the dispute. Romulus went up on to the Palatine Hill and Remus to the Aventine in order to make their observations. Remus is said to have seen six vultures and Romulus double that number; though some declared that Remus did truly see his number and that Romulus only pretended to see his. Others declared that Romulus had seen the twelve vultures, though they had appeared after the six seen by Remus, but that the gods undoubtedly favoured him because to him had appeared double the number seen by his brother. Angry words passed between the two brothers, and then Remus

> contemptuously jumping over the newly raised walls was forthwith killed by the enraged Romulus, who exclaimed: "So shall it be henceforth with everyone who leaps over my walls." Romulus thus became sole ruler, and the city was called after him, its founder.

Thus, according to tradition, was Rome founded, on the twenty-first day of April in the year 753 B.C., and that day of their country's birthday was kept by ancient Rome and is still kept in Rome today as a national holiday.

The Assassination of Julius Caesar

By Plutarch

Julius Caesar was born in Italy in 100 B.C. He spent most of his life as a soldier, honing his military skills—and his popularity—with each war he fought to bring territory and glory to the Roman Republic. This popularity helped him begin a second career as a politician.

Although Rome had long been ruled by a sophisticated republican system in which elected senators and other officials acted on behalf of the people, that system changed dramatically because of Caesar. Throughout Rome's history, there had been frequent civil wars that pitted different political factions against each other. Caesar, like his fellow Romans, had suffered through this long period of disunity. As he began to gain political power—and eliminate his enemies in civil wars of his own—he worked to win the unified support of the Roman people.

Caesar's enormous popularity made it easy for him to win increasing amounts of power, as well as new titles that were created just for him. Eventually, however, it began to appear both to the jealous senators and to the people themselves that Caesar's ultimate goal was to be named king. To stop this from happening, and to increase their own power, a large group of Roman senators conspired to assassinate Caesar.

After the deed was done, the plotters believed they would have the support of the Roman people. But when the people learned that Caesar had left each citizen a generous amount in his will, they turned on the senators and began to hold the dead Caesar in higher esteem than ever. Caesar became a symbol for worship, almost on the same level as a god. As a result, the republic was, over time, replaced by an empire ruled by Julius Caesar's nephew, Augustus.

Plutarch was a historian who lived from A.D. 46 to 120. His major work was an impressive collection of biographies of famous figures from both Greek and Roman history. In this selection, Plutarch recounts the assassination of Julius Caesar, which took place on March 15—the Ides of March, of which a soothsayer had warned Caesar to beware—in 44 B.C.

Plutarch, "Caesar," *The Lives*, A.D. 100.

F ate . . . is to all appearance more unavoidable than unexpected. For many strange prodigies and apparitions are said to have been observed shortly before this event.[1] As to the lights in the heavens, the noises heard in the night, and the wild birds which perched in the Forum, these are not perhaps worth taking notice of in so great a case as this. Strabo, the philosopher, tells us that a number of men were seen, looking as if they were heated through with fire, contending with each other; that a quantity of flame issued from the hand of a soldier's servant, so that they who saw it thought he must be burnt, but that after all he had no hurt. As [Julius] Cæsar was sacrificing, the victim's heart was missing, a very bad omen, because no living creature can subsist without a heart. One finds it also related by many that a soothsayer bade him prepare for some great danger on the Ides of March [March 15]. When this day was come, Cæsar, as he went to the senate, met this soothsayer, and said to him by way of raillery, "The Ides of March are come," who answered him calmly, "Yes, they are come, but they are not past." The day before his assassination he supped with [Roman politician] Marcus Lepidus; and as he was signing some letters according to his custom, as he reclined at table, there arose a question what sort of death was the best. At which he immediately, before any one could speak, said, "A sudden one."

Calpurnia's Premonition

After this, as he was in bed with his wife, all the doors and windows of the house flew open together; he was startled at the noise and the light which broke into the room, and sat up in his bed, where by the moonshine he perceived Calpurnia [his wife] fast asleep, but heard her utter in her dream some indistinct words and inarticulate groans. She fancied at that time she was weeping over Cæsar, and holding him butchered in her arms. Others say this was not her dream, but that she dreamed that a pinnacle, which the senate, as [Roman historian] Livy relates, had ordered to be raised on Cæsar's house by way of ornament and grandeur, was tumbling down, which was the occasion of her tears and ejaculations. When it was day, she begged of Cæsar, if it were possible,

1. The people of the Roman Republic put great stock in omens, which were interpreted by prophets called soothsayers. This practice of divination was called augury. The people also found symbolic meaning in nature, such as comets or animals. Dreams, too, were considered glimpses of future events.

not to stir out, but to adjourn the senate to another time; and if
he slighted her dreams, that she would be pleased to consult his
fate by sacrifices and other kinds of divination. Nor was he himself without some suspicion and fears; for he never before discovered any womanish superstition in Calpurnia, whom he now
saw in such great alarm. Upon the report which the priests made
to him, that they had killed several sacrifices, and still found them
inauspicious, he resolved to send Antony to dismiss the senate.

The Senators Deceive Caesar

In this juncture, Decimus Brutus, surnamed Albinus, one whom
Cæsar had such confidence in that he made him his second heir,
who nevertheless was engaged in the conspiracy with the other
Brutus and Cassius, fearing lest if Cæsar should put off the senate to another day the business might get wind, spoke scoffingly
and in mockery of the diviners, and blamed Cæsar for giving the
senate so fair an occasion of saying he had put a slight upon
them, for that they were met upon his summons, and were ready
to vote unanimously that he should be declared king of all the
provinces out of Italy, and might wear a diadem in any other
place but Italy, by sea or land. If any one should be sent to tell
them they might break up for the present, and meet again when
Calpurnia should chance to have better dreams, what would his
enemies say? Or who would with any patience hear his friends,
if they should presume to defend his government as not arbitrary
and tyrannical. But if he was possessed so far as to think this day
unfortunate, yet it were more decent to go himself to the senate,
and to adjourn it in his own person.

Brutus, as he spoke these words, took Cæsar by the hand, and
conducted him forth. He was not gone far from the door, when
a servant of some other person's made towards him, but not being able to come up to him, on account of the crowd of those
who pressed about him, he made his way into the house, and
committed himself to Calpurnia, begging of her to secure him
till Cæsar returned, because he had matters of great importance
to communicate to him.

Artemidorus, a Cnidian, a teacher of Greek logic, and by that
means so far acquainted with Brutus and his friends as to have
got into the secret, brought Cæsar in a small written memorial
the heads of what he had to depose. He had observed that Cæsar,
as he received any papers, presently gave them to the servants who

attended on him; and therefore came as near to him as he could, and said, "Read this, Cæsar, alone, and quickly, for it contains matter of great importance which nearly concerns you." Cæsar received it, and tried several times to read it, but was still hindered by the crowd of those who came to speak to him. However, he kept it in his hand by itself till he came into the senate. Some say it was another who gave Cæsar this note, and that Artemidorus could not get to him, being all along kept off by the crowd.

All these things might happen by chance. But the place which was destined for the scene of this murder, in which the senate met that day, was the same in which Pompey's statue stood, and was one of the edifices which Pompey had raised and dedicated with his theatre to the use of the public, plainly showing that there was something of a supernatural influence which guided the action and ordered it to that particular place. Cassius, just before the act, is said to have looked towards Pompey's statue, and silently implored his assistance, though he had been inclined to the doctrines of Epicurus. But this occasion, and the instant danger, carried him away out of all his reasonings, and filled him for the time with a sort of inspiration. As for Antony, who was firm to Cæsar, and a strong man, Brutus Albinus kept him outside the house, and delayed him with a long conversation contrived on purpose.

The Senators Carry Out Their Plot

When Cæsar entered, the senate stood up to show their respect to him, and of Brutus's confederates, some came about his chair and stood behind it, others met him, pretending to add their petitions to those of Tillius Cimber, in behalf of his brother who was in exile; and they followed him with their joint applications till he came to his seat. When he was sat down, he refused to comply with their requests, and upon their urging him further began to reproach them severely for their importunities, when Tillius, laying hold of his robe with both his hands, pulled it down from his neck, which was the signal for the assault.

Casca gave him the first cut in the neck, which was not mortal nor dangerous, as coming from one who at the beginning of such a bold action was probably very much disturbed; Cæsar immediately turned about, and laid his hand upon the dagger and kept hold of it. And both of them at the same time cried out, he that received the blow, in Latin, "Vile Casca, what does this mean?" and he that gave it, in Greek, to his brother, "Brother, help!"

Upon this first onset, those who were not privy to the design were astonished, and their horror and amazement at what they saw were so great that they durst not flee, nor assist Cæsar, nor so much as speak a word. But those who came prepared for the business enclosed him on every side, with their naked daggers in their hands. Which way soever he turned he met with blows, and saw their swords levelled at his face and eyes, and was encompassed, like a wild beast in the toils, on every side.

For it had been agreed they should each of them make a thrust at him, and flesh themselves with his blood; for which reason Brutus also gave him one stab in the groin. Some say that he fought and resisted all the rest, shifting his body to avoid the blows, and calling out for help, but that when he saw Brutus's sword drawn, he covered his face with his robe and submitted, letting himself fall, whether it were by chance, or that he was pushed in that direction by his murderers, at the foot of the pedestal on which Pompey's statue stood, and which was thus wetted with his blood. So that Pompey himself seemed to have presided, as it were, over the revenge done upon his adversary,[2] who lay here at his feet, and breathed out his soul through his multitude of wounds, for they say he received three-and-twenty. And the conspirators themselves were many of them wounded by each other, whilst they all levelled their blows at the same person.

When Cæsar was despatched, Brutus stood forth to give a reason for what they had done, but the senate would not hear him, but flew out of doors in all haste, and filled the people with so much alarm and distraction, that some shut up their houses, others left their counters and shops. All ran one way or the other, some to the place to see the sad spectacle, others back again after they had seen it. Antony and Lepidus, Cæsar's most faithful friends, got off privately, and hid themselves in some friends' houses.

Brutus and his followers, being yet hot from the deed, marched in a body from the senatehouse to the capitol with their drawn swords, not like persons who thought of escaping, but with an

2. Gnaeus Pompey was a Roman general and political leader who lived from 106 to 48 B.C. At one time, Pompey and Caesar served as co-leaders of Rome. Both men, however, wanted ultimate power over the republic, and eventually they competed for control of Rome. The former colleagues became bitter enemies. With the aid of foreign allies, Caesar was able to defeat Pompey, who was beheaded by the Egyptians as a demonstration of loyalty to Caesar. It was considered noteworthy that at his death, Caesar fell at the feet of his old enemy's statue.

air of confidence and assurance, and as they went along, called to the people to resume their liberty, and invited the company of any more distinguished people whom they met. And some of these joined the procession and went up along with them, as if they also had been of the conspiracy, and could claim a share in the honour of what had been done. . . .

The day after, Brutus with the rest came down from the capitol and made a speech to the people, who listened without expressing either any pleasure or resentment, but showed by their silence that they pitied Cæsar and respected Brutus. The senate passed acts of oblivion for what was past, and took measures to reconcile all parties. They ordered that Cæsar should be worshipped as a divinity, and nothing, even of the slightest consequence, should be revoked which he had enacted during his government. At the same time they gave Brutus and his followers the command of provinces, and other considerable posts. So that all the people now thought things were well settled, and brought to the happiest adjustment.

Caesar's Legacy

But when Cæsar's will was opened, and it was found that he had left a considerable legacy to each one of the Roman citizens, and when his body was seen carried through the market-place all mangled with wounds, the multitude could no longer contain themselves within the bounds of tranquillity and order, but heaped together a pile of benches, bars, and tables, which they placed the corpse on, and setting fire to it, burnt it on them. Then they took brands from the pile and ran, some to fire the houses of the conspirators, others up and down the city to find out the men and tear them to pieces, but met, however, with none of them, they having taken effectual care to secure themselves.

Augustus and the Golden Age of the Roman Empire

By Augustus Caesar

Augustus Caesar became the first emperor of Rome in 27 B.C. He created the Roman state and managed it so well that he ensured its continued existence and expansion. Although he was one of the greatest national leaders of all time, he was not modest: He ordered that a list of his accomplishments be inscribed on bronze pillars following his death. Portions of this list, the Res gestae, *are excerpted here. Although the list is accurate, Augustus implies that the republican institutions were still at full strength under his regime; in fact, most of the real power was in his hands.*

Below is a copy of the accomplishments of the deified Augustus by which he brought the whole world under the empire of the Roman people, and of the moneys expended by him on the state and the Roman people, as inscribed on two bronze pillars set up in Rome.

1] At the age of nineteen, on my own initiative and my own expense, I raised an army by means of which I liberated the Republic, which was oppressed by the tyranny of a faction. For which reason the senate, with honorific decrees, made me a member of its order in the consulship of Gaius Pansa and Aulus Hirtius [43 B.C.], giving me at the same time consular rank in voting, and granted me the *imperium* [power of command]. It ordered me as propraetor, together with the consuls, to see to it that the state suffered no harm. Moreover, in the same year, when both consuls had fallen in war, the people elected me consul and a triumvir for the settlement of the commonwealth.

Augustus Caesar, "Res Gestau," *Roman Civilization: Selected Readings*, edited by Naphtali Lewis and Meyer Reinhold. New York: Columbia University Press, 1951–1955.

2] Those who assassinated my father [his adoptive father, Julius Caesar], I drove into exile, avenging their crime by due process of law; and afterwards when they waged war against the state, I conquered them twice on the battlefield [at Philippi, in Greece, in 42 B.C.].

3] I waged many wars throughout the whole world by land and by sea, both civil and foreign, and when victorious I spared all citizens who sought pardon. Foreign peoples who could safely be pardoned I preferred to spare rather than to extirpate. About 500,000 Roman citizens were under military oath to me. Of these, when their terms of service were ended, I settled in colonies or sent back to their own municipalities a little more than 300,000 and to all of these I allotted lands or granted money as rewards for military service. I captured 600 ships, exclusive of those which were of smaller class than triremes.

Various Honors Bestowed on Me

4] Twice I celebrated ovations, three times curule triumphs, and I was acclaimed *imperator* [supreme commander] twenty-one times. When the senate decreed additional triumphs to me, I declined them on four occasions. I deposited in the Capitol laurel wreaths adorning my *fasces*, after fulfilling the vows which I had made in each war. . . .

5] The dictatorship offered to me in the consulship of Marcus Marcellus and Lucius Arruntius [22 B.C.] by the people and by the senate, both in my absence and in my presence, I refused to accept. In the midst of a critical scarcity of grain I did not decline the supervision of the grain supply, which I so administered that within a few days I freed the whole people from imminent panic and danger by my expenditures and efforts. The consulship, too, which was offered to me at that time as an annual office for life, I refused to accept.

6] In the consulship of Marcus Vinicius and Quintus Lucretius [19 B.C.], and again in that of Publius Lentulus and Gnaeus Lentulus [18 B.C.], and a third time in that of Paullus Fabius Maximus and Quintus Tubero [11 B.C.], though the Roman senate and people unitedly agreed that I should be elected sole guardian of the laws and morals with supreme authority, I refused to accept any office offered me which was contrary to the traditions of our ancestors. The measures which the senate desired at that time to be taken by me I carried out by virtue of the tribunician power. In this power I five times voluntarily requested and was given a colleague by the senate.

7] I was a member of the triumvirate for the settlement of the commonwealth for ten consecutive years [43–33 B.C.]. I have been ranking senator for forty years, up to the day on which I wrote this document. I have been *pontifex maximus* [chief state priest], augur, member of the college of fifteen for performing sacrifices, member of the college of seven for conducting religious banquets [and a member of various other distinguished religious orders].

8] In my fifth consulship I increased the number of patricians, by order of the people and the senate. Three times I revised the roll of senators. And in my sixth consulship, with Marcus Agrippa as my colleague, I conducted a census of the people. I performed the *lustrum* [census] after an interval of forty-two years. At this *lustrum* 4,063,000 Roman citizens were recorded. Then a second time, acting alone, by virtue of the consular power, I completed the taking of the census in the consulship of Gaius Censorinus and Gaius Asinius. At this *lustrum* 4,233,000 Roman citizens were recorded. And a third time I completed the taking of the census in the consulship of Sextus Pompeius and Sextus Appuleius, by virtue of the consular power and with my son Tiberius Caesar as my colleague. At this *lustrum* 4,937,000 Roman citizens were recorded. By new legislation which I sponsored I restored many traditions of our ancestors which were falling into desuetude in our generation; and I myself handed down precedents in many spheres for posterity to imitate. . . .

10] My name was inserted, by decree of the senate, in the hymn of the Salian priests. And it was enacted by law that I should be sacrosanct in perpetuity and that I should possess the tribunician power as long as I live. I declined to become *pontifex maximus* in place of a colleague [the former triumvir, Marcus Lepidus] while he was still alive, when the people offered me that priesthood, which my father had held. A few years later, in the consulship of Publius Sulpicius and Gaius Valgius, I accepted this priesthood, when death removed the man who had taken possession of it at a time of civil disturbance; and from all Italy a multitude flocked to my election such as had never previously been recorded at Rome. . . .

13] The temple of Janus Quirinus, which our ancestors desired to be closed whenever peace with victory was secured by sea and by land throughout the entire empire of the Roman people, and which before I was born is recorded to have been closed only twice since the founding of the city, was during my principate three times ordered by the senate to be closed.

14] My sons [actually adopted grandsons] Gaius and Lucius Caesar, whom fortune took from me in their youth, were, in my honor, made consuls designate by the Roman senate and people when they were fifteen years old, with permission to enter that magistracy after a period of five years. The senate further decreed that from the day on which they were introduced into the Forum they should attend its debates. . . .

15] To the Roman plebs I paid 300 sesterces apiece in accordance with the will of my father; and in my fifth consulship I gave each 400 sesterces in my own name out of the spoils of war; and a second time in my tenth consulship I paid out of my own patrimony a largess of 400 sesterces to every individual; in my eleventh consulship I made twelve distributions of food out of grain purchased at my own expense; and in the twelfth year of my tribunician power for the third time I gave 400 sesterces to every individual. These largesses of mine reached never less than 250,000 persons. In the eighteenth year of my tribunician power and my twelfth consulship I gave sixty *denarii* to each of 320,000 persons of the urban plebs. And in my fifth consulship I gave out of the spoils of war 1,000 sesterces apiece to my soldiers settled in colonies. This largess on the occasion of my triumph was received by about 120,000 persons in the colonies. In my thirteenth consulship I gave sixty *denarii* apiece to those of the plebs who at that time were receiving public grain; the number involved was a little more than 200,000 persons. . . .

17] Four times I came to the assistance of the treasury with my own money, transferring to those in charge of the treasury 150,000,000 sesterces. And in the consulship of Marcus Lepidus and Lucius Arruntius I transferred out of my own patrimony 170,000,000 sesterces to the soldiers' bonus fund, which was established on my advice for the purpose of providing bonuses for soldiers who had completed twenty or more years of service.

18] From the year in which Gnaeus Lentulus and Publius Lentulus were consuls, whenever the provincial taxes fell short, in the case sometimes of 100,000 persons and sometimes of many more, I made up their tribute in grain and in money from my own grain stores and my own patrimony.

The Buildings I Erected

19] I built the following structures: the senate house and the Chalcidicum adjoining it; the temple of Apollo on the Palatine with its porticoes; the temple of the deified Julius; the Lupercal; the portico at the Circus Flaminius, which I allowed to be called Octavia after the name of the man who had built an earlier portico on the same site; the state box at the Circus Maximus; the temples of Jupiter the Smiter and Jupiter the Thunderer on the Capitoline; the temple of Quirinus; the temples of Minerva and Queen Juno and of Jupiter Freedom on the Aventine; the temple of the Lares at the head of the Sacred Way; the temple of the Penates on the Velia; the temple of Youth and the temple of the Great Mother on the Palatine.

20] I repaired the Capitol and the theater of Pompey with enormous expenditures on both works, without having my name inscribed on them. I repaired the conduits of the aqueducts which were falling into ruin in many places because of age, and I doubled the capacity of the aqueduct called Marcia by admitting a new spring into its conduit. I completed the Julian Forum and the basilica which was between the temple of Castor and the temple of Saturn, works begun and far advanced by my father, and when the same basilica was destroyed by fire, I enlarged its site and began rebuilding the structure, which is to be inscribed with the names of my sons; and in case it should not be completed while I am still alive, I left instructions that the work be completed by my heirs. In my sixth consulship I repaired eighty-two temples of the gods in the city, in accordance with a resolution of the senate, neglecting none which at that time required repair. In my seventh consulship I reconstructed the Flaminian Way from the city as far as Ariminum, and also all the bridges except the Mulvian and the Minucian.

21] On my own private land I built the temple of Mars Ultor and the Augustan Forum from spoils of war. On ground bought for the most part from private owners I built the theater adjoining the temple of Apollo which was to be inscribed with the name of my son-in-law Marcus Marcellus. In the Capitol, in the temple of the deified Julius, in the temple of Apollo, in the temple of Vesta, and in the temple of Mars Ultor I consecrated gifts from spoils of war which cost me about 100,000,000 sesterces....

22] I gave a gladiatorial show three times in my own name,

and five times in the names of my sons or grandsons; at these shows about 10,000 fought. Twice I presented to the people in my own name an exhibition of athletes invited from all parts of the world, and a third time in the name of my grandson. I presented games, in my own name four times, and in addition twenty-three times in the place of other magistrates. On behalf of the college of fifteen, as master of that college, with Marcus Agrippa as my colleague, I celebrated the Secular Games in the consulship of Gaius Furnius and Gaius Silanus. In my thirteenth consulship I was the first to celebrate the Games of Mars, which subsequently the consuls, in accordance with a decree of the senate and a law, have regularly celebrated in the succeeding years. Twenty-six times I provided for the people, in my own name or in the names of my sons or grandsons, hunting spectacles of African wild beasts in the circus or in the Forum or in the amphitheaters; in these exhibitions about 3,500 animals were killed.

23] I presented to the people an exhibition of a naval battle across the Tiber where the grove of the Caesars now is, having had the site excavated 1,800 feet in length and 1,200 feet in width. In this exhibition thirty beaked ships, triremes or biremes, and in addition a great number of smaller vessels engaged in combat. On board these fleets, exclusive of rowers, there were about 3,000 combatants. . . .

How I Expanded the Empire

26] I extended the frontiers of all the provinces of the Roman people on whose boundaries were peoples subject to our empire. I restored peace to the Gallic and Spanish provinces and likewise to Germany, that is to the entire region bounded by the Ocean from Gades to the mouth of the Elbe river. I caused peace to be restored in the Alps, from the region nearest to the Adriatic Sea as far as the Tuscan Sea, without undeservedly making war against any people. My fleet sailed the Ocean from the mouth of the Rhine eastward as far as the territory of the Cimbrians, to which no Roman previously had penetrated either by land or by sea. The Cimbrians, the Charydes, the Semnones, and other German peoples of the same region through their envoys sought my friendship and that of the Roman people. At my command and under my auspices two armies were led almost at the same time into Ethiopia and into Arabia which is called Felix [what is now

Yemen]; and very large forces of the enemy belonging to both peoples were killed in battle, and many towns were captured. In Ethiopia a penetration was made as far as the town of Napata, which is next to Meroe; in Arabia the army advanced into the territory of the Sabaeans to the town of Mariba.

27] I added Egypt to the empire of the Roman people. Although I might have made Greater Armenia into a province when its king Artaxes was assassinated, I preferred, following the precedent of our ancestors, to hand over this kingdom, acting through Tiberius Nero, who was then my stepson, to Tigranes, son of King Artavasdes and grandson of King Tigranes. And afterwards, when this same people revolted and rebelled, after I subdued it through my son Gaius, I handed it over to the rule of King Ariobarzanes, son of Artabazus, king of the Medes, and after his death to his son Artavasdes. When the latter was killed, I dispatched to that kingdom Tigranes, a scion of the royal family of Armenia. I recovered all the provinces extending beyond the Adriatic Sea eastward, and also Cyrenae, which were for the most part already in the possession of kings, as I had previously recovered Sicily and Sardinia, which had been seized in the slave war.

28] I established colonies of soldiers in Africa, Sicily, Macedonia, in both Spanish provinces, in Achaea, Asia, Syria, Narbonese Gaul, and Pisidia. Italy, moreover, has twenty-eight colonies established by me, which in my lifetime have grown to be famous and populous.

29] A number of military standards lost by other generals I recovered, after conquering the enemy, from Spain, Gaul, and the Dalmatians. The Parthians I compelled to restore to me the spoils and standards of three Roman armies and to seek the friendship of the Roman people as suppliants. The standards, moreover, I deposited in the inner shrine of the temple of Mars Ultor.

30] Through Tiberius Nero, who was then my stepson and legate, I conquered and subjected to the empire of the Roman people the Pannonian tribes, to which before my principate no army of the Roman people had ever penetrated; and I extended the frontier of Illyricum to the bank of the Danube River. An army of the Dacians which had crossed to our side of the river was conquered and destroyed under my auspices, and later on, my army crossed the Danube and compelled the Dacian tribes to submit to the orders of the Roman people. . . .

How I Became "Father of the Country"

34] In my sixth and seventh consulships [28 and 27 B.C.], after I had put an end to the civil wars, having attained supreme power by universal consent, I transferred the state from my own power to the control of the Roman senate and people. For this service of mine I received the title of Augustus by decree of the senate, and the doorposts of my house were publicly decked with laurels, the civic crown was affixed over my doorway, and a golden shield was set up in the Julian senate house, which, as the inscription on the shield testifies, the Roman senate and people gave me in recognition of my valor, clemency, justice, and devotion. After that time I excelled all in authority, but I possessed no more power than the others who were my colleagues in each magistracy.

35] When I held my thirteenth consulship, the senate, the equestrian order, and the entire Roman people gave me the title of "father of the country" and decreed that this title should be inscribed in the vestibule of my house, in the Julian senate house, and in the Augustan Forum on the pedestal of the chariot which was set up in my honor by decree of the senate. At the time I wrote this document I was in my seventy-sixth year.

Emperor Constantine and the Spread of Christianity

By Don Nardo

Italy was not only the heartland of the Roman Empire, but also the focus of Christianity's rapid rise to political power and influence in the fourth century, an event that profoundly affected the later course of cultural developments in Europe and other sections of the globe. In this essay, classical historian Don Nardo, who has published numerous books about ancient Roman history and culture, tells how the Christian revolution in Italy and beyond was initiated by the emperor Constantine and carried on by his successors.

During the roughly five-hundred-year period that began with Augustus Caesar's creation of the state that came to be called the Roman Empire (in the 20s B.C.) and ended with the deposition of the last Roman emperor (in A.D. 476) Italy was the political and cultural focal point of Europe and the Mediterranean world. And not surprisingly, the era of the Empire marked one of Italy's two great high-water marks in history. (The other was the Italian Renaissance, lasting from about 1300 to 1600, in which Italy often dominated European economic and cultural endeavors.) Rome bequeathed a rich cultural heritage to the medieval and modern worlds, including Roman law and the Latin language. But no single cultural development or achievement in that heritage proved to be more influential to later generations in all corners of the globe than the triumph of Christianity. The rapid rise of that faith to the status of Rome's

Don Nardo, "Constantine and the Christian Revolution," unpublished article, 2003. Reproduced by permission.

official religion reshaped Italian culture (as well as European culture in general) in the Empire's final years. And after Rome's demise, Christianity survived and proceeded to exert a powerful influence over the minds and hearts of hundreds of millions of people in the succeeding fifteen centuries.

These developments would in all likelihood not have occurred, or at least not in the same way, had it not been for the deeds of one of the most accomplished of all the Roman emperors—Constantine I, known as "the Great," who ruled from 306 to 337. When the Christians were still a distrusted, persecuted group, he granted them religious toleration and economic and other privileges; later, he converted to the faith, an act that gave it much legitimacy and social acceptance in Roman society. After Constantine's death, the revolution he had initiated continued and expanded, thanks to the contributions of some other devout and committed individuals, most notably Constantine's sons and Ambrose, bishop of Milan, who strongly influenced the policies of several later Roman emperors. Thus, it can be argued that, though Christianity was first born in Palestine, it was in Italy that it gained the acceptance, legitimacy, and political power it needed to triumph and survive to the present.

The Great Persecution

It appears that the relationship between Constantine and the Christian sect, which was so important to the group's survival and ultimate success, began when he was quite young. The date of his birth is uncertain but was probably some time in the early 270s. Constantine's father, Constantius I Chlorus, was a noted military leader and close associate of the emperor Diocletian, who ascended the throne in 284. In 293, when Constantine was about twenty, Diocletian appointed Constantius to a position in the tetrarchy, a coalition of four men who governed the Empire for the next several years (with Diocletian as the senior partner). Constantius had control of Gaul and Britain and for his regional capital chose the city of Trier, in northern Gaul. Sometime during Constantine's youth, he, and perhaps his whole family, likely developed a positive relationship with some local Gallic Christians. It is otherwise hard to explain why both Constantius and Constantine treated the Christians so humanely during the worst of Rome's Christian persecutions.

As for how that persecution came about, in the years of Dio-

cletian's reign the Christians were still a relatively small minority
in the Roman population, making up less than 10 percent of the
population, and more probably less than 5 percent. They were, as
they had been for more than two centuries, widely hated, mis-
trusted, and suspected of criminal behavior, which included
killing babies and eating them during their secret religious rites.
Despite these suspicions, which were later proven groundless,
Diocletian tolerated the Christians at first, although he worried
that their supposed crimes might anger the traditional gods and
turn them against Rome. He finally decided to act in 303 following a traditional state religious ceremony in which the livers
of the slaughtered animals did not look right to the priests.
Someone suggested that some Christians had cast an evil spell.
And the emperor's second in command, Galerius, who had a particular hatred of Christians, convinced Diocletian to close the
Christian churches. Soon, numerous Christian writings were
burned and many members of the sect were either killed or
thrown into prison.

These acts of persecution were confined mainly to the eastern part of the Roman realm, the power base of Diocletian and
Galerius. In the west, by contrast, Constantius showed the Christians mercy. He closed some churches, perhaps to make it look
like he was following the party line, but took no further action.
Moreover, when Constantine eventually succeeded his father, he
treated the Christians in Gaul and Britain no differently than he
did any other Roman citizens. This kindly treatment of the
Christians would later have huge consequences for Constantine's
career and the realm as a whole.

The Vision and the Milvian Bridge

The next and perhaps the pivotal connection between Constantine and the Christians occurred after Diocletian abdicated the
throne in 305. Before stepping down, the emperor formed a second tetrarchy, hoping its four partners would get along and maintain the peace. But the plan did not go as he had wished. In the
next few years, a power struggle erupted among the tetrarchs and
some of their sons and soon there was a full-blown civil war in
which several different men proclaimed themselves emperor (or
were proclaimed by their troops) while fighting major battles all
over the Empire. Among these claimants was Constantine.

The climax of this round of conflict came in 312, when Constantine marched his army into Italy with the goal of unseating one of the imperial claimants, Maxentius, who had illegally declared himself emperor and seized the city of Rome. Hoping to intercept and destroy the approaching enemy, Maxentius led his own troops out of the city via the Milvian Bridge. But soon he found his route blocked by Constantine's soldiers, whose shields bore a strange insignia—what looked like the letter X superimposed over a letter I with its top twisted into a loop. Maxentius did not realize that this insignia was a Christian symbol, composed of Chi and Rho, the first two letters of *Christos,* the Greek version of Christ's name. According to Constantine's contemporary biographer, the Christian bishop Eusebius, the day before, Constantine had been praying, when

> a most marvelous sign appeared to him from heaven.
> . . . He said that at about noon, when the day was already beginning to decline, he saw with his own eyes the trophy of a cross of light in the heavens, above the sun, and an inscription, CONQUER BY THIS, attached to it. At this sight he himself was struck with amazement, and his whole army also, which followed him on his expedition and witnessed the miracle. He said, moreover, that he doubted within himself what the import of this apparition could be. And while he continued to ponder and reason on its meaning, night overtook him; then in his sleep the Christ of God appeared to him with the same sign which he had seen in the heavens, and commanded him to make a like of that sign which he had seen in the heavens, and to use it as a safeguard in all engagements with his enemies. At the dawn of day he arose, and communicated the marvel to his friends; and then, calling together the workers in gold and precious stones, he sat in the midst of them, and described to them the figure of the sign he had seen, bidding them [to] represent it in gold and precious stones.

The truth of this account is questionable at best. The most probable explanation (assuming it was not completely fabricated) is that Constantine saw a solar halo, caused by sunlight reflecting off ice crystals in the upper atmosphere, and that Eusebius later embellished the tale to strengthen the image of the Christians

and their god. Whatever Constantine's motivation for adopting
the Christian symbol, he seems to have earnestly believed that its
power had won the day for him. Maxentius retreated back to the
Milvian Bridge, where the two armies clashed and he and several
thousand of his men died in a bloodbath. The next day, October
29, 312, Constantine entered Rome in triumph.

The Unconquered Sun and Edict of Milan

Constantine's victory and belief that the Christian god had played
a key role in it seem satisfactorily to explain the favor and support he showed the Christians thereafter. Like nearly all other
people of his day, he was both deeply religious and highly superstitious. (Besides believing in various gods, the Romans took
for granted the existence of magic and also put great store in
dreams and omens, which they thought prophesied future
events.) He could therefore be expected not only to attribute his
win to the Christian god, but also to repay that deity handsomely
by helping its followers. It must be emphasized that Constantine
did not actually convert to the faith at this moment. For a long
time he remained a pagan who accepted the existence of and
showed favor and gratitude to the Christian god along with a
number of traditional gods.

To some degree at least, Constantine now associated the
Christian god with one he had long showed particular favor—
the Unconquered Sun. An eastern religious import, the cult of
the Sun had grown increasingly popular in the third century; and
during Diocletian's reign the faith grew rapidly, attracting many
Roman notables, including Constantine. Therefore, it seems likely
that religious syncretism (the merging of two belief systems) may
have played an important role in the events surrounding the battle at the Milvian Bridge. If Constantine did indeed see a solar
halo in the sky near the sun, it would have been ample evidence
in his mind for associating the Unconquered Sun with the Christian god. And this would explain how he could favor and endorse
the latter deity without actually becoming a Christian. Constantine evidently did not yet fully appreciate that the Christian divinity did not tolerate partners or competitors; and for the time
being, his Christian friends, who were extremely grateful for his
support, did not want to risk losing it by emphasizing the point.

The first major boon Constantine granted the Christians was
toleration. The official decree was known as the Edict of Milan,

named for a meeting held in that northern Italian city in February 313 between Constantine, now firmly in control of the western part of the realm, and Valerius Licinius, master of most of the eastern part. The Edict stated in part:

> [We] give both to Christians and to all others free facility to follow the religion which each may desire. All restrictions which were previously put forward in official pronouncements concerning the sect of the Christians should be removed, and . . . each one of them who freely and sincerely carries out the purpose of observing the Christian religion may endeavor to practice its precepts without any fear or danger.

Continued Support for the Faith

The good relations Constantine and Licinius established at Milan did not last long. The two rulers clashed in still another civil war and on July 3, 324, Constantine won an overwhelming victory. During the remaining thirteen years of his reign, he was the Empire's sole ruler.

During these years, Constantine continued to support the Christians and help them gain acceptance in Roman society. He also played a chief role in church affairs as the mediator of several serious disputes that arose among the bishops, whom he recognized as the faith's political, as well as spiritual, leaders. Now that Christianity was considered a legitimate religion, it was only natural that he would assume such a role. By tradition, the Roman government, and in particular the emperor, had the duty of maintaining good relations between the Roman nation and the gods.

Constantine performed another important service for Christianity, as well as for the Empire itself, by establishing Constantinople, "the city of Constantine." His initial reasons were probably self-glorification and the need to establish a strong base from which to defend the Empire's eastern sphere against attacks from the north and east. Its location on the Bosporus strait (the site of the Greek town of Byzantium) was a strategically strong position for the command and defense of Greece in the west, Asia Minor in the east, and the Black and Aegean Seas. However, because of the emperor's support for the Christians and their increasing power and influence, Constantinople also grew into a mighty Christian bastion. Indeed, at the inaugural festivities on May 11,

330, the emperor dedicated the city to the Virgin Mary and Holy Trinity.

Constantine also poured vast sums of money into church-building programs, both in Constantinople and many other cities across the realm.

The final service Constantine rendered to the Christian cause was an act he performed on his deathbed. Shortly before Easter in 337, he became seriously ill and, feeling that death was near, asked to be baptized. Available evidence suggests that by this time he was a committed Christian, and the fact that he received this sacrament so late in life does not mean that he still harbored doubts about the faith. At the time, baptism was considered a very serious step to take and many people waited as long as possible to be baptized so that they would be less likely to commit a mortal sin before dying and meeting their maker.

Growth by Leaps and Bounds

After Constantine's passing, Christianity underwent nothing less than spectacular growth, partly because of his efforts on its behalf and also due to the staunchly pro-Christian policies of his successors. His three sons—Constantine II, Constantius II, and Constans—were all pious and committed Christians. They confirmed and extended the privileges their father had given Christian clergymen, including exempting them from the poll tax; they also made bishops immune from prosecution by secular courts, allowing them to be tried by their fellow bishops. In addition, Constantine's sons frowned on pagan sacrifices and demolished some pagan temples, although most such temples and their worship remained untouched for the moment.

At the same time, the ceremonial trappings of the Roman imperial court exerted increasing influence in Christian ceremony. For example, churchmen began using incense, long employed at court as a sign of respect for the emperor. And bishops received bows and other gestures of respect traditionally shown to the emperor by his courtiers. High-ranking clergymen also started dressing in more luxurious garments. (The ceremonial outfits worn by Catholic bishops and other church leaders today are adaptations of the formal wear of late Roman nobles.)

Along with these gains and changes, the sheer number of Christians in the Empire grew by proverbial leaps and bounds. The reasons for such huge numbers of conversions in so short a time span are somewhat unclear. Certainly, some pagans were drawn to the faith for the same reasons they had been in prior ages—the promise of salvation and eternal life in heaven, the inspirational example of courageous martyrs, the faith's embracing of the poor, sick, and downtrodden, and so forth. But there were other motives for conversion in the fourth century besides such spiritual, unselfish ones. Because the emperors now endorsed the faith, it had become a source of prestige and possible social mobility. Eusebius complained about the "hypocrites" who joined the church merely to gain favor at the court; and the later Christian writer Augustine was equally critical of large numbers of "feigned" or "half-way" Christians who still clung to many pagan ways and ideas. But whether their reasons for calling themselves Christians were admirable or self-serving, in the long run the converts' overall effect on Roman society was the same. After the "transitional" generations of the fourth and early fifth centuries, most Romans were born and brought up as Christians and the act of conversion become rarer and less of an issue.

Attacks on Pagan Beliefs and Worship

It must be emphasized that paganism was far from dead in these transitional years. At least until the early fifth century, a majority of Romans were still pagans, even if many of them worshiped in secret to avoid the wrath of the Christians. And indeed, paganism found itself increasingly under attack. It was not uncommon for militant Christians, sometimes with the approval of church leaders, to smash pagan statues and vandalize or even destroy pagan temples. At the same time, zealous Christian priests denounced pagan beliefs from the pulpit and prominent bishops gained steadily increasing influence over the emperors and other government officials.

The most influential of these bishops was Ambrose of Milan (ca. 340–397), who was stubborn and uncompromising in defending and promoting Christian beliefs. In 382, he convinced the emperor Gratian (who ruled in the west from 367 to 383) to give up the post of *pontifex maximus,* chief priest of the state religion, traditionally held by the emperors. Also at Ambrose's urgings, Gratian confiscated the funds of the state priesthood and removed the time-honored statue of the goddess Victory from Rome's Senate House.

The removal of the statue stirred up a storm of protests from leading non-Christians, who viewed the act as intolerant and insensitive. They eventually asked Quintus Aurelius Symmachus, a respected nobleman and senator, to plead their case to Gratian's coemperor, Valentinian II. "The glory of these times makes it suitable that we defend the institutions of our ancestors and the rights and destiny of our country," Symmachus began.

> We demand then the restoration of that condition of religious affairs which was so long advantageous to the state. . . . We beseech you, as old men, to leave to posterity what we received as boys. The love of custom is great. . . . We ask, then, for peace for the gods of our fathers and of our country. It is just that all worship should be considered as one. We look on the same stars, the sky is common [to all], the same world surrounds us. What difference does it make by what pains each seeks the truth? We cannot attain to so great a secret by one road.

Ambrose personally answered this plea, saying:

> [Symmachus] complains with sad and tearful words, asking . . . for the restoration of the rites of [the] ancient ceremonies. . . . Your sacrifice is a rite of being sprinkled with the blood of beasts. Why do you seek the voice of God in dead animals? . . . By one road, says he, one cannot attain to so great a secret. What you know not . . . we know by the voice of God. And what you seek by fancies, we have found out from the very Wisdom and Truth of God. Your ways, therefore, do not agree with ours. . . . You worship the works of your own hands; we think it an offense that anything which can be made should be esteemed God. God wills not that He should be worshipped in stones.

Ambrose prevailed. The statue was never returned to the Senate and the affair was widely viewed as a major victory of Christianity over paganism.

Living Links with the Past
This was only part of Ambrose's antipagan offensive. He also persuaded the emperor Theodosius I (sole ruler of the Empire from 392 to 395) to abolish all pagan sacrifices and cults and officially

close all pagan temples. (Some temples were demolished, others turned into museums, and still others transformed into Christian churches.) Though the number of pagans in the realm remained considerable, their days were numbered. In astonishingly little time, the Christians had skillfully capitalized on the boost Constantine had given them and managed to achieve a controlling influence over the political and religious apparatus of the Roman state.

Less than a century later, that state would no longer exist. But Christianity would handily survive in Italy and beyond. It would salvage what it could from the Empire's wreckage and go on profoundly to shape the destiny of European civilization. When Rome fell, Italy largely lapsed into obscurity until the Renaissance. In contrast, Christianity survived not only in Italy but all over Europe and remains today, along with Roman law, a living link with the past, a potent reminder that part of ancient Roman society never died.

The Fall of the Roman Empire

By Edward Gibbon

Edward Gibbon was an English historian who wrote The Decline and Fall of the Roman Empire, *first published in the 1700s. The following excerpt was taken from the section entitled "General Observations on the Fall of the Roman Empire in the West." Gibbon concludes that many causes contributed to the Empire's collapse: It had grown too large and complex to govern itself effectively, and the upper classes had become self-indulgent. In addition, internal divisions and barbarian invasions had weakened the Empire. Finally, Christianity, with its pacifist teachings, had undermined the military's fighting spirit.*

The Greeks, after their country had been reduced into a province, imputed the triumphs of Rome, not to the merit, but to the FORTUNE, of the republic. The inconstant goddess, who so blindly distributes and resumes her favours, had *now* consented (such was the language of envious flattery) to resign her wings, to descend from her globe, and to fix her firm and immutable throne on the banks of the Tyber [the Tiber River, which flows near Rome; i.e., the gods have now come to favor Rome over Greece]. A wiser Greek [Polybius, who wrote a history of Rome in the second century B.C.], who has composed, with a philosophic spirit, the memorable history of his own times, deprived his countrymen of this vain and delusive comfort, by opening to their view the deep foundations of the greatness of Rome. The fidelity of the citizens to each other, and to the state, was confirmed by the habits of education, and the prejudices of religion. Honour, as well as virtue, was the principle of the republic; the ambitious citizens laboured to deserve the solemn glories of a triumph; and the ardour of the Roman youth was kindled into active emulation, as often as they beheld the domestic images of their ancestors. The temperate struggles of the patricians and plebeians had finally established the firm and equal balance of the constitution, which united the freedom of popular assemblies, with the authority and wisdom of a senate, and the executive powers of a regal magistrate. When the consul displayed the standard of the republic, each citizen bound himself, by the obligation of an oath, to draw his sword in the cause of his country, till he had discharged the sacred duty by a military service of ten years. This wise institution continually poured into the field the rising generations of freemen and soldiers; and their numbers were reinforced by the warlike and populous states of Italy, who, after a brave resistance, had yielded to the valour, and embraced the alliance, of the Romans. The sage historian [again Polybius], who excited the virtue of the younger Scipio, and beheld the ruin of Carthage, has accurately described their military system; their levies, arms, exercises, subordination, marches, encampments; and the invincible legion, superior in active strength to the Macedonian phalanx of Philip and Alexander. From these institutions of peace and war, Polybius has deduced the spirit and success of a people, incapable of fear, and impatient of repose. The ambitious design of conquest, which might have been defeated by the seasonable conspiracy of mankind, was attempted and achieved; and the perpetual violation of justice was maintained by the political virtues of prudence and courage. The arms of the republic, sometimes vanquished in battle, always victorious in war, advanced with rapid steps to the Euphrates, the Danube, the Rhine, and the Ocean; and the images of gold, or silver, or brass, that might serve to represent the nations and their kings, were successively broken by the *iron* monarchy of Rome.

Division and Decay

The rise of a city, which swelled into an empire, may deserve, as a singular prodigy, the reflection of a philosophic mind. But the decline of Rome was the natural and inevitable effect of immoderate greatness. Prosperity ripened the principle of decay; the causes of destruction multiplied with the extent of conquest; and as soon as time or accident had removed the artificial supports, the stupendous fabric yielded to the pressure of its own weight. The story of its ruin is simple and obvious; and instead of inquiring *why* the Roman empire was destroyed, we should rather be surprised that it had subsisted so long. The victorious legions, who, in distant wars acquired the vices of strangers and mercenaries, first oppressed the freedom of the republic, and afterwards violated the majesty of the Purple [i.e., the authority of the emperors]. The emperors, anxious for their personal safety and the public peace, were reduced to the base expedient of corrupting the discipline which rendered them alike formidable to their sovereign and to the enemy; the vigour of the military government was relaxed, and finally dissolved, by the partial institutions of Constantine; and the Roman world was overwhelmed by a deluge of Barbarians.

The decay of Rome has been frequently ascribed to the translation of the seat of empire; but this history has already shewn, that the powers of government were *divided*, rather than *removed*. The throne of Constantinople was erected in the East; while the West was still possessed by a series of emperors who held their residence in Italy, and claimed their equal inheritance of the legions and provinces. This dangerous novelty impaired the strength, and fomented the vices, of a double reign: the instruments of an oppressive and arbitrary system were multiplied; and a vain emulation of luxury, not of merit, was introduced and supported between the degenerate successors of Theodosius. Extreme distress, which unites the virtue of a free people, embitters the factions, of declining monarchy. The hostile favourites of Arcadius and Honorius betrayed the republic to its common enemies; and the Byzantine court beheld with indifference, perhaps with pleasure, the disgrace of Rome, the misfortunes of Italy, and the loss of the West. Under the succeeding reigns, the alliance of the two empires was restored; but the aid of the Oriental Romans was tardy, doubtful, and ineffectual; and the national schism of the Greeks and Latins was enlarged by the perpetual difference of language and manners, of interest, and even of religion. Yet the salutary event approved in some measure the judgment of Constantine. During a long period of decay, his impregnable city repelled the victorious armies of Barbarians, protected the wealth of Asia, and commanded, both in peace and war, the important streights which connect the Euxine [Black] and Mediterranean seas. The foundation of Constantinople more essentially contributed to the preservation of the East, than to the ruin of the West.

As the happiness of a *future* life is the great object of religion, we may hear without surprise or scandal, that the introduction, or at least the abuse, of Christianity, had some influence on the decline and fall of the Roman empire. The clergy successfully preached the doctrines of patience and pusillanimity [cowardice]; the active virtues of society were discouraged; and the last remains of military spirit were buried in the cloyster: a large portion of public and private wealth was consecrated to the specious demands of charity and devotion; and the soldiers pay was lavished on the useless multitudes of both sexes, who could only plead the merits of abstinence and chastity. Faith, zeal, curiosity, and the more earthly passions of malice and ambition, kindled the flame of theological discord; the church, and even the state, were distracted by religious factions, whose conflicts were sometimes bloody, and always implacable; the attention of the emperors was diverted from [military] camps to synods [church meetings]; the Roman world was oppressed by a new species of tyranny; and the persecuted sects became the secret enemies of their country. Yet party-spirit, however pernicious or absurd, is a principle of union as well as of dissention. The bishops, from eighteen hundred pulpits, inculcated [taught] the duty of passive obedience to a lawful and Orthodox sovereign; their frequent assemblies, and perpetual correspondence, maintained the communion of distant churches; and the benevolent temper of the gospel was strengthened, though confined, by the spiritual alliance of the Catholics. The sacred indolence of the monks was devoutly embraced by a servile and effeminate [unmanly] age; but if superstition had not afforded a decent retreat, the same vices would have tempted the unworthy Romans to desert, from baser motives, the standard of the republic. Religious precepts are easily obeyed, which indulge and sanctify the natural inclinations of their votaries; but the pure and genuine influence of Christianity may be traced in its beneficial, though imperfect, effects on the Barbarian proselytes of the North. If the decline of the Roman empire was hastened by the conversion of Constantine, his victorious religion broke the violence of the fall, and mollified the ferocious temper of the conquerors.

Medieval Italy and the Church

Charlemagne Enters Rome

By Harold Lamb

During the Middle Ages, Italy was not one nation, but a group of cities and territories. The Church, to which all the people belonged, afforded the only real unity Italy knew. Although the pope was the spiritual leader for Italy and other Christians around the world, he lacked the military might to protect the independence of all the territories under his power.

As a result, regions of Italy frequently fell victim to invaders from the north. Among the most feared of those were the Lombards, Germanic people who had settled close to Italy and often made raids into the Italian peninsula to claim new territories for their own. During the 500s and 600s, the Lombards had taken control of many pieces of Italy, including the strategic city of Pavia.

When the Lombards appeared to be a threat once again in 753, the pope issued a plea to the one group he thought might help him—the Carolingian family. The Carolingians were the leaders of the Franks, another Germanic people who often opposed the Lombards. In response to the pope's call, Pippin III, the Frankish leader, was able to use his military strength to win back some of Italy's territories and to negotiate an agreement that would force the Lombards to leave Italy.

Once Pippin departed though, the Lombards slowly began to reassert their power. By 773, the pope appealed once again to the Carolingians for help. This time, the man who answered the call was Pippin's son, Charles, who would later be known as Charlemagne, or Charles the Great. Through a series of military campaigns, Charles was able to remove the Lombards, regain much of Italy's territory, and unite the peninsula under his power. Over time, Charles was to create an empire of which Italy was just one part. In 800, perhaps in gratitude for Charles's help in fighting off Italy's invaders, Pope Leo II crowned Charles as Roman emperor in the West. He would now be in control, in title at least, of all the regions under the sway of the Western church. He would be the political leader, while the pope would remain the spiritual leader.

Harold Lamb, *Charlemagne: The Legend and the Man*. Garden City, NY: Doubleday & Company, 1954. Copyright © 1954 by Harold Lamb. Reproduced by permission of Doubleday, a division of Random House, Inc.

Years later, Charles's coronation would, in turn, lead to the founding of
the Holy Roman Empire, which would survive for centuries.

After he had defeated the Lombards in 773, Charles, on impulse, de-
cided to march with his forces toward Rome. Although Pope Hadrian
had asked for Charles's help, he and the people of the city were appre-
hensive when they learned that the conquering Frank was approaching.
Hadrian worried that Charles would not stop at protecting Italy, but
would instead decide to dominate Italy as a harsh ruler. This selection is
by well-known twentieth-century biographer Harold Lamb, whose wide-
spread travels helped him write books on many historical figures, includ-
ing Genghis Khan and Alexander the Great. In this passage, Lamb re-
counts Charles the Great's journey to Rome and his historic meeting
with Pope Hadrian.

Once these Lombards—the Longbeards or Langobards—
had been the proudest if not the most formidable of
the German migrants who had settled forcibly within
the Roman Empire. They had been pushed into Italy by the
pressure of the more savage Avars. Then for some two centuries
they had kept to their tribal ways and tradition and speech. After
that they moved into the cities.

Only in the last two generations had the former Longbeards
abandoned their clan grouping and traditions while beginning to
speak the lingua Romana of the country.... Oddly, while taking
at last to urban life, and intermarrying with the natives, the Lombard overlords insisted upon the local people adopting their cos-
tume of trousers and mantles, with beards and forehead hair
grown long, and the backs of the heads shaved. Their pride
turned into conceit, their ferocity into cunning.

Nevertheless the strongest of their kings . . . had sought to
unite the Italian peninsula from the Venetian isles to sunny Benevento under their single rule. Even the crafty Desiderius [the last
Lombard king in Italy] when he pounded at the gates of Rome
the year before, seemed on his way to possess Italy entire, as
Theodoric the great Goth had once possessed it.

Pope Hadrian Tries to Protect Rome

In that endeavor he [Desiderius] had been opposed only by
Hadrian, who locked the doors of St. Peter's and sealed up the
city gates, to defy him. Hadrian the Pope held to the memory of
the vanished Roman world empire, to the glory of his half-

ruined city, and to the firm conviction that the vicar of St. Peter could never be made the subject of an earthly monarch. Hadrian's gesture had been one of spirit rather than force because he had only the unruly city guards to defend him. (Then Charles had mustered his expedition at Geneva, and Desiderius had fared north with his son to the mountain passes.)

Formidable as the mighty cities of Lombardy seemed to the Franks—who thought of Italy as "Lombardy"—there was weakness in the rule of Desiderius. The richest cities such as Benevento, Spoleto, or Friuli (Forum Julii) were occupied by self-seeking *Gastalds* busied in building up their own domains, and strongly resistant to any central authority. So much Charles soon discovered.

Charles Comes to Italy

While he [Charles] must have doubted . . . the ability of his army to hew its way through a battle, he was not at all disposed to allow his *fideles* to feast slothfully in their tents. Moreover, the sun-warmed grandeur of the Po valley, with vineyards and fruit orchards clustered beneath gray castles and basilicas, excited this restless rover of untilled woodlands. Why, here the paved roads crossed streams on stone bridges, and beggars picked out their lice on mosaic floors of Roman baths! Never before had he beheld the wonders of urban life. . . .

In setting out so impulsively for the Holy City, he [Charles] failed to notify Hadrian, the Pope, of his coming. But he did not fail to take along his serviceable spearhead of chosen horsemen.

Merrily his cavalcade threaded through the hills of Tuscany, down to the Roman plain where stone aqueducts strode like inanimate giants across the marshes. At the last night's camp Charles saw to it that his nobles donned their blue and crimson mantles, while he girded on a sword with a hilt of gold. His middle had swelled with the good Italian food. He remembered that he was, by title, a Patrician of Rome. "Dear and valiant brothers," he cautioned his nobles, "I will hold faithless and fit for the swine any one of you who falls drunk at this Easter feast." . . .

Beside him paced the standard-bearers of the churches. At such splendor and harmony, Charles' heart expanded. Dismounting, he went forward on foot. Never before had a king of Frankland set eyes on this Holy City, behind its massive brown wall.

Nearing it, watching to see that his following did not straggle,

Charles was led aside by his palm-bearing guides. "This is the way of triumph. Will the Great Clemency of the Franks proceed upon this path of the ancient victorious Caesars?"

In this manner they led him away from the city gate toward the church of St. Peter. Happily, Charles walked on, listening to the hymn singing so much more tuneful than the hoarse chanting of his Frankish clerics.

Hadrian had resolved not to let him march into the city.

Hadrian Reacts to Charles' Arrival

According to the author of his life [the pope's biographer], Hadrian had fallen at the news of Charles' immediate arrival "into an ecstasy of amazement."

The truth is, the Pope was stunned.

Hadrian came of a distinguished Roman family. A man of poise, determination—rather than clerical learning—and wide political experience, he had squelched and punished black conspiracy within the cliques of Rome, had fought a one-man battle against the wiles of Desiderius, while he dreamed of rebuilding the shattered monuments of his city. He was that rare combination, a diplomat of great force of character.

The problem he faced seemed almost insoluble. Cut off from the eastern patriarch in Constantinople, this bishop, traditional successor to St. Peter, had become by circumstances sole master of riotous and impoverished Rome, city of his distinguished ancestors, supplying itself precariously with food and a little money by the lands of the Roman duchy. He was, himself, the last vestige of the *Respublica Romana*. As such, he existed by sufferance of the Lombards, who were, at the worst, more refined and outwardly devout than other barbarian kings. To sustain his enfeebled city, Hadrian must have more territory in Italy—which he claimed as the patrimony of St. Peter—territory that neither the covetous Desiderius, nor the independent dukes, nor the distant emperor in Constantinople would think of yielding up. So Hadrian prepared to defend his walls of Rome desperately with priests, militia, and pilgrims, when the advent of the Franks across the Alps relieved the Lombard pressure.

Not only that. Charles' seizure of Verona decided the southern Lombard dukes to make their peace with the least menacing power of the three contending for Italy, with Hadrian himself. From Benevento, Spoleto, and other cities they hurried to St. Peter's to be shaven of their beards and long hair and to offer their fealty to this apostolic lord before the Frankish king or the Lombard, as the fate of Pavia [the Lombards' capital city in the north of Italy, which was under siege by Charles's troops and defended

EINHARD'S BIOGRAPHY OF CHARLEMAGNE

Einhard was a member of Charlemagne's court, so he was an eyewitness to most of the major events of the emperor's reign. His admiring biography, which includes many personal details about the legendary king, first came out around A.D. 830.

[Charlemagne]... cherished the Church of St. Peter the Apostle at Rome above all other holy and sacred places, and heaped its treasury with a vast wealth of gold, silver, and precious stones. He sent great and countless gifts to the popes, and throughout his whole reign the wish that he had nearest at heart was to re-establish the ancient authority of the city of Rome under his care and by his influence, and to defend and protect the Church of St. Peter, and to beautify and enrich it out of his own store above all other churches....

The Romans had inflicted many injuries upon the Pontiff Leo, tearing out his eyes and cutting out his tongue, so that he had been compelled to call upon the King for help. Charles accordingly went to Rome, to set in order the affairs of the Church, which were in great confusion, and passed the whole winter there. It was then that he received the titles of Emperor and Augustus, to which he at first had such an aversion that he declared that he would not have set foot in the Church the day that they were conferred, although it was a great feastday, if he could have foreseen the design of the Pope.

Einhard, *The Life of Charlemagne.* Ann Arbor: University of Michigan Press, 1960.

by Desiderius] might decide, could crush them. These dukes were present in Rome as devout and suddenly submissive pilgrims, and Hadrian was beholding the territory he needed thrust, as it were, into his hand when he heard that the barbarian Frank was riding, unannounced, into Rome. . . .

Hence he [Hadrian] sent for his guides and welcomers to lead Charles aside, to quarter the armed Franks safely beyond the walls in the Field of Nero, and to conduct Charles himself to the portal of St. Peter's.

Charles and Hadrian Meet

There, since dawn Hadrian waited anxiously, at the head of his clergy with the massed Benedictines. Thither strode Charles, with a flicker of gold from the hilt of his sword and crown circlet. On his knees he climbed the steps, laboring up the weight of his great body. He kissed the hand that Hadrian held out to him with the greeting, "Blessed is he that comes in the name of the Lord."

For a moment the prelate studied the towering barbarian. Charles beamed with exultation when the thronged monks chanted a prayer. He felt as if he had come into a great and festive hall. Gripping Hadrian's hand, he was led through the atrium into the very door of the apostle's church, up the nave between ninety-six columns, to the altar where a hundred lighted candles shone above the holy tomb. The light gleamed on plates of silver and gold, and the mosaic wall pictures. Never had Charles imagined such splendor. . . .

He heard Hadrian's voice, when they rose, saying that he had laid low the heads of proud enemies and had served St. Peter by his strength. What was he minded to do at Rome?

Charles murmured that he wished to visit the shrines during the four Easter days, and then depart.

Hadrian was not quite ready to believe that. He kept at Charles' side, a gracious host serving his uninvited guest.

Frankly he asked Charles to pledge faith and comradeship in peace with him. After doing so, Charles bade all his Frankish nobles and clerics take the same oath. Hadrian was satisfied, but he kept at the warrior's side.

"Yours is a joyous entry," he said at the gate. . . .

For three days Hadrian puzzled over this man with the eager mind of a boy, who might become either the master or the protector of Rome. In Charles he sensed a stubborn will, and a disposition to accept responsibility. The Frank had a trick of picking up his crippled boy to show the child anything that pleased him. Thereafter Hadrian always asked if Charles would do a thing, never if he could do it; he pleaded for protection against enemies rather than for aid to himself.

The observant Hadrian came close to guessing the secret of Charles' personality. But that the powerful barbarian kept hidden, because it came from a suppressed and terrifying fear. Fear, to Charles, was a shameful thing and he fought against revealing it.

Hadrian did wonder, silently, at the way Charles haunted the spots of sacred tradition—the crypt of Peter's prisoning, the stones of the apostle's confessional, the golden reliquaries. No ordinary pilgrim wanted so to carry off a fragment of stone. Then, too, the Frank's joy seemed overmastering when he pushed his big frame into such a spot. He seemed to be hilarious with relief. Briefly Hadrian wondered if he were trying to escape, physically, from some fancied pursuit. But that did not seem possible.

Charles and Hadrian Make an Agreement

After the third day's Mass at St. Paul's outside the walls, the Franks prepared to depart. But before they could do so on the fourth day, Hadrian requested them to meet—he realized now that Charles never liked to be separated from his family and liegemen—again at St. Peter's altar. There, quietly, he reminded Charles of the promise his father Pepin had given . . . the promise of certain cities and lands to be handed over to St. Peter and his vicars. He then asked Charles if he and his nobles would confirm the promise so made.

Readily, Charles assented. Had he not crossed the Alps to redeem that very pledge?

Then Hadrian had a secretary read the written items of Pepin's donation. Charles could not follow the swift intoned Latin too well.

". . . from the isle of Corsica . . . thence to Mount Bardo, to Parma . . . from thence to Mantua and Mount Silicis, together with the whole . . . of Ravenna, as it was in old time, and the provinces of Venetiae with Istria . . . and the whole of Spoletium and Beneventum."

Many of the names Charles did not know. Only the roads over which he had ridden in Italy were familiar to him. He had never laid eyes on a map. So he could not have realized that the recited boundaries took in two thirds of Italy.

Understanding that this was what Hadrian needed to have bestowed, he agreed readily. Some who watched the scene say that Charles had his chaplain copy the list, and that he himself placed the script of the copy beneath the Gospels that lay on the tomb under the altar.

The resolute Hadrian had been promised more than he ever hoped to possess. . . .

When his Franks swarmed into the gates [of Pavia], Charles rode in as victor, admiring the long colonnades and warm spring baths of this city of palaces. . . . Pavia was his. In high good humor he watched the treasures sorted out, ordering them given entire to his liegemen, who had besieged the walls so long. Delighted, they shouted approval of Charles' generosity and luck in gaining a profitable victory with so little bloodshed. From that day he signed himself "Charles, king by the grace of God of the Franks and the Lombards, and Patrician of the Romans.". . .

No burden of Frankish law or tribute did he lay upon the other Lombards, nor did he claim aught of their lands or cities for himself. He was merely king "of the Lombards," not of their country. They could manage as they had done before.

Then he was off, swiftly for his homeland. . . .

To the Lombard nobles, deserted by their conqueror, such heedless mercy seemed fantastic. One of them wrote, "The king of the Franks, who could have destroyed our possessions, showed himself merciful and indulgent."

That had never happened before in Italy.

The Struggle Between the Popes and the Emperors

By James Walston

Although the establishment of the Holy Roman Empire helped unite Italy and protect its territory from invaders, it also opened the door to power struggles between the pope and the emperor. Both leaders struggled to gain more power, and rarely did both agree on which aspects of the empire's affairs each should handle.

The popes and emperors were not the only ones who disagreed. Many of Italy's people also became involved in the dispute, taking the side of one leader over the other. Factions developed. The Guelphs supported the pope and opposed the emperor, who was usually from Germany, not Italy. The Ghibellines supported the emperor. At times, warfare erupted over who should control the empire.

In 1167, a group of people came together to form a league that was designed to fight the German emperor, Frederick Barbarossa, and to protect the independence of the cities or territories in which they lived. As author James Walston, professor of Italian politics and history at the American University in Rome, explains, this association of allies, which was known as the Lombard League, is believed to have signed its pact at a monastery called Pontida.

Through the league's military efforts, the Guelphs were able to defeat Frederick Barbarossa and bring about a peace treaty in which Barbarossa agreed to recognize the authority of the pope. Because of the league's ultimate success, Walston argues, it is appropriate that the abbey at Pontida is revered as a place where men fought for freedom and independence.

An event that may or may not have taken place . . . [at the abbey of Pontida] eight hundred and forty years ago was celebrated in the 19th century as a presage of the unity

James Walston, "Recycling a Symbol," *Italy Italy*, Year XX, 2002, pp. 35–39.

of Italy, only to be discarded as being too pro-Church in the anticlerical Risorgimento. In World War I, the story was revived and used as a symbol of allied unity against Germany. Today, it is trumpeted as the essence of the North against the rest of Italy.

On April 7, 1167, representatives of [the cities of] Bergamo, Brescia, Cremona, Mantua and Milan, calling themselves the Lombard League, are supposed to have gathered together at the abbey to swear the oath of Pontida. They were Guelphs [people who opposed German emperors], and supported Pope Alexander III against Holy Roman Emperor Frederick I Barbarossa and the Ghibelline faction. But they were fighting mainly to protect their cities' autonomy.

The Abbey of Pontida

The Benedictine monastery in Pontida on the banks of the Adda River was founded by Alberto da Prezzate, who fought on the side of Bergamo. When he was wounded, he vowed to enter a religious order if he survived. He did, and Pontida was the result. Alberto himself was beatified.

The monastery flourished in the later Middle Ages and became a center of wealth and culture. It was to be involved in another conflict between religious and secular power. The ruler of Milan, Matteo Visconti, planned to dispose of his enemy Pope John XXII by sending him a poisoned statue. Visconti used a Pontida man in the plot but it came to nothing. Not long after, in 1373, his successor, Bernabo Visconti, devastated the monastery, which was then rebuilt. Like most big religious houses, Pontida was suppressed during the French revolutionary period, and from 1798 to 1910 there were no monks. Despite the abbey's centuries-long history and impressive art, it is that day in 1167 that gives the place its fascination.

The Struggle Between the Pope and the Emperor

For most of the later Middle Ages, Italy was split between Guelphs and Ghibellines, the Pope and the Emperor. That apparently simple frontier masked a thousand other divides. Families and cities supported one side or the other, sometimes changing parties for short-term advantage. The conflict was not a religious one, though some popes did not hesitate to use excommunications and interdicts as weapons in their conflicts with the emperors. There were no distinctions of behavior (or misbehavior) on the battlefield or in negotiations. Both sides were Christian and they recognized the pope's spiritual hegemony, and most recognized the emperor's at least nominal temporal sovereignty. It was in the practice that problems arose.

Frederick Barbarossa

Frederick of Hohenstaufen, called Barbarossa in Italy, had become [Holy Roman] emperor in 1152 and soon realized that his main task would be keeping order in Italy rather than in Germany. In 1162, Milan surrendered to Frederick and he reckoned that he would have no more trouble in Italy, especially as his Lombard allies thought they would be able to share the spoils made available by Milan's defeat.

Instead, the emperor's representatives made them pay for privileges that had previously been rights. So two years later a league was formed in Verona to fight the emperor. The Guelphs and Alexander III had made a comeback and forced Frederick to return to Italy in 1166. Lombard cities wanted to imitate the Verona league even though they paid lip service to imperial power. They resolved to form a common defense, while remaining faithful to the emperor.

The Formation of the Lombard League

In December 1167, the papal legate in Milan put together a new league of sixteen cities whose first act was to found a new city strategically located where the rivers Tanaro and Bormida meet. It was called Alessandria in honor of Pope Alexander. Each city was represented by special ambassadors. In 1167, rectors were named and swore to uphold the rules established by the cities. They dealt with all the operational matters of the war against the emperor and were able to raise taxes and administer justice.

The practical result of the League was more trouble for Frederick. In 1174 he made his fifth journey to Italy. Many aristocrats returned to the Ghibelline fold, so he decided to take final action. He moved on Alessandria but failed to take it. In May 1176, he started out from Como with a small force, intending to meet up with the main body of imperial forces at Pavia.

Frederick Is Defeated

A large force of League troops moves out from Milan to try to prevent the union. At [the city of] Legnano, their vanguard meets

Italy's City-States

Through all the struggles between popes and emperors over the control of Italy, the city-states took advantage of the situation. Using their trade connections and relations with other cities, they won political and economic power that was sometimes stronger than that of either the pope or the emperor.

The disorganization of the Holy Roman Empire, its ongoing dispute with the papacy over the extent of Church authority in secular government and absentee foreign overlords left Italians largely self-governing within their communes. At the start of the fourteenth century, Italy was a patchwork of independent towns and small principalities whose borders were drawn and redrawn by battles, diplomatic negotiations and marriage alliances. During the fourteenth and fifteenth centuries, many of these petty principalities consolidated into five major political units that precariously balanced power on the Italian peninsula: the kingdoms of Naples and Sicily, the Papal States and the three major city-states of Florence, Venice and Milan. The other minor city-states which coexisted with these larger powers made political stability in Italy even more tenuous as their loyalties shifted from one main force to another. . . .

The ultimate success of a city-state as an autonomous

the imperial troops who push them back, not realizing that the main force was backing them up. There is a terrible melee around the Lombard center, the *carroccio,* a battlewagon full of military force and city pride. It is defended by the most dedicated soldiers, a Milan militia led by the legendary Alberto da Giussano. Frederick himself is unhorsed and wounded and for a time thought to be dead. The imperial standard bearer falls, the standard and Frederick's shield are captured, and "the Germans pursued for eight miles."

The result was that Frederick was forced to recognize Alexandria and negotiate the Peace of Venice with the pope, estab-

power was dependent on whether it could acquire the economic wherewithal to exist. It had to gain control over a sufficiently large [area] . . . to both provide a defensive zone and to generate adequate food and taxes. This process of urban expansion began in the twelfth century and by the thirteenth and fourteenth centuries, several city-states had acquired sufficient dominance to be considered major political powers and their influence was felt not only within Italy but throughout Europe. . . .

While the history of each Italian city-state is, of course, unique, the history of Italian politics is most significantly the history of the despots. In Italy, they achieved amazing levels of preeminence and the tools of diplomacy and espionage that they developed to retain their power set the standard for international relations throughout the Renaissance and into our own Modern era. Although Italy opened the door to the enlightenments of the Renaissance and the eyes of Europe turned to her for artistic guidance, her rulers continued to be split by their own squabbles. This lack of unity left Italy incapable of mounting successful defenses against the foreign invasions and occupations that were to come in the sixteenth century.

Kelly L. Morris, "Italy's City-States," *The End of Europe's Middle Ages.* Applied History Research Group/University of Calgary, 1997.

lishing an equilibrium that endured for the rest of their reigns. More lasting was the image of the Milanese carroccio. It was a cart with four ironclad wheels drawn by four yokes of oxen covered in drapes with the red and white cross of Saint Ambrose, Milan's patron. In the middle stood a forty-five-foot pole, like a ship's mast, topped with a gilded globe and a bell. There was an altar where mass was said before the battle. During the battle, the cart became a sort of command and control center. In peacetime, the carroccio was kept in the cathedral and was a major symbol of civic loyalty and pride. . . .

For many centuries the story of Pontida and Legnano did not

figure highly in either Lombard or Italian memories. The oath of Pontida is first mentioned by a chronicler two centuries after the event. Most of the story of Alberto da Giussano is a late addition. In any case, Milan later was in fact loyal to the empire, first the Holy Roman one, then that of the Hapsburgs.

All this changes in the age of Romanticism and nationalism. In the 1840s the neo-Guelph movement fights for the unity of Italy under the pope. Verdi writes an opera about the battle of Legnano that is premiered in Rome in 1848, when the then pope is still considered a potential leader of Italian unification. Alexander III became a model for the 19th century, so much so that a massive 1885 mural of Pontida in the Siena town hall celebrates the Siena-born pope also as an icon of Italian unity.

The use of Pontida's image during World War I was pretty straightforward; it was easy to project an alliance of free cities against German invaders in the 12th century onto the 20th-century alliance of sovereign states against Germany and Austria.

Today, Pontida has been given a new role to play as the symbol of the independence of all of the North against another presumed invader: Rome and the rest of Italy. Umberto Bossi's Northern League, a political party, has been in Italy's cabinet since 2001 but still holds its rallies at Pontida, in a show of freedom. When a group broke away from the League, they went to Pontida to declare that they were the real carriers of the spirit of the oath.

Saints and Cities in Medieval Italy

By Diana Webb

After the fall of the Roman Empire, the church was the only institution that still held real influence over the entire territory of Italy, which remained a loosely organized collection of cities. For most Italians, faith went beyond a belief in the main figures of the church—God the Father, Jesus Christ, and the Holy Spirit. People also relied heavily on their beliefs in the power of saints to help people on earth.

So strong was the people's faith in patron saints that many cities in Italy were actually founded around the worship of a particular saint. In those places, the people held special celebrations to honor the life of their saint, and often, a city's heavenly patron became so important that a virtual cult grew up around him or her.

Author Diana Webb is an expert on medieval Italian religious history who lectures at King's College in London. In this selection, she explores the relationship between certain Italian cities and their chosen patrons. She also shows the interesting effects such saint worship had on religion as well as on the political and economic interaction of the different city-states.

A round the year 1530 an Italian humanist succinctly explained the concept of the patron saint:

> We can see that by a great gift of Heaven it has come about that every city has been divinely allotted some saint as guardian and protector. Rightly it awards him honour and worship at all times, but it has especial recourse to him as protector and defender in uncertain or dangerous circumstances. This is so well known in all cities that there is no need to give examples. For although it can be believed that all those blessed spirits

Diana Webb, "Saints and Cities in Medieval Italy," *History Today*, July 1993, pp. 15–22. Copyright © 1993 by History Today Limited. Reproduced by permission.

which enjoy eternity with the angels care for Christians everywhere, it is nonetheless piously to be believed that there are very many of them who exercise
a special care and protection over those places in which
they were born, or where they lived for a long time, or
suffered dire tortures and death for Christ, with happy
results; or there are those, albeit foreigners, whom the
cities themselves have chosen as their patrons with a
special cult and devotion.

The basic idea of patronage, of powerful and influential beings who offer help and protection to their clients, does not, perhaps, need much explanation. But the vocabulary in which patron saints were described and invoked in medieval Europe
derived from ancient Rome. . . . The saints were high in the
favour of God, and a community which had exclusive possession
of a saint (whether the community consisted of the inmates of
a monastery, or the inhabitants of a settlement clustered about a
church, or both) imagined that, in return for their obedience and
offerings and the proper upkeep of the shrine, the saint would
show a particular tenderness for their needs and sufferings. . . .

Patron Saints in the City-States

The saints functioned as patrons in the Italian cities basically just
as they did elsewhere. The distinctive character of government
in the city states, however, had profound repercussions on the
cult. The associations of notable citizens who after about 1100,
constituted communes and claimed to exercise jurisdiction over
the city and its dependent territory, often won power in opposition to the bishop. The inhabitants of the city, the bishop's ten-
ants, and the clergy of the diocese were accustomed to express
their obedience to the bishop's authority in processions and offerings on the feast-day of the cathedral's patron saint. When the
commune superseded the bishop, was it also to appropriate the
bishop's patron saint and make his or her feast-day a demonstration of obedience to the secular authorities as well as (or even
more than) to the church? Or was the commune to seek a saint,
and a celebration, of its own?

Siena and Its Patron

Different answers were found in different places. At Siena, as in
many other cities, the citizens could hardly improve on the Vir-

gin [Mary], who already ruled the cathedral, and the Feast of the Assumption (August 15th) became the commune's great day as well as the cathedral's. Rural communities and individual nobles who had submitted to Sienese rule appeared to pay tribute and make a ceremonial offering of a stipulated quantity of wax at her altar in the cathedral.

Already in the early thirteenth century, the ancestor of the famous horse-race, the palio, that is such a tourist attraction today, was being run on this day for a prize provided by the commune, in the midst of the plagues of the fourteenth century it was resolved that the palio must still be run, despite the unpropitious circumstances, in order to woo the Virgin's favour. The Virgin was in fact often hailed as the actual ruler of Siena. This conception drew strength from the legends that grew up around the battle of Montaperti, on September 4th, 1260, in which the Sienese inflicted an unexpected and bloody defeat on the Guelfs of Tuscany, headed by the Florentines. It came to be believed that the Virgin had intervened to protect the city and its army, and later tradition related in detail how the citizens had on the eve of the battle mounted a great penitential procession which culminated in their formal submission to the Virgin as their ruler.

Other City-States and Their Patrons

In other Tuscan cities the commune opted for a cult of its own. The Venetians might be regarded as having furnished the prototype, for St Mark was the patron of the doge and the city, and his church did not become the cathedral of Venice until the early nineteenth century. It would, however, be difficult to prove that the Venetian example was consciously imitated elsewhere. The Florentine commune adopted St John the Baptist, patron not of the cathedral but of the adjacent Baptistery. At Lucca, St Martin of Tours, to whom the cathedral was dedicated, did not receive a legally prescribed offering from the officials of the commune until the mid-fourteenth century.

The great Lucchese civic festival from the late twelfth century, took place on September 14th, the Feast of the Exaltation of the Cross. Citizens and subject communities were bound by law to make their offerings to the miraculous crucifix, the Volto Santo or Holy Face, which had its own altar and chapel in the cathedral. According to legend it had been brought to Lucca in the year 782, but there is in fact no evidence for its cult before the

1090s, when we have it on good authority that William Rufus of England liked to swear by it. Lucca was strategically sited on a major pilgrimage route to Rome, and Rufus' oaths are among the evidence for the European fame of the Volto Santo.

At neighbouring Pistoia it seems that the bishop himself took steps to obtain the relics which provided the foundation of the citizens' special cult. Bishop Atto in 1138 excommunicated the consuls of the commune for violating the sacristy of his church. A few years later, however, he sent letters to the archbishop of Compostela by two Pistoiese citizens who were going there on pilgrimage, and obtained from him a portion of the relics of the apostle James. These were installed in a chapel in the cathedral of Pistoia, and within a few years James had his own hospital and his own office of works, the statutes of which ranked with those of the commune and people, and survive in several versions— Latin and vernacular—from the fourteenth century. This was a lay body, which administered the fabric of the chapel and had complete charge of the festivities held in honour of the saint. James was the civic patron, and his day was the chief civic festival of the year; St Zeno remained the patron saint of the cathedral. An incoming podesta (chief executive officer of the commune) did reverence at Zeno's altar on taking office, the captain of the people at James'.

Citizens and the City-States

The experience of these citizen bodies, which managed either to appropriate the management of the episcopal cult, or to promote one of their own, or both, can be contrasted with what happened in one city north of the Alps. The burghers of the new town at Tours, the Chateauneuf, failed to throw off the authority of the canons of St Martin who ruled them (with the backing of the kings of France) and largely dictated the terms on which the profits of the pilgrimage traffic, including such items as the income from taverns, were divided. The burghers neither successfully appropriated St Martin nor installed their own saint as the emblem of the urban community. If Italian citizens were often more successful in achieving autonomy, this was in part because so many of the cities were simply larger and richer, but also because of the absence of an effective central authority, which might have underwritten the authority of the bishop and clerical establishment.

In the fourteenth century, in fact, city-state governments often increased the amount of official homage that was paid to the ancient patrons of the bishopric. At Lucca, for example, it became customary for the commune to pay every year for the robing and adornment of the sculpted group of St Martin and the Beggar which stood high on the facade of the cathedral. At Pistoia, a procession was instituted in honour of St Zeno, at which the attendance of all citizens was required. The Florentine authorities recognised their duty to do public homage to the ancient bishop-saint Zenobius and the martyr Reparata, to whom the cathedral was dedicated. In 1351, they tried to obtain the arm of Santa Reparata from the abbey of Teano in the kingdom of Naples, but the abbess of Teano palmed them off with a fake made in wood and gesso, which was only discovered some years later, in 1353 the priors did some research to discover why the cathedral was dedicated to Reparata, and why by ancient custom a palio was run on her day. The story went that it was on her feast-day that Florence had, in the fifth century, been delivered by the forces of the emperor, Honorius, from the threat of barbarian hordes. It was declared that henceforth the prize for her palio should consist of twelve braccia of fine scarlet cloth, worth up to forty florins.

Multiple Patrons

Such developments suggest that by the fourteenth century the rulers of the communes had nothing to fear from symbols of episcopal authority, and in fact wished to advertise their pious regard for all the saints who were historically associated with the city, especially if their bodily remains were present. Multiple patronage was in fact both possible and praiseworthy: the ancient bishop-martyr, Rufinus, remained (and is still) patron of both the cathedral and commune of Assisi, despite the appearance of St Francis and St Clare in the thirteenth century. Four ancient martyrs (Ansanus, Crescenzius, Victor and Savinus), whose relics lay in the cathedral of Siena, began around 1300 to be celebrated in works of art commissioned by the civic authorities. The two greatest Sienese painters of the age, Duccio and Simone Martini, both painted representations of the Virgin in Majesty in which these four martyrs were depicted as suppliants kneeling on either side of the Virgin's throne, conveying to her the wishes and prayers of the Sienese people. In 1413 they were declared to be the official 'advocates' of the city, and their feast-days became public holidays. Later in the century they were joined as 'advocates' of Siena by the Franciscan preacher, Bernardino, canonised in 1450, and the dyer's daughter, Catherine, canonised in 1461.

The Law and Patron Saints

Governments composed of laymen thus managed and manipulated the cult of the saints, publishing laws which regulated it, and using it to display both their piety and their authority. The patron's feast-day was often marked by the release of one or more carefully selected prisoners from the city's gaols; the commune would pay for small candles for them to offer at the saint's altar. Informers who reported on citizens who failed to offer on the prescribed occasions were rewarded with a share of the fine; there might be penalties for disorderly conduct on major feast-days. The authority exercised by the city-state over the surrounding countryside, which was so notable a feature of the Italian scene, was visibly symbolised by the annual rendering of tribute by the city's rural subjects at the shrine of the patron. In the 1240s the Lucchese mounted an armed expedition to punish the failure of the inhabitants of the region called the Garfagnana to make their offering to the Volto Santo. This discipline extended to cities that were subjected to the rule of other, more powerful, cities. When in 1400 Florence achieved total control over its small neighbour, Pistoia, it required its new subjects to send a palio every year for the feast of St John, as Arezzo and many other Tuscan towns already had to do; but when the rural communes that were subject to Pistoia tried to avoid sending their offerings to St James, the Florentine authorities intervened to insist that they should fulfil their obligations.

Patron Saints and War

Warfare had its influence in shaping the civic cult. The carrozzo, an ox-drawn cart decked with holy emblems, was used by Archbishop Aribert of Milan already in the early eleventh century to serve as a rallying-point and inspiration for the citizen body at war; the Milanese took their carrozzo, with an image of St Ambrose, into battle against the Emperor Frederick Barbarossa at Legnano in 1176. Typically the carrozzo was kept wherever the patronal cult was allocated, for example in the Baptistery at Florence, to be brought forth when the communal troops went forth to war. Prisoners of war were paraded through the streets to the patron's altar, and might be ceremonially released there.

From the late thirteenth century, victory on the battlefield was commemorated with increasing frequency by the institution of official celebrations and offerings to the saint on whose day the event had taken place. Many of the earliest examples were associated with successes scored by Guelf forces after the death of the emperor, Frederick II, in 1250. In June 1256 a crusading army under the Archbishop of Ravenna was preparing to assault Padua, ruled by the notorious tyrant, Ezzelino da Romano. The chronicler, Salimbene, himself a Franciscan, tells how a lay-brother in the army encouraged all its members to put their faith in the Franciscan St Antony, canonised in 1232 and intimately associated with Padua. The crusaders carried the suburbs on June 19th and the city itself the following day, which was the octave (the eighth day after) Antony's feast-day. As a consequence, Salimbene says, the Paduans kept Antony's octave and its vigil with more solemnity than they did his feast-day itself, and the Paduan statutes bear him out.

On June 11th, 1289, the feast-day of the apostle Barnabas, the Florentines won a great victory over Arezzo at Campaldino. As a result, all Florentines, and especially the Guelf party, were supposed to venerate Barnabas. A cardinal and nephew of Pope Clement V got to know of the Florentines' devotion to Barnabas, and in 1310 sent them a gift of relics of the saint from the papal court, which were joyously received and installed in the Baptistery. A race was run in Barnabas' honour, which was still a feature of the Florentine social calendar in the late fifteenth century. Similar victory celebrations were inaugurated in many cities of northern and central Italy. The author of a description of the city of Pavia around the year 1330 commented that at several churches a palio and offerings were presented not out of custom, but because of some special devotion, or because of a victory won on that day'.

Other Celebrations

A deliverance from tyranny or change of regime might be treated in the same manner as a triumph on the battlefield. Both St Anne and St Victor (Pope Victor I) are depicted among Florence's patrons in an altarpiece of the Coronation of the Virgin which the Florentine office of the Mint, the Zecca, commissioned from Ja-

copo di Cione on October 20th, 1372. Anne is shown holding a
model of the city, an artistic device expressive of a specially pro-
tective role, which was often used in representations of bishop-
patrons like Petronius of Bologna or San Gimignano, patron of
both Modena and the little Tuscan town which bore his name.
Anne was so depicted because, in July 1343, she had helped rid
Florence of the short-lived tyranny of Walter de Brienne, Duke
of Athens. By expelling the tyrant on her feast-day, Anne, mother
of the Virgin, avenged the insult done to her daughter, on the
feast of whose nativity he had seized power in September the
previous year. Just over twenty years later, on July 29th, 1364,
Florence obtained a victory over Pisa which was both so complete and so unexpected, according to a chronicler, that the Guelf
party decreed the annual celebration of St Victor, whose day it
was, as of a patron of the Guelfs' like St Barnabas in the altarpiece, therefore, Victor holds both the palm of his martyrdom
and the bays of the victory he had brought Florence. Barnabas is
also present, as is Bishop Zenobius, with a fleur-delys on his vest-
ments, Reparata, who carries the communal standard, a red cross
on white, St Matthew as patron of the Mint, and of course the
Baptist. Anne and Victor were both rewarded with races run on
their feast-days.

Conspicuous Offerings

In the generation after the Zecca altarpiece was painted, several
more commemorative offerings were introduced but such innovation was firmly controlled. By an enactment of 1380 it was
strictly forbidden for officials of the guilds or of the merchant
college to institute any offering on a saint's day; the power to do
so was reserved to the officials of the commune. These officials
of course were foremost among the worshippers at the shrine of
the patron, and, often, other saints besides. They were not kings;
especially where a city succeeded in avoiding despotic rule, the
saint represented the monarchic principle in urban society,
supreme, undying, transcending mere mortal and temporary officials. Yet the offerings of the magistrates were conspicuous, and
all the world saw them process to the altar of the patron. In the
1330s it was declared that the Nine' of Siena would personally
attend the celebrations of the Feast of the Assumption, but no
other saint's day. Thus the identification of the city's supreme
magistracy with the supreme patron was underlined.

Jesus Christ as the Focus of Piety

From the late fourteenth century, however, a new ceremony demanded their presence. The ever-greater stress of late medieval
piety on Christ himself, as well as on his mother, exacted a public response from the leaders of the earthly society. The feast of
Corpus Christi, in Italy as everywhere in Europe, provided an irresistible occasion for them to associate themselves with the ultimate symbol of the divine embodied on earth, the Eucharist. To
walk immediately behind the sacrament as it was carried in public procession under a canopy demonstrated their status; to pay for
the candles that were borne about it, their piety; to take responsibility for the ordering of the procession, their authority. Neither
in Siena nor elsewhere in Italy did the rulers of the Italian cities,
whether princes or magistrates, fail to grasp this opportunity.

THE HISTORY OF NATIONS
Chapter 3

The Italian
Renaissance

Art and Ideas Flourish in the Italian Renaissance

By Susan Fegley Osmond

The term renaissance *comes from the French word for "rebirth." Although the name may have come from France, it was Italy that pioneered the great artistic and cultural movement so named that swept Europe in the fifteenth and sixteenth centuries.*

The Renaissance was a collection of new ideas in almost every aspect of human life, from medicine to religion to astronomy. It is probably best known, though, for the incredible art it produced. During this period many of history's greatest artists lived and worked, including Botticelli, Raphael, Michelangelo, and Leonardo da Vinci. As they branched out from traditional artistic styles that depicted people almost solely in relation to God, Renaissance artists forever changed old notions about the place people hold in the universe. New philosophies of the day, particularly humanism, insisted people were inherently good rather than sinful and declared that people could strive to become perfect with some success. In response to this revolutionary thinking, a new school of artists began to focus on more realistic and natural subjects, in which they, too, showed how human beings had the power to shape their world.

Author Susan Fegley Osmond, an art editor for the periodical World & I, *describes the vast changes that took place in the world of art during the Renaissance in this selection. Highlighting the radical differences in the way religious themes were treated, Osmond also explores how the humanist movement within Italy's artistic community spread across Europe to help inspire an expanded Renaissance.*

Renaissance (from the French for "rebirth") is a term coined in the nineteenth century originally to denote the revival of art and letters under the influence of ancient Roman and Greek models. This revival began in Italy in the fourteenth century, flourished in the fifteenth, and in the sixteenth reached apogee [peak] and then crisis in Italy while it spread through most of Europe. But humanism's classical learning alone cannot account for the immense changes that took place during these centuries; moreover, movements originating in the North also contributed to these changes. Therefore the term Renaissance has also come to denote the era in general and its overriding spirit, in which desires intrinsic to human nature, generally repressed under medieval feudalism, burst forth with new fervor and resulted in a new culture.

Characteristics of the Renaissance

Understood as an era and also as an inspiritus [spirit] of awakening, the Renaissance includes both the movement of humanism that emanated from Italy and the northern-based Reformation (and its precursors in England and Bohemia [in today's western Czech Republic] in the fourteenth and fifteenth centuries). These two developments should by no means be equated with each other, but they had in some respects a common root and exerted a powerful influence on each other. The era is also characterized by increasing secularization, burgeoning trade (run by a powerful merchant class), the expanding power of northern European monarchies and of vying Italian city-states, and the beginnings of the age of exploration and the scientific revolution.

It seems that the Renaissance sprang forth in response to the need for outlets through which some basic human desires, generally denied in the medieval order of things, could be expressed and find fulfillment. One sees during the Renaissance a marked increase in individual freedom and autonomy, and the acceptance of physical existence and of the desire to pursue a happy, practical life. Renaissance thinkers stressed man's intrinsic value and dignity as a being created in the image and likeness of God. Related to this was a pervasive desire to pursue a direct relationship with the Divinity founded on personal mystical experience and/or the study of Scripture, early church writings, and even pagan texts reinterpreted in Christian terms. Also fundamental to the era was the desire to understand and master nature through direct observation and the discovery of its laws and structure.

As in any period, remnants of the old worldview coexisted with and to some extent helped shape the new. In northern Europe, Gothic art and culture (as it was derisively named by Italian humanists) held sway into the sixteenth century, and, as a result, the Renaissance there had a strongly religious cast. . . .

City-States and the Spread of Individuality

Political developments in Italy played a significant part in the emergence of artists such as Giotto, who were confident to assert individual styles based on the observation of nature rather than the perpetuation of medieval traditions. During the eleventh and twelfth centuries, a number of independent city-states, fortified by their powerful European-wide trade and banking, formalized their governments as republics (Venice had even been a republic since the eighth century). These qualified democracies were governed ad hoc [improvisedly] by guilds—associations of merchants, bankers, artisans, and other professionals. The unformalized nature of the city constitutions enabled men greedy for power to manipulate the quasi-democratic governments; relics of the nobility or great merchant oligarchs tended to lead the communes into despotism at the hands of a family or a clique (the fifteenth century saw the most virulent forms of this). Nonetheless, these republics—particularly Florence—offered guild-member citizens unprecedented freedom. Fourteenth-century frescoes reveal that individuality was not only evident but already prized in the Italian city-republics.

But burgeoning individuality and naturalism were not unique to Italians. In the region today known as the Netherlands and Belgium there had also sprung up prosperous cities that were semi-independent and run on republican lines by guilds. Haarlem-born Claus Sluter, an outstanding sculptor, shows the elevation of individuality in his powerfully characterized, strikingly realistic figures for the *Well of Moses* (1395–1403) in Dijon.

It is in the early to mid fifteenth century that we see the real flowering of the Renaissance, evident in both Italy and Flanders. In Italy a new breed of artists arose with strong, independent personalities. They knew they were forging a new art and indeed a new culture, and strove to rival and even surpass the brilliance of classical antiquity.

A New Artistic Perspective

During this time . . . there occurred in the service of naturalism a development that was to revolutionize art. Indeed, it defined most painting up to the twentieth century (and still holds sway in realistic painting). This was the discovery of linear or vanishing-point perspective in Florence. The principles of it were first demonstrated around 1413 by architect Filippo Brunelleschi (who later gained fame for the technical feat of designing and erecting the immense dome of Florence Cathedral). But it was architect and man of letters Leon Battista Alberti who first described the underlying geometry and a simple method in his treatise *On Painting* in 1435. This system was further refined by Piero della Francesca, Leonardo, and [Albrecht] Durer.

Early pioneers devised a system of looking at the world as if through a framed window, in which the painting's panel (or picture plane) is the "glasspane." They even devised frames with grids through which the artist looked at (and could even trace)

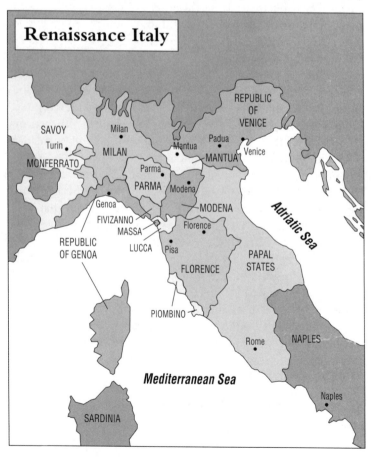

Renaissance Italy

the subject to be depicted. This was not a very scientific approach, but it allowed the artist to observe and gauge the phenomenon of foreshortening. Artists had previously noticed that if, say, . . . one gazes at the interior of a long room, the sides of the room appear to move inward, while the floor appears to move up and the ceiling down, so the wall at the far end of the room appears to be smaller than a theoretical wall on the spot where . . . the viewer stands.

What Brunelleschi and Alberti discovered was that—to take our example—while your side walls are in reality parallel, if in your drawing you extend the lines of their receding top and bottom edges to a horizontal line denoting the far horizon opposite your eye level, the lines of the walls all appear to meet in a single vanishing point. With the further help of geometry they developed a system to measure "depth" in the picture. Thus it became possible to depict objects with exact dimensions placed in a measurable three-dimensional space and to draw all objects to proper scale. The result is a rendition of visual reality quite like what you see with one eye closed, or like that produced in a photograph. It is not exactly the way humans see, for we have stereoscopic vision, among other things. But it presents a convincing, readable, and systematic two-dimensional representation of three-dimensionality.

Early systems of linear perspective used a single vanishing point in the center of the picture. The system for working out the depth easily resulted in the checkerboard floors and street-grounds often found in Early Italian Renaissance paintings. But the single vanishing point system works only for simple scenes in which all planes depicted in depth are parallel to each other and all planes depicted in width are parallel to the picture plane. Any plane at a different angle would result in another vanishing point. To obtain greater naturalism, a system evolved years later that used two vanishing points (or even more) to achieve round-the-corner or up hill and down dale effects.

When linear perspective was first introduced, Florentine artists seized upon it with fervor, for here they not only had a method to render a scene in correct perspective, re-creating almost exactly what the eye sees, but they felt they had found the key to unlock the divine order of the cosmos. Since at least the time of [philosopher and mathematician] Pythagoras in ancient Greece, people had believed that the universe was ordered—was held together, in a sense—by sacred numerical relationships and proportions, by sacred geometry. Here the artist-architects of the Renaissance seemed to have found basic principles underlying the structure of reality. No wonder they had such confidence that man as a creative being was capable of achieving divinity. Here they could experience and vicariously participate in the very process of the mathematical creation of the universe through the re-creation of "worlds" of harmony in their own works. . . .

Attention to Atmosphere

In Italy the originator of atmospheric perspective and chiaroscuro (light and shadow) modeling was Massacio. This and his pioneering work in linear perspective make him a watershed figure in the history of art—a fact well appreciated by painters of the Italian Renaissance. His cycle of frescoes in the Branacci Chapel in the Church of Santa Maria del Carmine in Florence was the manifesto of the new pictorial style and became the model for all Florentine artists, including Michelangelo, who personally studied the frescoes to learn the new art of chiaroscuro.

The greatest Renaissance master of modeling and atmospheric perspective, however, was Leonardo. He developed sfumato ("smoke") modeling, the transition of tone from light to dark so gradual as to be imperceptible. (A version of this is previously apparent in [Flemish painter Hubert] van Eyck, but Leonardo expanded the tonal spectrum to include more dramatic darks, while van Eyck accurately observed the effects of not only the shadows cast by a primary light but reflected light playing in these shadows.) In works such as his first version of *Virgin of the Rocks* (1483–85), we can see Leonardo using sfumato modeling and atmospheric perspective to soften the overall image into a unity and also to impart a mood of gentle yet profound gravity. The harmonizing of all elements—with figures arranged in geometric forms (in Leonardo's case usually the pyramid) and all proportions in careful balance—is integral to the Renaissance ideal of beauty. But in his sfumato and delicate atmospherics Leonardo goes beyond geometrics to produce harmony through something that connotes intuitive perception. His approach—not only combining the outward expression of well-proportioned forms but harmonizing three inward ways of knowing: the intellectual, the empirical, and the emotional-intuitive—epitomizes the ideal balance achieved during the all too brief High Renaissance.

The Mannerist painters [of the late sixteenth century] would continue to utilize chiaroscuro modeling and atmospheric perspective to convey an impression of profundity as well as spacial depth, but in their unbalanced paintings—such as those of [Jacopo] Tintoretto—the techniques are manipulated to heighten the rather hysteric [excessive] emotional effect. Nonetheless, when one looks back to see how far painting had come from medieval times, . . . a radical increase in the sensitivity to and honesty about emotion [is seen], and atmospheric effects are an important part of this. A sense of mood does not exist in medieval painting, but it becomes primary in later sixteenth-century Italian and especially seventeenth-century Dutch, Spanish, and Italian painting.

Renaissance Individualism

One of the most distinguishing characteristics of the Renaissance is the emergence of individualism. . . . The unique value of the individual is implied in linear perspective. Individualism is also revealed, perhaps more blatantly, in the care with which each of the outstanding artists of the era cultivated a unique style. It is also demonstrated in the increasing depiction of human figures as unique, complex individuals.

Although there was discernible originality in artists of the 1300s, with the fifteenth century, in both Italy and the Low Countries, [there was] . . . a quantum leap in the intensification of personal style among the luminaries of the day. The manifesto for this was Donatello's marble *St. Mark* (1411–15) in Florence. Art historian Frederick Hartt has said, "It has been rightly claimed that this statue represents so abrupt a break with tradition that it should be considered a mutation—a fundamental declaration of the new Renaissance position with respect to the visible world."

What makes the *St. Mark* revolutionary is its decidedly classical gravitas [seriousness] and moral grandeur. The full-bodied figure stands in natural contrapposto [the twisting of a figure to turn the limbs in different directions] that has nothing to do with the artificial grace of the Gothic International Style exemplified, for example, in the nearly contemporary *St. John the Baptist* and *St. Matthew* by Lorenzo Ghiberti. (These, like the *St. Mark*, occupied niches on the outside of Florence's grain exchange, the Orsanmichele, which was also a shrine.) *St. Mark*'s clothing, too, is not the usual study in late Gothic decorative lyricism but is completely realistic, revealing the contours of a solid body beneath its weighty folds. (Vasari tells us of a technique, apparently originated by Donatello, in which the sculptor, making his preparatory model, would make a clay nude and then dip sheets

LEONARDO DA VINCI: RENAISSANCE MAN

A universal, or "Renaissance," man is someone who has talent in many different fields and is equally skilled in all of them. Leonardo da Vinci—the artist, scientist, musician, and athlete who lived from 1452 to 1519—fit this description. Biographer Giorgio Vasari (1511–1574) wrote about Leonardo with a great deal of admiration.

The greatest gifts often rain down upon human bodies through celestial influences as a natural process, and sometimes in a supernatural fashion a single body is lavishly supplied with such beauty, grace, and ability that wherever the individual turns, each of his actions is so divine that he leaves behind all other men and clearly makes himself known as a genius endowed by God (which he is) rather than created by human artifice. Men saw this in Leonardo da Vinci, who displayed great physical beauty (which has never been sufficiently praised), a more than infinite grace in every action, and an ability so fit and so vast that wherever his mind turned to difficult tasks, he resolved them completely with ease. His great personal strength was joined to dexterity, and his spirit and courage were always regal and magnanimous. And the fame of his name spread so widely that not only was he held in high esteem in his own times, but his fame increased even more after his death. . . .

Leonardo's Many Talents

Possessing so divine and wondrous an intelligence, and being a very fine geometrician, Leonardo not only worked in sculpture but in architecture. In his youth, he made in clay the heads of some women laughing, created through the craft of plaster-casting, as well as the heads of some children,

of cloth in clay slip and drape them on the figure.)

But even more revolutionary than this is the psychological re-alism that Donatello brought to his depiction of the saint. Michelangelo said of the statue, "No one could fail to believe the

which seemed to have issued forth from the hand of a mas-ter; in architecture, he made many drawings of both ground-plans and other structures, and he was the first, even though a young man, to discuss making the River Arno a canal from Pisa to Florence. He drew plans for mills, fulling machines, and implements that could be driven by water-power; and since painting was to be his profession, he carefully studied his craft by drawing from life, and sometimes by fashioning models or clay figures. . . . There was infused in this genius so much divine grace, so formidable and harmonious a com-bination of intellect and memory to serve it, as well as so great an ability to express his ideas through the designs of his hands, that he won over with arguments and confounded with reasonings the boldest minds.

Leonardo, the Man

Leonardo was so pleasing in his conversation that he won everyone's heart. And although we might say that he owned nothing and worked very little, he always kept servants and horses; he took special pleasure in horses as he did in all other animals, which he treated with the greatest love and patience. For example, when passing by places where birds were being sold, he would often take them out of their cages with his own hands, and after paying the seller the price that was asked of him, he would set them free in the air, restor-ing to them the liberty they had lost. As a result, Nature so favoured him that, wherever he turned his thought, his mind, and his heart, he demonstrated such divine inspiration that no one else was ever equal to him in the perfection, liveliness, vitality, excellence, and grace of his works.

Giorgio Vasari, *The Lives of the Artists*, trans. Julia Conaway Bondanella and Peter Bondanella. New York: Oxford University Press, 1991.

word of such a sincere man." The most compelling thing about the figure is the concentrated power of the face, with its alert tension, assessing dangers from without while summoning inner resources to deal with them. Hartt comments, "This noble face with its expression of severe determination—the Italian term *terrible* is how the Renaissance would describe it—can be thought of as a symbolic portrait of the ideal Florentine under stress. . . . It is a summation of the virtues demanded in an age of crisis."

More than any of his contemporaries, Donatello showed fascination with the inner life of his subjects. He remained an innovator throughout his career. His bronze *David* (c. 1440) was the first nude rendition of this biblical character. (In the Middle Ages and Renaissance, nudity symbolized the nakedness of the soul before God; in Donatello this was combined with the humanists' admiration of the body as the encapsulation of ideal beauty.) The sinuous figure was also possibly the first freestanding statue since antiquity—quite literally the embodiment of republican individualism. In later years, the long-lived artist developed a highly expressionistic style, and it appears he forsook the humanistic ideals of his youth during a time of religious reaction in Florence dominated by its archbishop. His harrowing *Mary Magdalene* (c. 1453–55) is unforgettable evidence of this.

During the fifteenth century, the portrayal of convincingly individual character is sporadic, both in the South and the North. It became more pervasive during the sixteenth century.

The Popularity of Portraits

Perhaps the best vehicle for communicating the individuality of human beings in art was the revival of the ancient art of portraiture. Portraits were almost always commissioned by patrons, and the fact that they wanted to leave some lasting memorial to themselves itself is evidence of a new attitude. In Italy, early pictorial portraits tended to be profiles, and often they recorded little more than the outward visage of the sitter. It was in Flanders [a region bordering the Netherlands and France] that portraiture became the revelation of personality, in the art of van Eyck and [Rogier] van der Weyden. Van Eyck's *Man in a Red Turban* (1433), possibly a self-portrait, was the first in which the sitter turned his gaze directly to meet that of the viewer. Here we see a man of the world, a person of unmistakable intelligence who has his own opinions and is not about to change them. He takes things as they come and suffers no illusions. His middle-aged face, with wrinkles surrounding the skeptical eyes and thin lips, is recorded in every particular, down to the graying stubble on his chin.

In Italy, portraiture as a window onto character later reached great heights in such works as Raphael's *Baldasarre Castiglione* (1514–15), Leonardo's enigmatic *Mona Lisa* (c. 1503–1506), and many works by Titian, including *The Young Englishman* (c. 1540–45). . . .

The Dignity of Man

All of this shows that there was a new concept of man at work in the Renaissance. This view extolled the intrinsic value and dignity of man as the supreme creation of God and the microcosm of the world. In 1451–52, Florentine humanist Giannozzo Manetti wrote a treatise titled *On the Dignity and Excellence of Man*, in which he refuted the claims of medieval theologians that man was worthless in the sight of God. Instead, Manetti declared man "lord and king and emperor in the whole orb of the World, and not unworthy to dominate and to reign and to rule." He argued that there is nothing the human intelligence cannot encompass, no mystery of the cosmos it cannot fathom.

A later humanist, Giovanni Pico della Mirandola, stressed both the freedom and the responsibility of the individual. In his influential *Oration on the Dignity of Man* (1486), Pico has God speaking to Adam: "The nature of all other beings is limited and constrained within the bounds of laws prescribed by Us. Thou, constrained by no limits, in accordance with thine own free will, in whose hand We have placed thee, shalt ordain for thyself the limits of thy nature." Pico exclaims: "O highest and most marvelous felicity of man! To him it is granted to have whatever he chooses, to be whatever he wills." He warns that, depending on which aspects of his nature one chooses to cultivate, one moves either downward into the bestial or upward toward perfection. "Let a certain holy ambition invade our souls," he exhorts, "so that, not content with the mediocre, we shall pant after the highest and (since we may if we wish it) toil with all our strength to obtain it." Through the proper cultivation of love and reason, one may ultimately reach that state where he "is in God and God in him, nay, rather, God and himself are one."

. . . The latter view [was clearly] at work in Durer's 1500 self-portrait. In general, however, the belief in the godlike dignity of man was exemplified through the depiction of the nude human form, and this was most prevalent in humanist Italy. Some artists, such as Michelangelo and Botticelli, did not even concern themselves much with placing figures in clearly delineated three-dimensional space.

Throughout Michelangelo's long career, his main interest was the life of the human soul as expressed through the body. He often called the human body the mortal veil of divine intention. His colossal *David* (1501–1504) is the epitome of the heroic style for which he is best known, celebrating the nobility of the human form and the power of human will.

But the *Creation of Adam* (1511–12), from his grand cycle of frescoes covering the ceiling of the Sistine Chapel in the Vatican, is the epigrammatic statement of the divine potential of man. Here the massive, beautiful, receptive figure of Adam lifts his hand—that modus of creation—to receive from the hand of a most virile yet venerable God the . . . [gift] of life: a divine soul. The tiny space that separates the fingers human and divine has given rise to centuries of rumination. But what is undeniably clear is that this is Father and Son. Adam is no mere vessel but an Incarnation, and God Himself shows tense concentration and excitement as He brings to life this culmination of His creation, His second self. Here we have what is perhaps posterity's greatest inheritance from the Renaissance—the confident assertion of man's everlasting destiny, though impeded by the Fall [from grace in the Garden of Eden], to become the child, companion, and embodiment of God.

The Italian People Explore Their World

BY JACOB BURCKHARDT

Jacob Burckhardt was a Swiss historian who lived from 1818 to 1897. He was working as a professor at Basel University when he decided to write an expansive study of the Middle Ages that would trace Italian history from Constantine through the Renaissance. He traveled widely to research his topic and devoted years to its writing. Burckhardt's first volume—the one that would be last chronologically in his proposed study— was published in 1860 under the title The Civilization of the Renaissance in Italy. *At the time, it was not well accepted. Over the years, however, Burckhardt's work has become a classic example of historical writing. In fact, Burckhardt is known today as perhaps the greatest art historian of the nineteenth century, because he was the first in his field to point out the shift from the values of medieval society to the modern spirit of humanism and individuality.*

In this selection from The Civilization of the Renaissance in Italy, *Burckhardt discusses the role of exploration in Renaissance culture. He discusses how explorers brought new ideas to Italy from the places they visited. It was because the Italian people were so receptive to these new cultural and intellectual practices that Italy became the home of the Renaissance.*

Freed from the countless bonds which elsewhere in Europe checked progress, having reached a high degree of individual development and been schooled by the teachings of antiquity, the Italian mind now turned to the discovery of the outward universe, and to the representation of it in speech and form.

Jacob Burckhardt, *The Civilization of the Renaissance in Italy*. London: Phaidon Press Ltd., 1860.

Early Exploration and the Voyages of Columbus

On the journeys of the Italians to distant parts of the world, we can here make but a few general observations. The Crusades [religious wars of the Middle Ages] had opened unknown distances to the European mind, and awakened in all the passion for travel and adventure. It may be hard to indicate precisely the point where this passion allied itself with, or became the servant of, the thirst for knowledge; but it was in Italy that this was first and most completely the case. Even in the Crusades the interest of the Italians was wider than that of other nations, since they already were a naval power and had commercial relations with the East. From time immemorial the Mediterranean Sea had given to the nations that dwelt on its shores mental impulses different from those which governed the peoples of the North; and never, from the very structure of their character, could the Italians be adventurers in the sense which the word bore among the Teutons [Germanic people]. After they were once at home in all the eastern harbours of the Mediterranean, it was natural that the most enterprising among them should be led to join that vast international movement of the Mohammedans [Muslims] which there found its outlet. A new half of the world lay, as it were, freshly discovered before them. Or, like [Marco] Polo of Venice, they were caught in the current of the Mongolian peoples, and carried on to the steps of the throne of the Great [Kublai] Khan. At an early period, we find Italians sharing in the discoveries made in the Atlantic Ocean; it was the Genoese who, in the thirteenth century, found the Canary Islands [off the coast of northwest Africa]. In the same year, 1291, when Ptolemais [a town in upper Egypt], the last remnant of the Christian East, was lost, it was again the Genoese who made the first known attempt to find a sea-passage to the East Indies. Columbus himself is but the greatest of a long list of Italians who, in the service of the western nations, sailed into distant seas. The true discoverer, however, is not the man who first chances to stumble upon anything, but the man who finds what he has sought. Such a one alone stands in a link with the thoughts and interests of his predecessors, and this relationship will also determine the account he gives of his search. For which reason the Italians, although their claim to be the first comers on this or that shore may be disputed, will yet retain their title to be pre-eminently the nation of discoverers for the whole latter part of the Middle Ages. The fuller proof of this assertion belongs to the special history of discoveries. Yet ever and again we turn with admiration to the august figure of the great Genoese, by whom a new continent beyond the ocean was demanded, sought and found; and who was the first to be able to say: 'il mondo è poco'—the world is not so large as men have thought. . . .

Science Helps Exploration

The development of geographical and allied sciences among the Italians must, like the history of their voyages, be touched upon but very briefly. A superficial comparison of their achievements with those of other nations shows an early and striking superiority on their part. Where, in the middle of the fifteenth century, could be found, anywhere but in Italy, such a union of geographical, statistical, and historical knowledge as was found in Æneas Sylvius [also known as Pope Pius II]? Not only in his great geographical work, but in his letters and commentaries, he describes with equal mastery landscapes, cities, manners, industries and products, political conditions and constitutions, whereever he can use his own observation or the evidence of eye-witnesses. What he takes from books is naturally of less moment. Even the short sketch of that valley in the Tyrolese [eastern] Alps where [Holy Roman Emperor] Frederick III had given him a benefice, and still more his description of Scotland, leaves untouched none of the relations of human life, and displays a power and method of unbiased observation and comparison impossible in any but a countryman of Columbus, trained in the school of the ancients. Thousands saw and, in part, knew what he did, but they felt no impulse to draw a picture of it, and were unconscious that the world desired such pictures.

In geography as in other matters, it is vain to attempt to distinguish how much is to be attributed to the study of the ancients, and how much to the special genius of the Italians. They saw and treated the things of this world from an objective point of view, even before they were familiar with ancient literature, partly because they were themselves a half-ancient people, and partly because their political circumstances predisposed them to it; but they would not so rapidly have attained to such perfection had not the old geographers shown them the way. The influence of the existing Italian geographies on the spirit and tendencies of the travellers and discoverers was also inestimable. . . .

Natural Science in Italy

The dispute as to the priority of particular discoveries concerns us all the less, since we hold that, at any time, and among any civilized people, a man may appear who, starting with very scanty preparation, is driven by an irresistible impulse into the path of scientific investigation, and through his native gifts achieves the most astonishing success. Such men were [mathematician] Gerbert of Rheims and [English philosopher and scientist] Roger Bacon. That they were masters of the whole knowledge of the age in their several departments was a natural consequence of the spirit in which they worked. When once the veil of illusion was torn asunder, when once the dread of nature and the slavery to books and tradition were overcome, countless problems lay before them for solution. It is another matter when a whole people takes a natural delight in the study and investigation of nature, at a time when other nations are indifferent, that is to say, when the discoverer is not threatened or wholly ignored, but can count on the friendly support of congenial spirits. That this was the case in Italy is unquestionable. The Italian students of nature trace with pride in the 'Divine Comedy' the hints and proofs of [poet] Dante's scientific interest in nature. On his claim to priority in this or that discovery or reference, we must leave the men of science to decide; but every layman must be struck by the wealth of his observations on the external world, shown merely in his picture and comparisons. He, more than any other modern poet, takes them from reality, whether in nature or human life, and uses them never as mere ornament, but in order to give the reader the fullest and most adequate sense of his meaning. It is in astronomy that he appears chiefly as a scientific specialist, though it must not be forgotten that many astronomical allusions in his great poem, which now appear to us learned, must then have been intelligible to the general reader. Dante, learning apart, appeals to a popular knowledge of the heavens, which the Italians of his day, from the mere fact that they were a nautical people, had in common with the ancients. This knowledge of the rising and setting of the constellations has been rendered superfluous to the modern world by calendars and clocks, and with it has gone whatever interest in astronomy the people may once have had. Nowadays, with our schools and handbooks, every child knows—what Dante did not know—that the earth moves round the sun; but the interest once taken in the subject itself has given place, except in the case of astronomical specialists, to the most absolute indifference.

Astrology, Science, and the Church

The pseudo-science which dealt with the stars proves nothing against the inductive spirit of the Italians of that day. That spirit was but crossed, and at times overcome, by the passionate desire to penetrate the future.

The Church treated this and other pseudo-sciences nearly always with toleration; and showed itself actually hostile even to genuine science only when a charge of heresy together with necromancy [sorcery] was also in question—which certainly was often the case. A point which it would be interesting to decide is this: whether and in what cases the Dominican (and also the Franciscan) [Catholic] Inquisitors in Italy were conscious of the falsehood of the charges, and yet condemned the accused, either to oblige some enemy of the prisoner or from hatred to natural science, and particularly to experiments. The latter doubtless occurred, but it is not easy to prove the fact. What helped to cause such persecutions in the North, namely, the opposition made to the innovators by the upholders of the received official, scholastic system of nature, was of little or no weight in Italy. [Physician and philosopher] Pietro of Abano, at the beginning of the fourteenth century, is well known to have fallen a victim to the envy of another physician, who accused him before the Inquisition of heresy and magic; and something of the same kind may have happened in the case of his Paduan contemporary, Giovannino Sanguinacci, who was known as an innovator in medical practice. He escaped, however, with banishment. Nor must it be forgotten that the inquisitorial power of the Dominicans was exercised less uniformly in Italy than in the North. Tyrants and free cities in the fourteenth century treated the clergy at times with such sovereign contempt that very different matters from natural science went unpunished. But when, with the fifteenth century, antiquity became the leading power in Italy, the breach it made in the old system was turned to account by every branch of secular science. Humanism, nevertheless, attracted to itself the best strength of the nation, and thereby, no doubt, did injury to the inductive investigation of nature. Here and there the Inquisition suddenly started into life, and punished or burned physicians as blasphemers or magicians. In such cases it is hard to discover what was the true motive underlying the condemnation. But even so, Italy, at the close of the fifteenth century, with Paolo Toscanelli, Luca Pacioli and Leonardo da Vinci, held incomparably the highest place among European nations in mathematics and the natural sciences, and the learned men of every country, even [astronomer] Regiomontanus and [Polish astronomer Nicolaus] Copernicus, confessed themselves its pupils. This glory survived the Counterreformation, and even today the Italians would occupy the first place in this respect if circumstances had not made it impossible for the greatest minds to devote themselves to tranquil research.

Plant and Animal Studies

A significant proof of the widespread interest in natural history is found in the zeal which showed itself at an early period for the collection and comparative study of plants and animals. Italy claims to be the first creator of botanical gardens, though possibly they may have served a chiefly practical end, and the claim to priority may be itself disputed. It is of far greater importance that princes and wealthy men, in laying out their pleasure-gardens, instinctively made a point of collecting the greatest possible number of different plants in all their species and varieties. . . . This is evidently something very different from the score or two of familiar medicinal plants which were to be found in the garden of any castle or monastery in Western Europe. Along with a careful cultivation of fruit for the purposes of the table, we find an interest in the plant for its own sake, on account of the pleasure it gives to the eye. We learn from the history of art at how late a period this passion for botanical collections was laid aside, and gave place to what was considered the picturesque style of landscape-gardening.

The collections, too, of foreign animals not only gratified curiosity, but served also the higher purposes of observation. The facility of transport from the southern and eastern harbours of the Mediterranean, and the mildness of the Italian climate, made it practicable to buy the largest animals of the south, or to accept them as presents from the Sultans [Muslim kings]. The cities and princes were especially anxious to keep live lions, even where a lion was not, as in Florence [in central Italy], the emblem of the State. The lions' den was generally in or near the government palace, as in Perugia [in central Italy] and Florence; in Rome, it lay on the slope of the Capitol. The beasts sometimes served as executioners of political judgements, and no doubt, apart from this, they kept alive a certain terror in the popular mind. Their condition was also held to be ominous of good or evil. . . .

By the end of the fifteenth century, however, true menageries [zoos] (serragli), now reckoned part of the suitable appointments of a court, were kept by many of the princes. 'It belongs to the position of the great,' says [historian Graziani] Matarazzo, 'to keep horses, dogs, mules, falcons, and other birds, court-jesters, singers, and foreign animals.' The menagerie at Naples, in the time of Ferrante, contained even a giraffe and a zebra, presented, it seems, by the ruler of Baghdad [now in Iraq]. Filippo Maria Visconti [ruler of Milan] possessed not only horses which cost him each 500 or 1,000 pieces of gold, and valuable English dogs, but a number of leopards brought from all parts of the East; the expense of his hunting-birds, which were collected from the countries of Northern Europe, amounted to 3,000 pieces of gold a month. King Emanuel the Great of Portugal knew well what he was about when he presented Leo X with an elephant and a rhinoceros. It was under such circumstances that the foundations of a scientific zoology and botany were laid.

The Holy League Fights France

By Francesco Guicciardini

Francesco Guicciardini was born in Florence in March 1483. He came from a distinguished family that supported the famous Medici ruling family of that city-state. As he grew up and became involved in politics, Guicciardini witnessed instability and violence both within the city and outside as the governments of city-states changed hands and foreign nations tried to exert their own influence on Italian politics. He devoted the last three years of his life—from 1537 to 1540—to writing a book that he called The History of Italy.

In this selection from his book, Guicciardini discusses the frequent invasions Italy faced because of its disorganization and weakness. To try to strengthen Italy's defenses, Pope Julius II set up a Holy League in 1511 as an attempt to keep foreigners—or barbarians, as the Italians called them—away from the peninsula. The pope was able to secure the cooperation of other nations, including Spain and England, both of which hoped to limit the expanding power of France.

Together, the troops of the Holy League fought the French at a battle near Ravenna, in northern Italy, on Easter Sunday, April 11, 1512. Although the French ultimately defeated the Holy League, France's military suffered significant losses in the battle, which cost ten thousand lives.

Not all of Italy's territories took part in the Holy League's war to drive out the French. The city-state of Florence was among those remaining neutral. By that time, the Medicis had been driven from Florence by the people, who demanded popular rule. Under the new system, the city-state was ruled by a group under the leadership of an officer called a gonfaloniere. *After the war, the pope forced the city-state to allow the Medici family to return. Because the people had already demonstrated how much they disliked the Medici rulers, the family's return was meant to be a punishment for Florence's refusal to support the Holy League.*

Francesco Guicciardini, *The History of Italy*, translated and edited by Sidney Alexander. Princeton, NJ: Princeton University Press, 1984. Copyright © 1969 by Sidney Alexander. Reproduced by permission.

This [Holy] League made by the Pope for the purpose of liberating Italy from the barbarians aroused various interpretations in the minds of men, according to the diversity of their passions and their judgments. Many, beguiled by the magnificence and splendor of the title of the League, extolled up to the very heaven with the highest praises so lofty an aim, declaring that it was truly a statement of purpose worthy of the pontifical majesty, and that [Pope] Julius' greatness could not have taken upon itself a more generous enterprise, and that his wisdom was no less than his magnanimity, since by his efforts, he had set the armies of the barbarians against each other. Whence, shedding more foreign than Italian blood against the French, not only would spare our blood, but once one of the enemies had been expelled, it would be much easier for Italian armies to expel the others which would be already weakened and enervated.

Concerns About the Holy League

But others, perhaps considering the substance of things more deeply, nor allowing their eyes to be dazzled by the League's splendid title, feared that wars begun with the intention of driving the barbarians out of Italy would cause much more harm to the vital spirits of that body than those which had begun with the avowed purpose and resolute retention of subjugating it; and that it was more rash than wise to hope that Italian arms—lacking in skill, discipline, captains of authority and reputation; its princes devoid of common purpose or will—would be sufficient to drive the victor out of Italy. For when all other remedies might fail him, the conqueror could always fall back on the possibility of joining with the conquered to the common ruination of all Italy. Hence, there was much more to fear that these new military agitations might provide other nations with an opportunity to pillage Italy, rather than to hope that the union of the Pope and the Venetians would be likely to subdue [invaders] . . .

But the Pope, who felt otherwise, his spirits roused to greater ardor and inflamed all the more by the new confederation he had formed . . . declared that the cardinals of Santa Croce, of San Malò, of Cosenza, and of Bayeux were stripped of the dignity of the purple and had incurred all those penalties to which heretics and schismatics were subject. Besides this, he published an admonition of the same form against the Cardinal of San Severino, whom he had not threatened up to that time; and with the same violence he proceeded to plan for his war, continually calling for the coming of the Spaniards, and having more than anything else in mind a desire to launch a war against the Florentines, re-establishing the government in the hands of the Medici [who had been driven into exile], and no less to satisfy his boundless hatred against Piero Soderini, the gonfaloniere [leader of Florence], whom he felt was responsible for the fact that the Florentines had never wished to break away from the King of France . . .

Opponents of the League

[The French King] hoped that his army would conquer all or parts of the Romagna [a district of northern Italy] before the Spaniards approached; and then his forces would either march far-ther as opportunities offered themselves, or sustain the war in the territories of others until the spring. At that time, he would per-sonally cross into Italy with all the forces of his kingdom, hope-ful that his army would prove superior to the enemy in every way. While these matters were being planned, the deliberations . . . proceeded more slowly than perhaps they should have, given the circumstances; and the King [was] unwilling to lay up great supplies and especially to enlist new footsoldiers because he was instinctively loathe to spend money . . .

England Supports the League

At that time the war planned by . . . King [Henry VIII] of En-gland [against France] was already beginning to make itself man-ifest, although that King had earlier specifically denied it and then beclouded his intentions with uncertainties. Nevertheless, the true and very different nature of the facts could no longer be con-cealed. For the news came from Rome that King Henry's ratifi-cation of the League had finally arrived by a long maritime route; and it was known that men and ships were being mobi-lized, and that in Spain an armada was being rigged to sail to En-gland [to join them] and that the minds of all peoples were en-flamed to make war against France . . .

And now it leaked out that it had been secretly agreed that the King of England with his maritime forces should attack the coasts of Normandy and Brittany [in France], and that he should send eight thousand footsoldiers into Spain to join the armies of the King of Aragon and make war against the duchy of Guyenne.

The King of France was greatly afflicted by this suspected action, because knowing how fearful his people were of the English, remembering their ancient wars, he realized that their danger was all the greater now that Spanish armies were joined with those of England; and particularly because he had sent all his men-at-arms, except two hundred lances, into Italy, and if he summoned back either all or part of them, the duchy of Milan, which he prized so much, would be left in manifest danger. . . .

The Battle of Ravenna

[T]he air resounded with the sound of trumpets and drums and the joyful exclamations of the entire army, as the French began to move toward the enemy camp, less than two miles away from the place where they had crossed the stream. The armies of the Holy League were stretched out along the riverbank to their left [at Ravenna, in northern Italy], in front of which they had dug as deep a ditch as they could in the brief time available. Winding clockwise, this trench encircled the entire camp, except for a space of about twenty cubits which they had left open in front of the ditch so that the cavalry could ride out for skirmishing. As soon as they heard the French begin to cross the river, the armies of the League placed themselves in the following battle-order: the vanguard of eight hundred men-at-arms led by Fabrizio Colonna was disposed along the riverbank, with a squadron of six thousand footsoldiers joined with them on the right. Behind the vanguard, also along the river, was the main body of six hundred lances, flanked by a squadron of four thousand footsoldiers, led by the Viceroy [of Naples, Raimondo de Cardona] together with the Marquis della Palude. The Cardinal de' Medici was also part of this army, although he was naturally very weak-sighted and mild mannered. The Cardinal wore no battle dress and was, both in demeanor and behavior, utterly unlike the Cardinal of San Severino. Also along the riverbank, following the main forces, was the rear guard of four hundred men-at-arms, led by Carvajal, a Spanish captain; alongside them was a squadron of four thousand footsoldiers, and the light cavalry whose captain-general was Fernando Davalos, Marquis of Pescara, still very young but one of whom great things were expected. His forces were posted to the right, back of the footsoldiers, as reinforcements wherever they were needed. The artillery were planted in front of the men-at-arms; and Pedro Navarro, who with five hundred chosen footsoldiers, was not assigned to any particular post, had drawn up along the ditch in front of the infantry, thirty wagons similar to the scythed war chariots of the ancients, loaded with small artillery pieces and with a very long spear on top, in order to more easily bear the brunt of the French assault. In this order they stood firm-ranked within the stronghold of the ditch waiting for the enemy attack: and just as this disposition of forces did not prove successful at the end, similarly, it seemed very harmful at the beginning. For Fabrizio Colonna had advised them to charge the enemy when he began to cross the stream, judging the advantage of engaging in combat with only part of the enemy to be greater than that of having a little ditch in front of them. But Pedro Navarro disagreed, and since his counsels were accepted almost like oracles by the Viceroy, it was very un-wisely agreed to permit the enemy to cross.

Therefore, the Frenchmen kept coming on and were already about two hundred cubits [300 feet; 91.44 meters] from the trench; but when they saw that their enemies were standing firm and didn't want to issue forth out of their position, the French halted in order not to give them that advantage which they sought to have. Thus both armies remained motionless for more than two hours, the artillery shooting from both sides all this time; the French infantry, especially, suffered not a little from this exchange of fire, since Navarro had planted his artillery pieces very effectively. But the Duke of Ferrara, who had been hauling part of the artillery behind the army, quickly brought it up and had it emplaced at the point in the French battle-order where the archers were disposed; and since the army had been arrayed in a crescent, this point was almost at the shoulders of the enemy when they now began to batter furiously along the flank. The cavalry of the League especially suffered great losses from this at-tack, but the Spanish footsoldiers could not be struck, because, at Navarro's orders, they had been withdrawn to a low-lying spot along the riverbank and ordered to stretch out flat upon the ground. Fabrizio cried aloud and sent many messengers, impor-tuning the Viceroy to enter into the battle without waiting un-til they were all destroyed by artillery fire. But Navarro was op-posed, motivated by his perverse ambition, for he presupposed that even though all the others should perish, he would emerge victorious because of the valor of his Spanish footsoldiers, be-lieving that the more losses suffered by the army, the greater would be his glory. But the French artillery had already created such havoc among the men-at-arms and light horse that they could hold out no longer. And now there was a most miserable spectacle: horrible cries, and soldiers and horses falling dead to the ground, and heads and arms sundered from the rest of the body, flying up into the air. . . .

[A]t Ravenna everyone was intermingled in the battle which was being fought in a flat countryside without any impediments of waters or shelter which might hinder the action, or any place to take cover. Here two armies fought stubbornly for victory or death, enflamed not only by danger, glory and hope but also by the hatred of nation against nation. And it was a memorable spectacle, when in the encounter of the German and Spanish footsoldiers, two very famous captains, Jakob Empser, a German, and Zamudio, a Spaniard, marched out in front of their squadrons and fought almost as if it were a duel, the Spaniard emerging victorious, killing his enemy. Ordinarily the cavalry of the League were not equal to the French cavalry, and since their ranks had been so decimated and torn that day by the enemy artillery, they had become even more inferior; therefore, since they had stood off the enemy attack for some time, with stout hearts rather than by strength of arms . . . and now that Fabrizio Colonna had already been captured by the soldiers of the Duke of Ferrara while he was valorously fighting, the cavalry of the League could no longer hold out, and they turned their backs and fled. In this they were only following the example of their captains, because the Viceroy and Carvajal, without making a final test of the valor of their men, had already fled, taking almost the entire third squadron with them, as well as Antonio de Leva, a man at that time of very humble position, but who subsequently served in all ranks of the militia for many years and became a famous captain. All the light cavalry had already been routed, and their captain, the Marquis of Pescara, captured, all covered with blood and wounds. Also taken captive was the Marquis della Palude who had led the second squadron into battle with great disorder through a field full of ditches and briars. The terrain was strewn with dead men and horses; nevertheless, the Spanish infantry, abandoned by their cavalry, continued to fight with incredible ferocity; and although at the first encounter with the German footsoldiers, the Spaniards had been somewhat thrown by the firm and close order of the pikes, later coming to swords' point, many of the Spaniards, protected by their shields, had stabbed their way with daggers amidst the legs of the Germans, and managed to penetrate with very great slaughter almost to the center of the squadron. Near them, the Gascon footsoldiers, having occupied the space between the river and the bank, had assailed the Italian infantry who, although artillery fire had raked their ranks, nevertheless would have repulsed them to their great honor had not Yves d'Allègre with a company of horsemen thrust in amongst them with greater valor than fortune. For almost immediately Yves saw his son Nivarais slaughtered before his very eyes, and not wishing to live after so doleful a loss, hurled himself with his horse amidst the thickest swirl of the enemy, where fighting as a great captain should, and after slaying a great many, he was himself slain. The Italian footsoldiers gave way, not being able to hold out against so great a number, but part of the Spanish infantry, racing to their aid, kept them in the battle; and the German footsoldiers, being pressed on the other side by the Spaniards, could scarcely resist any longer. . . .

Nothing is more uncertain than the number of those dying in a battle; nevertheless, among the various opinions, the most common was that both armies counted at least ten thousand men dead, one-third of the French and two-thirds of their enemies; others say the figures are much greater, but undoubtedly almost all of the most valorous and choicest soldiers; among the ecclesiastical forces, Raffaello de' Pazzi, a famous condottiere, was killed; and a great many men wounded. . . .

The victorious [French] army having returned to their camp, the people of Ravenna immediately sent representatives to offer up their surrender; but either while they were meeting or had already met, and were waiting to order provisions to be sent to the camp, they neglected to maintain their vigilance in guarding the walls, and German and Gascon footsoldiers entered through the breach in the wall which had been broken down to the ground and cruelly sacked the town; incited to the greatest cruelties because of their fury at the loss which they had received during that day, as well as by their natural hatred against the Italians. . . .

The soldiers . . . were involved in distributing and dispatching to safe places the goods which they had plundered; and so weakened and dispirited were they by the victory which they had won with such expenditure of blood, that they seemed more like the conquered than the conquerors.

Political Advice for Lorenzo de Medici

By Niccolò Machiavelli

Niccolò Machiavelli was born in 1469 in the city of Florence. As he grew up, he was a witness to the flourishing Renaissance as well as the violence and intrigue of Italian politics. Machiavelli served in several government positions in which he had the opportunity to observe up close how the state and the church ran their affairs. In 1504, he spent several months in France on a diplomatic mission. There, he saw how efficiently the French king was able to control the political dealings of his nation, compared to the disorganized leaders of Italy.

In 1513, Machiavelli took the knowledge he had gained from his years in politics and diplomacy and wrote The Prince, *from which the following selection is taken. The book was written as a set of suggestions for Lorenzo de Medici, a powerful Italian ruler, to help him keep his influence.*

Today many people criticize The Prince, *objecting to its political philosophy that "the end justifies the means." For example, Machiavelli holds up Pope Julius II, who ruled from 1503 to 1513, as an example of an effective leader. Without worrying about the possible response of foreign nations, and without trying to make diplomatic agreements to create peaceful international relations, Julius made Italy more powerful with the wars he carried out quickly and with ferocious force. In his admiration of Julius, Machiavelli shows that fear is often a leader's best weapon.*

Because of such passages, The Prince *is sometimes considered an immoral work that advocates violence and corrupt political tactics. However, Machiavelli wrote it when Italy was being subjected to invasions by foreign powers; the country was desperate to find a way to avoid being conquered. In* The Prince, *Machiavelli tried to create a plan to do just that.*

A new prince is far more closely observed in his activities than is a hereditary prince; and when his deeds are recognized as skillful they attract men much more and bind

Niccolò Machiavelli, *The Prince*, 1513.

111

them to him more strongly than does ancient blood. For men are much more taken by present concerns than by those of the past; and when they find the present good they enjoy it and seek nothing more; in fact, they will seize every measure to defend the new prince as long as he is not lacking in his other responsibilities. And thus he will have a double glory: that of having given birth to a new principality and of having decorated it and strengthened it with good laws, good arms, and good examples; as that one will have double shame who, having been born a prince, loses his principality on account of his lack of prudence.

Why Italian Rulers Failed

And if one will consider those rulers in Italy that have lost their states in our times, such as the King of Naples, the Duke of Milan, and others, one will discover in them, first, a common defect insofar as arms are concerned . . . and then, one will see that some of them either will have had the people as their enemy or, if they have had the people as their friend, they will not have known how to secure themselves against the nobles; for without these defects states are not lost which have enough nerve to take an army into battle. . . .

Therefore, these princes of ours who have been in their principalities for many years, and who have then lost them, must not blame Fortune but instead their own idleness: for, never having thought in peaceful times that things might change (which is a common defect in men, not to consider in good weather the possibility of a tempest), when adverse times finally arrived they thought about running away and not about defending themselves; and they hoped that the people, after having been angered by the insolence of the victors, would recall them. This policy, when others are lacking, is good; but it is indeed bad to have disregarded all other solutions for this one; for you should never wish to fall, believing that you will find someone else to pick you up; because whether this occurs or not, it does not increase your security, that method being a cowardly defense and one not dependent upon your own resources. And only those defenses are good, certain, and lasting that depend on yourself and on your own ability.

Fortune's Role in Politics

It is not unknown to me that many have held, and still hold, the opinion that the things of this world are, in a manner, controlled by Fortune and by God, that men with their wisdom cannot control them, and, on the contrary, that men can have no remedy whatsoever for them; and for this reason they might judge that they need not sweat much over such matters but let them be governed by fate. This opinion has been more strongly held in our own times because of the great variation of affairs that has been observed and that is being observed every day which is beyond human conjecture. Sometimes, as I think about these things, I am inclined to their opinion to a certain extent. Nevertheless, in order that our free will not be extinguished, I judge it to be true that Fortune is the arbiter of one half of our actions, but that she still leaves the control of the other half, or almost that, to us. And I compare her to one of those ruinous rivers that, when they become enraged, flood the plains, tear down the trees and buildings, taking up earth from one spot and placing it upon another; everyone flees from them, everyone yields to their onslaught, unable to oppose them in any way. And although they are of such a nature, it does not follow that when the weather is calm we cannot take precautions with embankments and dikes, so that when they rise up again either the waters will be channeled off or their impetus will not be either so disastrous or so damaging. The same things happen where Fortune is concerned: she shows her force where there is no organized strength to resist her; and she directs her impact there where she knows that dikes and embankments are not constructed to hold her. And if you will consider Italy, the seat of these changes and the nation which has set them in motion, you will see a country without embankments and without a single bastion: for if she were defended by the necessary forces, like Germany, Spain, and France, either this flood would not have produced the great changes that it has or it would not have come upon us at all. And this I consider enough to say about Fortune in general terms.

Why Some Rulers Succeed and Others Fail

But, limiting myself more to particulars, I say that one sees a prince prosper today and come to ruin tomorrow without having seen him change his character or any of his traits. I believe that this comes about, first, because of the reasons that have been discussed at length earlier; that is, that a prince who relies completely upon Fortune will come to ruin as soon as she changes; I also believe that the man who adapts his course of action to the nature of the times will succeed and, likewise, that the man who sets his course of action out of tune with the times will come to grief. For one can observe that men, in the affairs which lead them to the end that they seek—that is, glory and wealth—proceed there in different ways; one by caution, another with impetuousness; one through violence, another with guile; one with patience, another with its opposite; and each one by these various means can attain his goals. And we also see, in the case of two cautious men, that one reaches his goal while the other does not; and, likewise, two men equally succeed using two different means, one being cautious and the other impetuous: this arises from nothing else than the nature of the times that either suit or do not suit their course of action. From this results that which I have said, that two men, working in opposite ways, can produce the same outcome; and of two men working in the same fashion one achieves his goal and the other does not. On this also depends the variation of what is good; for, if a man governs himself with caution and patience, and the times and conditions are turning in such a way that his policy is a good one, he will prosper; but if the times and conditions change, he will be ruined because he does not change his method of procedure. Nor is there to be found a man so prudent that he knows how to adapt himself to this, both because he cannot deviate from that to which he is by nature inclined and also because he cannot be persuaded to depart from a path, having always prospered by following it. And therefore the cautious man, when it is time to act impetuously, does not know how to do so, and he is ruined; but if he had changed his conduct with the times, Fortune would not have changed.

Rulers and Their Styles

Pope Julius II [who ruled from 1503 to 1513] acted impetuously in all his affairs; and he found the times and conditions so apt to this course of action that he always achieved successful results. Consider the first campaign he waged against Bologna [in northern Italy]. . . . The Venetians were unhappy about it; so was the King of Spain; Julius still had negotiations going on about it with France; and nevertheless, he started personally on this expedition with his usual ferocity and lack of caution. Such a move kept Spain and the Venetians at bay, the latter out of fear and the former out of a desire to regain the entire Kingdom of Naples; and at the same time it drew the King of France into the affair, for when the king saw that the Pope had already made this move, he judged that he could not deny him the use of his troops without obviously harming him, since he wanted his friendship in order to defeat the Venetians. And therefore Julius achieved with his impetuous action what no other pontiff would ever have achieved with the greatest of human wisdom; for, if he had waited to leave Rome with agreements settled and things in order, as any other pontiff might have done, he would never have succeeded, because the King of France would have found a thousand excuses and the others would have aroused in him a thousand fears. I wish to leave unmentioned his other deeds, which were all similar and which were all successful. . . .

The Terrible State of Italian Politics

Considering, therefore, all of the things mentioned above, and thinking to myself about whether the times are suitable, at present, to honor a new prince in Italy, and if there is the material that might give a skillful and prudent prince the opportunity to form his own creation that would bring him honor and good to the people of Italy, it seems to me that so many circumstances are favorable to such a new prince that I know of no other time more appropriate. And if . . . it was necessary that the people of Israel be slaves in Egypt in order to recognize Moses' ability, and it was necessary that the Persians be oppressed by the Medes to recognize the greatness of spirit in Cyrus, and it was necessary that the Athenians be dispersed to realize the excellence of Theseus, then, likewise, at the present time, in order to recognize the ability of an Italian spirit, it was necessary that Italy be reduced to her present condition and that she be more enslaved than the Hebrews, more servile than the Persians, more scattered than the Athenians; without a leader, without organization, beaten, despoiled, ripped apart, overrun, and prey to every sort of catastrophe.

And even though before now some glimmer of light may have shown itself in a single individual, so that it was possible to believe that God had ordained him for Italy's redemption, nevertheless it was witnessed afterward how at the height of his career he was rejected by Fortune. So now Italy remains without life and awaits the man who can heal her wounds and put an end to the plundering of Lombardy, the ransoms in the Kingdom of Naples and in Tuscany, and who can cure her of those sores which have been festering for so long. Look how she [Italy] now prays to God to send someone to redeem her from these barbaric cruelties and insolence; see her still ready and willing to follow a banner, provided that there be someone to raise it up. Nor is there anyone in sight, at present, in whom she can have more hope than in your illustrious house [the Medici family], which, with its fortune and ability, favored by God and by the Church, of which it is now prince, could make itself the head of this redemption. This will not be very difficult if you keep before you the deeds and the lives of those named above. And although those men were out of the ordinary and marvelous, they were nevertheless men; and each of them had less opportunity than the present one; for their enterprises were no more just, nor easier, nor was God more a friend to them than to you. Here justice is great: "Only those wars that are necessary are just, and arms are sacred when there is no hope except through arms." Here there is a great willingness; and where there is a great willingness there cannot be great difficulty, if only you will use the institutions of those men I have proposed as your target. Besides this, we now see extraordinary, unprecedented signs brought about by God: . . . everything has converged for your greatness. The rest you must do yourself. God does not wish to do everything, in order not to take from us our free will and that part of the glory which is ours.

The Strengths and Weaknesses of Italy

And it is no surprise if some of the Italians mentioned previously were not capable of doing what it is hoped may be done by your illustrious house, and if, during the many revolutions in Italy and the many campaigns of war, it always seems that her military ability is spent. This results from the fact that her ancient institutions were not good and that there was no one who knew how to discover new ones; and no other thing brings a new man on the rise such honor as the new laws and the new institutions discovered by him. These things, when they are well founded and have in themselves a certain greatness, make him revered and admirable. And in Italy there is no lack of material to be given a form: here there is great ability in her members, were it not for the lack of it in her leaders. Consider how in duels and skirmishes involving just a few men the Italians are superior in strength, dexterity, and cunning; but when it comes to armies they do not match others. And all this comes from the weakness of her leaders; for those who know are not followed; and with each one seeming to know, there has not been to the present day anyone who has known how to set himself above the others, either because of ingenuity or fortune, so that others might yield to him. As a consequence, during so much time and many wars fought over the past twenty years, whenever there has been an army made up completely of Italians it has always made a poor showing. . . .

Encouragement for the Possible Leader

Therefore, if your illustrious house desires to follow these excellent men who redeemed their lands, it is necessary before all else, as a true basis for every undertaking, to provide yourself with your own native troops, for one cannot have either more faithful, more loyal, or better troops. And although each one separately may be brave, all of them united will become even braver when they find themselves commanded, honored, and well treated by their own prince. It is necessary, therefore, to prepare yourself with such troops as these, so that with Italian strength you will be able to defend yourself from foreigners. And although Swiss and Spanish infantry may be reputed terrifying, nevertheless both have defects, so that a third army could not only oppose them but be confident of defeating them. For the Spanish cannot withstand cavalry and the Swiss have a fear of foot soldiers they meet in combat who are as brave as they are. . . . As the defects of both these kinds of troops are recognized, a new type can be instituted which can stand up to cavalry and will have no fear of foot soldiers: this will come about by creating new armies and changing battle formations. And these are among those matters that, when newly organized, give reputation and greatness to a new prince.

This opportunity, therefore, must not be permitted to pass by so that Italy, after so long a time, may behold its redeemer. Nor can I express with what love he will be received in all those provinces that have suffered through these foreign floods; with what thirst for revenge, with what obstinate loyalty, with what compassion, with what tears! What doors will be closed to him? Which people will deny him obedience? What jealousy could oppose him? What Italian would deny him homage? This barbarian dominion stinks to everyone! Therefore, may your illustrious house take up this mission with that spirit and with that hope in which just undertakings are begun; so that under your banner this country may be ennobled and, under your guidance, those words of [the poet] Petrarch may come true:

Discipline over rage
Will take up arms; and the battle will be short.
For ancient valor
In Italian hearts is not yet dead.

THE HISTORY OF NATIONS
Chapter 4

Italy in Transition: The Seventeenth and Eighteenth Centuries

Italy in the Face of Foreign Domination

By Giuliano Procacci

Through the years of the Renaissance, Italy was the center of art and culture. Still, it had remained under the domination of foreign nations. By the end of the sixteenth century, however, the balance of power in Europe was shifting. Nation-states were forming, and the people of Italy, on the fringe of activity, envisioned autonomy from Spain.

Over the next century, Italy remained outside the power struggles of the more organized nations with stronger militaries. By the start of the seventeenth century, Spain and its rival European nations were losing power. Because Italy played no real role in the wars that occupied the rest of Europe, it was able to retain the little power it had.

Author Giuliano Procacci is a professor of modern history who has taught at the University of Caligari and the University of Florence. He has written several books on Italy that focus on the Renaissance and post-Renaissance periods. In this selection, he shows how Italy's noncompetitiveness as a world power was, in some ways, helpful during the seventeenth and eighteenth centuries, because it gave Italy time to make the transition from a dominated territory to a nation at the forefront of intellectual change.

Towards the end of the sixteenth century, . . . the international situation had changed and there were signs that Spain's prestige had begun to decline. [A] rebellion of the Dutch provinces was followed by the resounding defeat of the Invincible [Spanish] Armada, and this by the accession of [French king] Henri IV, and France's dramatic return to its position as antagonist of the Habsburgs [ruling family] of Madrid and Vienna.

Giuliano Procacci, *History of the Italian People*, translated by Anthony Paul. New York: Harper & Row, 1968. Copyright © 1968 by Librairie Artheme Fayard. English translation copyright © 1970 by George Weidenfeld and Nicolson, Ltd. Reproduced by permission of HarperCollins Publishers and George Weidenfeld and Nicolson, Ltd.

Some Italian princes took advantage of the new situation by trying to loosen the bonds of subjection and protectorate that bound them to Spain, and to win back a wider margin of autonomy and political initiative. When Ferdinando de'Medici negotiated the marriage of his daughter Maria with Henri IV, and sought to persuade Clement VIII to recognize the new King of France, he showed clearly that, as far as the circumstances and the Spanish domination of Italy allowed him, he was keen to resume the traditional line of friendship with France that the Florentine Republic had followed. Carlo Emanuele I of Savoy [in southeastern France, on the Italian border] went further, and in 1610 formed a league with Henri IV, committing himself to a joint attack on Lombardy [in northern Italy]; but this plan was frustrated by the French King's unexpected death. . . .

The Thirty Years War

By this stage the international picture had again altered: Henri IV's death had meant a shrinking of France's counter-balancing presence, and now the accession of Ferdinand II, a pupil of the Jesuits, to the Viennese throne marked the resurgence of the militant Counter-Reformation, and the start of the Thirty Years War.

The first stage of this conflict was favourable to the Habsburgs, in Italy as elsewhere. Spain's domination of the key position of the Valtellina both assured the connection of Lombardy with the Habsburg territories of Austria, and completed Venice's geographic isolation. Her resistance, helped once again by Carlo Emanuele I and by France, could not alter the situation; also in vain were Savoy's attempts, encouraged by conspiracies within the city, to gain control of Genoa, most pro-Spanish of Italian cities.

Even the vicissitudes of the Thirty Years War—the general pattern being one of French counter-offensive until the victorious peace of Westphalia [that ended the war in 1648]—brought about no significant changes in the political and territorial arrangement of the [Italian] peninsula, except in Savoyard Piedmont [in southeastern France and northwestern Italy], which had joined the Habsburg camp, and found itself in consequence invaded by the armies of [the French general] Richelieu and for many years reduced practically to the status of a French protectorate. The anti-Spanish revolts of Sicily and Naples were . . . repressed; and at the date of the treaty of Westphalia Italy still lay mainly within the orbit of Spain's influence. But by that time

Spain was no longer a great power, and so, as far as the Italian states were concerned, the disadvantages of political dependence or semi-dependence were not even balanced by the advantages of an effective protectorate. Little by little, during the second half of the century, the decline of the Spanish Empire became more and more evident, and Italy came to the notice of the new rising political star of Europe, the France of Louis XIV . . .

The Pope and Italy

The Papacy's . . . loss of authority as an international arbitrator, and the eclipse of its prestige serve better than anything to symbolize and summarize the marginal rôle Italy was reduced to in the new Europe of the nation-states. None of the protests raised by Pope Innocent X against the religious clauses of the Treaty of Westphalia was taken into consideration by the European powers, while in the second half of the century no one was very surprised to see Louis XIV laying down the law to the conclaves. In his *Siècle de Louis XIV* [French writer and philosopher] Voltaire wrote: 'Certain rights, many claims, a political tradition, a little patience: that is all that today remains to Rome of ancient power, who six centuries ago wished to subjugate the Empire and Europe . . .'

Anti-Spanish Revolts

Of all the Spanish dominions in Italy, the South was the one that had to contribute most massively to the Spanish monarchy's financial effort during the exhausting Thirty Years War. If Milan was the kingdom's rampart and as such felt the consequences of war directly, on her own soil, Naples had to pay for the privilege of having the war far from her own frontiers, by providing as many soldiers and as much money as she could. This was a constant rule of Spanish policy and of its great strategist of the moment, the Duke of Olivares. It was applied thoroughly. Raids were organized in the southern countryside, to procure the troops needed by the Habsburg armies. The men collected in this way were taken often in chains, to the ports of embarkation and to the fronts of Germany, the Valtellina, Flanders [on the coast of what is now Belgium and France]. But even more than men, the Spanish monarchy needed cash—enormous amounts of cash. This also it succeeded in procuring. According to the reliable accounts of a banker of Genoese descent, Cornelio Spinola, war contributions absorbed every year the enormous sum of three and a half million ducats; in only the first year and a half of his viceroyalty, the Duke of Medina managed to put together seven million ducats. Of these '*asistencias*' a considerable part was taken north to Milan, and thus constituted a clear loss for the southern economy.

To obtain the sums it needed, the central power naturally turned to the weapon of taxation, and wielded it vigorously. Between 1636 and 1644, ten new indirect taxes were imposed, and many extraordinary contributions were demanded. But little by little, as the number of heavy taxes grew, the amount collected by each one diminished. In an economic situation characterized, as we have seen, by a lasting stagnation of productive activity, there was in fact a limit to the contributive capacity of the kingdom, beyond which it was not possible to go. In these conditions the viceroy had no other way but to find private bankers ready for a financial operation with great risks attached to it, but with the incentive of possible profits of a highly speculative nature. . . .

[S]o long as they were able to face Madrid's financial demands, the Spanish viceroys who succeeded one another between 1620 and 1648 were willing to dispose of that part of sovereignty that was within their competence, and to put up for auction, to the profit of a privileged few, the state machine itself. So when taxation was at its highest, [Spain's] central organization was at its lowest: the severest oppression coincided with the greatest disorder. A further worsening of the situation, and disorganization and disorder would have become anarchy.

There had been previous warning signs of this tendency. In certain of the more turbulent and quarrelsome sectors of the nobility there flourished again the traditional spirit of dissidence, which had emerged in the familiar forms of aristocratic conspiracy . . . and of political flirtations with France, sworn enemy of Spain and the Habsburgs and protectress for many years of the southern baronial opposition. But these attempts were fairly easily repressed or absorbed: however bitterly some of the nobility might resent the current promotion of parvenus, the baronage in general had profited widely from the circumstances and speculations of the moment, and had indeed won large prizes in the lottery of rights, favours and concessions to which the state had been forced.

But from 1646 on, events moved faster, and control of the situation increasingly escaped the Spanish government. The viceroy, on the verge of bankruptcy, was compelled to arrest [former

merchant Bartolomeo] D'Aquino, attempting to make him a
scapegoat to general indignation. The manoeuvre only partially
succeeded, and a little later the same viceroy, realizing the extreme
precariousness of the situation, submitted his resignation. His successor found himself facing a situation that was by now explosive. On 17 July 1647, following the imposition of a new tax on
fruit, the people of Naples came out into the streets. From the
capital the insurrection spread into the provinces; and so began
what may be considered the most notable of the few revolutionary episodes of Italian history.

As always happens in upheavals of any magnitude, the forces
and interests set in motion were various, and their aims did not
always coincide. First were the common people of the capital,
with their improvised captains and tribunes, their desperate but
inconclusive radicalism, their anger and confusion. Then there
were the middle-class citizenry, with their more considered political aims and direction. To begin with, under the influence of
the aged Giulio Genoino, in his day counsellor of the Duke of
Ossuna, this class aimed at a 'reform of the kingdom' in a popular, anti-baronial sense; on this basis they were prepared to reach
a compromise with Spain. But Madrid's intransigence and the
consequent aggravation of the situation persuaded them, under
the leadership of the armourer Gennaro Annese, to take up pro-
gressively more extreme positions, culminating in the proclamation of a Republic in October. Another element was the diplomatic involvement of Mazarin's France, for whom the rebellion
was no more than one incident and front in the far wider anti-
Spanish struggle. Finally, linked with French policy, were the ill-
judged efforts of Duke Henry of Guise. After the proclamation
of the Republic, he arrived at Naples, and managed to get himself recognized as 'Duke' of the Republic itself. But his unexpected overtures to the baronage and his amateurism soon lessened his ephemeral popularity, and contributed to the loss of
direction and final defeat of the revolutionary camp. In August
1648 the Spanish, under the command of John of Austria, managed to regain control of Naples and snuff out the rebellion.

The Barons and the Peasants

There was . . . an extremely complex interweaving and interaction of forces. But it becomes simpler when one looks at the two
extremes of the forces and social classes involved in the struggle:

on the one hand the baronage, which had abandoned every whim of opposition and ranked itself solidly in defence of the king and its own privileges, and on the other, the antifeudal peasant movement in the provinces. These—barons and peasants—were the motive 'wings' of the opposed ranks of conservatism and revolt, and it was their frontal conflict that in the last analysis largely determined the outcome of the struggle.

This was most bitter. The peasants, drawn up and led by survivors of the battlefields of the Thirty Years War, gave proof both of their desperation and of their determination to fight and win. It was not merely a *jacquerie* [a peasants' revolt], but also a peasant war. Country and town were conquered, entire provinces put under peasant control, and the baronial military contingents defeated in many battles and skirmishes. . . . The dismay that these successes aroused among the barons appears clearly in the words of the most powerful and terrible of them, the Count of Conversano. *'Yo esto desperado'* ['I am desperate'] he wrote in January 1648, *'estamos perdidos'* ['we are lost']. But in the end, after the defeat of the revolt in Naples, even the peasant guerrillas had to submit, and the machine of feudal repression was able to move into action. The revenge was frightful and pitiless. Intended as a deterrent, it was determined to demonstrate that nothing had changed and nothing could change. And in fact that is how it was to be . . .

Italy and Europe

On the whole the political arrangement and internal frontiers of Italy had remained unchanged for almost a hundred and fifty years, and the irksome guardianship of Spain had kept the ambitions and initiative of particular states on a close rein. The French domination of Europe in the later seventeenth century had the same effect. . . . After the treaty of Cherasco in 1631, Piedmont, the most dynamic and warlike of Italian states, had been reduced to little more than a French protectorate.

This situation changed radically in the early years of the eighteenth century. The War of the Spanish Succession of 1700–13 reduced Spain to the rank of a secondary power, and put a constraint on the ambitions of France under Louis XIV: the doors of Italy were once again open to the play of widely-varied forces. . . . Italy's mosaic of little states and faded dynasties deprived of power made it a favourite field of action for the diplomacy of the great powers in their incessant work of adjusting and balancing the interests of various states. If any power had to make concessions, or if its candidate for this or that European throne was defeated by the candidate of some other power, there was always an Italian duchy or state in which the defeated candidate could be lodged. So there was hardly any international conflict, from the War of the Spanish Succession to those for the Polish and Austrian successions [1701–1713 and 1740–1748], which did not bring about some change in the political arrangement of Italy. Within a few decades, some Italian states passed several times from one master to another. Sicily, for example, passed from the house of Savoy to Austria, and then to the Bourbons of Naples, all between 1714 and 1734, while the duchy of Parma, where the Farnese dynasty expired in 1731, was held by the Bourbons, then by Austria and then by the Bourbons again, between 1734 and 1748. . . . [A]t the date of the treaty of Aquisgrana (1748), which concluded the War of the Austrian Succession, most of the Italian states were ruled by a different nation or dynasty from that which had ruled them at the beginning of the century. The state of Milan had passed from Spanish to Austrian rule; Mantua had lost its independence and had also been absorbed into Austrian Lombardy; Parma, formerly ruled by the Farnese family, was under the Bourbons; at Florence the Medici dynasty had expired in 1737, and the city was a Lorraine seigniory; Sicily and the Kingdom of Naples, after two hundred years of Spanish rule, had won back independence, under the Bourbons; and Sardinia no longer belonged to Spain, but to the house of Savoy. . . .

But the new dynasties and boundaries, and the changes these brought about in the power-relation of various states, were not the most important result of the upheavals Italy was subjected to in the first half of the eighteenth century, nor was even the shrinking of the area under foreign rule, now reduced to Lombardy. What mattered most was that the isolation and provincialism in which Spanish rule had kept Italy for two hundred years was now at an end. The new rulers of Florence, Naples and Parma may have been foreigners to the lands they had been assigned, but for this very reason they were a good deal more European and less provincial than the old ruling houses. As for the Austrian administrators of Lombardy, they were, as we shall see, infinitely abler and more modern in outlook than the previous Spanish rulers and viceroys. It is no accident that the Italian states that display the most vitality in this period are Austrian Lombardy and the other states ruled by new foreign dynasties. The others, such as Venice, Genoa, Piedmont and the Papal State, which kept their old rulers and systems, continued, to a greater or lesser extent, to decline, in provincial isolation.

But during the eighteenth century Italy was not merely brought politically further into the Europe of the age of balance and of family pacts; it was also economically integrated into a market at the centre of all the main trade-currents of the time. . . .

In this way Italy strengthened her economic bonds with Europe: her ports and Alpine coach-routes brought her firmly within the European circuit. But what must be particularly emphasized is that Italy became reintegrated within the European economy at a time when that economy was going through one of its most exuberant phases of expansion. The eighteenth century was of course the time of the 'agrarian revolution', which transformed wide areas of the European countryside, and it was also the eve of the great English industrial revolution. . . .

This was the Europe of which Italy was every day a more essential part, and this the prosperity she benefited from.

Italy and the French Revolution

By Raymond Grew

*In the early 1790s, Italy faced a crisis. The French Revolution, which be-
gan in July 1789, had grown radical and dangerous as the French citizenry seized power, executed their king, and installed a legislative government. As they looked on, Italy and the rest of Europe became
alarmed. France seemed intent on spreading its ideals to the rest of the
continent—by force, if necessary. European nations prepared to fight to
stop the French.*

*Italy, however, was still a loose group of independent kingdoms and
territories. It would have little chance to fight back if the French tried to
invade. Soon, Italy's fears were realized. Napoléon Bonaparte, a French
general who eventually rose to lead France as its emperor, marched his
troops into Italy and easily brought its territories under his control.*

*In this selection, Raymond Grew, a professor of history at the Univer-
sity of Michigan and the author of several books on European history
and culture, describes how Italy's people came together under Napoleonic
rule to help create a new sociopolitical system for their country, despite the
unwanted French invasion. Along with some of the competent leaders selected by Napoléon, Italians made some beneficial reforms, such as the establishment of new schools, public works programs, and improved trans-
portation. Although Italians gradually became hostile toward the French
occupation, Grew argues that the experience they gained in their united
political efforts during this time helped pave the way for later movements
that would demand freedom and independence for all of Italy.*

O n the whole, Italy received the [invading] French with
remarkable warmth in 1796; the elites of northern Italy
set about immediately, and enthusiastically, to write
constitutions for the Cispadane [south of the Po River] and
Cisalpine [on the south side of the Alps] republics. Their ener-

Raymond Grew, "Finding the Social Capital: The French Revolution in Italy,"
The Journal of Interdisciplinary History, vol. 29, Winter 1999, pp. 407–15. Copyright
© 1999 by Massachusetts Institute of Technology. Reproduced by permission.

getic participation in creating new political structures and re-
forming civil society spread with surprising ease (and French
arms) to Rome where the effort to establish civil authorities independent of church or aristocracy was widely welcomed—and
then to Naples, even if the republic there lasted only six months.
Subsequently, despite the dampening effect of Napoleonic rule,
the constrictions that accompanied continual warfare, and the exactions required to support it, the new institutions took root in
their Napoleonic forms so strongly that across the peninsula, the
restoration governments of 1815 kept the administrative, judicial,
military, fiscal, and educational systems that the French had introduced and Italians were operating. The lasting social effects of
this vast political and social transformation were essential to Italy's
Risorgimento [movement for unity] in the next century. A case
can be made that no European society outside France more readily accepted, or was more permanently affected by, the French
Revolution and Napoleon. . . .

Government and Civic Spirit

Italian governments had a long tradition of using public works,
especially monumental buildings, to appeal to civic pride and represent a beneficent regime. This use of culture may also have
helped to drown out issues of liberty or public policy, but the social and political significance of official culture could change. In
the sixteenth and seventeenth centuries, the governments of Italy
were nearly all more or less new and more or less imposed by
outside force. Their assertions of legitimacy—in statues, coins,
ceremonies, and rhetoric—thus made heavy use of symbols of
state that evoked memory and culture. In a regime still justifying
itself, the Tuscan grand duke could be credited with having
brought "all the sciences and arts [once again] to take up residence" in Florence. On a larger scale, Italy could be declared "the
most beautiful part of the world. It has the greatest number of
villages, towns, and cities with the greatest abundance of inhabitants; and its inhabitants are valorous [brave] and prudent in the
letters and arts, excellent in architecture, sculpture and painting
as well; trained and learned in the other liberal arts, diligent and
expert in agriculture."

Such praise from fawning clients at the turn of the sixteenth
century tended to become a call to civic spirit and national pride
at the turn of the eighteenth. By then, the colonades of the Uf-

fizi palace, which had stood empty for nearly three centuries, had been lined with statues of the great men of Florentine history, mainly artists and intellectuals, and the cathedrals of Milan and Florence at last got marble facades over their bare bricks, according to designs chosen in public competitions. Such works—examples of which were numerous throughout Italy on the eve of the French Revolution—now served a different purpose. They were not so much acts of patronage or praiseworthy proclamations of official values as conscious attempts by governments to appeal to a civic spirit that was assumed to be present already. . . .

Social Customs and Institutions

Social practice firmly rooted in Italian culture also facilitated Italy's adaptation to the new ways brought by the French. Multiple governments meant that Italy already had multiple bureaucracies, and Italy's many cities added another layer of governance, as well as sociability. So did its hierarchical church, which had bishops in every town of note, its own courts where permitted, and scores of religious orders. The point is not that these institutions operated efficiently but merely that they existed, literally training thousands and thousands of functionaries. In addition, Italy's many universities produced an unusually large number of lawyers, the majority of whom found employment in offices and courts that relied on a heavy and awkward proceduralism. Thousands of Italians were experienced in how to make legal formulae fit immediate pressures, how to collect data, and how to keep records. Many of them would take with ease to a more open political system that preserved, and even enhanced, their status, while increasing the importance and effectiveness of what they did.

Italian institutions sustained a great many consultative bodies, for Italy's old regime was full of talk. Everywhere residues remained of former parliaments and councils, and everywhere (but especially in Naples) constitutional treatises were a favorite genre, spelling out the importance of the law and of different forms of representation, attaching the principles of a strong legal tradition to memories of different regimes and the great revolt of 1647–1648. In eighteenth-century Naples, as [historian Benedetto] Croce noted, "Life in the law courts represented what, in different conditions in other times, was political life, because [that is where] issues between church and state, between holders of feudal rights and civil society were argued out and the new arrangements devised that advances in public economy and related theories made necessary." These traditions would show their value as social capital in the ease as well as the enthusiasm with which new constitutions were written once the French armies arrived. . . .

The Rise of a Civic Society

By the eighteenth-century, Italian society had nurtured a strong public sphere of talk and festivals, cafes and theaters, academies and newspapers, despite limited public politics. Nevertheless, the interest in law and in talk sustained a lively civic sense that, starting with local pride and familiar ritual, could be extended to a vision of civic education and a transformed civil society.

The looseness of the connection between reform and a vibrant urban life of promenades, parades, cafes, and ceremonies did not undermine the belief that they went together. In 1796, a famous competition offered a prize for the best treatise on the form of government most suitable for Lombardy. The winning essay declared that a good constitution would foster a society in which the rich and the poor mixed in balls, theaters, and festivals, and public ceremonies in piazzas and theaters would instill a sense of communal purpose. The Neapolitan constitution of 1799 called for theaters, national festivals, and public schools to provide civic training. In effect, statements about social capital, these programs—so attentive to custom and civic virtue—continued to avoid questions of power or social conflict.

This rising commitment to civic values is evident in the funerary [burial] inscriptions lining the walls of even the smallest Italian churches and cloisters. Previously in Latin, by the eighteenth century these inscriptions were more often written in lapidary [elegant] Italian. Miniature lessons in emulation, they listed not merely the honorable offices that a prominent figure had held but also the civic virtues that he had displayed while holding them. Similar values would later echo from the public platforms of every revolutionary republic (and be repeated throughout the Risorgimento). In a world of face-to-face relations, such commitments could be compelling as a basis for institutional reform. Antonio Genovesi, an eighteenth-century Neapolitan intellectual much admired in France, as well as Italy, for his concrete and detailed proposals for economic reform, built his philosophy around fede pubblica [public trust]. When one of Grand Duke Peter Leopold's councillors restated the case for granting Tuscany a constitution, he talked about civic freedom (onesta liberta civile). Vincenzo Cuoco, now remembered as the most penetrating critic of the [French] Revolution in Naples' naive adoption of French abstractions, held throughout his life to the idea of "liberta civile" that he had absorbed from eighteenth-century writers.

Such was the cultural capital available to those who supported revolution in Italy at the end of the eighteenth century—a conviction that an Italian culture existed despite the absence of a national state; belief in a glorious past; the political and public importance of high culture; active engagement with Enlightenment thought; a strong legal tradition with many lawyers; multiple administrations and bureaucracies; academies and gazettes at the heart of intellectual and social networks that reached across the peninsula; theaters and festivals where people of all classes encountered each other; and piazzas where townspeople occasionally performed civic or religious rituals, frequently met to discuss public affairs, and sometimes demonstrated their views to those in power.

Italy Embraces Revolution

Revolutionary events in France evoked a good deal of spontaneous enthusiasm in much of Italy from 1790 onward, including significant conspiratorial activity after 1794. In 1794–1795, there were revolutionary attempts in Piedmont, Bologna, Palermo, and Sardinia, frightening governments everywhere. In the sclerotic [rigid] old republic of Lucca, fear of the dynamic new one in France increased as word spread of changes occurring as nearby as Corsica. Authorities hastened to arrest Vincenzo Gherardi, an artisan, for declaring that a universal judgment that would make everyone equal was imminent. From 1796 to 1799, a distinctive Italian Jacobinism [radical revolutionary philosophy], mild by French standards, came to the fore, as revolutionary regimes were established under French aegis [protection].

The Italian experience of revolution was different from that of the French. Revolutionary ideology in Italy only rarely and briefly developed with the autonomous momentum and open contestation of Girondins and Jacobins [political parties in France]. Italians experienced much of France's revolutionary program, after Thermidor [the period when extremists led France] and in a different environment, without the violent tensions from which it had grown. The revolution in Italy was less insistently anticlerical (in Tuscany, especially, Jansenist priests were prominent among supporters of the revolution), sustained no systematic Reign of Terror [as had France], and was less divisive and less violent than its French model, making it easier for many Italians to hold a rather positive view of revolution as a way to effect change.

Diluted by distance, the Italian revolutions occurred in the presence of French armies that prevented the opponents of revolution from effectively fighting back (another reason for limited violence). Because the Italian revolutions remained closely tied to French arms, they occurred in two distinct phases. In the first, French forces were welcomed by support that had been bubbling up before their arrival. This period, which began with considerable excitement and spontaneity, was notable for the rapid spread of revolutionary symbols and rhetoric, the writing of constitutions, and the effective establishment of a new style of government. Disillusionment followed before long, however, as the French authorities revealed themselves to be much more concerned with their military strength and with extracting money and men from Italy than with fostering democracy. This initial phase, which ended in 1799 when allied armies drove the French from the peninsula, lasted from about three years in Lombardy to only a few months in most of Italy. . . .

Italy Under French Rule

The second phase of Italy's experience of the French Revolution was very different. This was revolution as reshaped by Napoleon's increasingly conservative policies. Institutionally and socially still a major transformation, it took place in a regime of order rather than radical democracy. Once again, the French were generally welcomed but now in the name of stability, and with the realization that exactions under the restored regimes had been no less great and repression much more brutal than under the French. . . . Before 1800, the conflict between radicals and moderates had been a critical problem for republicans everywhere, and that split may have been the principal reason for the short life of the republic established in Naples. Now, there was no room for radicals; and the issue that had divided Neapolitan republicans most sharply, the abolition of feudalism, was resolved by its elimination under [French general and king of Naples] Joachim Murat. The Neapolitan middle class at least found that the Napoleonic regimes suited them very well. . . .

The People See Benefits in French Rule

Official French declarations and the proclamations and constitutions written by Italians regularly referred to the "nation" while preserving the term's useful ambiguity. Recourse to the nation meant opposition to old privileges of church and aristocracy, and it meant the inclusion of the people in political affairs—a basis for legitimacy that remained radical even under the Napoleonic empire. It also meant efficient administration of the commonweal. Territorially, it could apply to the Cisalpine Republic, Tuscany, the Two Sicilies, or the whole peninsula (with an elasticity much like that in earlier discussions of Italian culture). In reality, revolution unleashed municipal patriotism, perhaps the strongest political loyalty of all in Italy. The restiveness—of Modena against Bologna; Arezzo, Siena, and Pisa against Florence; Vicenza and Padua against Venice; and the provinces and cities of the mezzogiorno against Naples—was a crucial dynamic in the replacement of the old regimes. Italians had many reasons for rallying to the tricolor [symbol of the French Revolution] and welcoming common measures, coins, and tariffs.

That Italian and French officials readily acknowledged the continuity between the new institutions and laws and those created, or at least described, in earlier reform programs undoubtedly helped to win the participation of a significant proportion of the ablest administrators and magistrates from the old regimes. Many Milanese nobles accepted public office and fought in the Napoleonic armies. The priest who had served as the Bourbon [French royal] regime's chief censor became the minister of the interior of the revolutionary republican government (and was tortured and executed when it fell). One of ablest officials of the Bourbon government, long an advocate of reform, ended up serving under the Napoleonic governments. [Vincenzo] Cuoco, who criticized the revolution in Naples as "passive" and its republic for failing to build a popular base, nevertheless went north after the fall of the Neapolitan republic to become editor of the *Giornale Italiano* [*Italian Journal*], published in Milan under Napoleon.

New Governments Are Formed

Even when their authority was circumscribed, a remarkable number of men of capacity and standing were willing to serve the new governments. In the spring of 1799, the French belatedly called for the establishment of municipal councils in eleven Tuscan towns. Although these councils had little power (their main responsibility was the formation of a national guard), prominent local lawyers, professors, doctors, and cultural figures sat in them alongside a few students, members of the clergy, and even some nobles. In a place like commercial Prato, where the revolution had been warmly received, a new political class of entrepreneurs, forged in these years, would lead the city into the Risorgimento.

These are the sorts of people who spent months writing detailed constitutions, and in their affectionate descriptions of electoral procedures and their confident consignment of decision making to parliament, one can sense the eagerness of authors who imagined themselves on the rostrums that they were creating. They believed in the importance of the new chairs in constitutional law established at the universities of Bologna, Pavia, and Ferrara in 1797–1798, and they were equally serious about instructing the people.

All of the new constitutions stressed education, and scores of patriotic societies took it upon themselves to instruct ordinary citizens on civic responsibility. In Florence, the society "of true friends of the patria" convened at the Accademia degli Armonici in Florence and agreed to meet every evening in order to educate the public, carefully changing moderators every ten days. The society, which published a monthly bulletin of public instruction, enjoyed important connections. Some of its leaders were clergymen, and it developed ties to older societies like the Georgofili. The Circolo d'Istruzione pubblica in Livorno met three times a week. The doctors and professors who formed a similar group in Siena added attention to charitable activities as well. The scores of newly founded newspapers declared that they fulfilled a similar responsibility. Theaters, which had flourished in the old regime, especially in Milan under [Austrian archduchess] Maria Theresa, reached a new peak after the revolution and continued to thrive under Napoleon (although Milan's Teatro Patriottico changed its name to the more generic Teatro dei Filodrammatici).

Propaganda and Ceremony

Revolutions, almost by definition, know how to make propaganda, and serious commitment is unmistakable in the symbol-laden letterheads printed for the newly established offices of government. The woodcuts of the period cannot be taken as what actually happened; but if the scenes of people from all classes (including clergy) cheering the entry of French soldiers into a city and celebrating around liberty trees seem too good to be true, they do capture the revolutionaries' pedagogical [educational] seriousness and their sense of theater in public spaces. The depictions of golden books of nobility discarded, of noble escutcheons [coats of arms] crumbling, and of figures from commedia dell'arte suffering. . . all speak to the ways in which the revolution connected with Italian society and culture.

In this sense, the triumphal arches, liberty trees, and symbols of aristocracy shattered deserve to be taken seriously, whatever proportion of public opinion they are thought to represent. As liberty trees were planted in the central squares of cities and towns, the accompanying rituals—speeches by prominant citizens, including priests; bands playing; and dancing—were familiar social capital with which to baptize a new order.

The revolutionaries continued something of the old ceremonial system, with public rites in assigned spaces, but celebrating revolutionary holidays, both French and local. These ceremonies underscored important changes: Old hierarchies were not maintained, and the aristocracy was largely absent from public affairs; the clergy were present to lend legitimacy to these occasions but were not their sponsors. Officials appeared less ex officio [lacking real authority] and more as representatives. These ceremonies remained visible expressions of community, but more a political act and less simply a matter of social custom. Whereas the old regime demonstrated power and hierarchy, while leaving decision making behind closed doors, the revolutionary governments intended their ceremonies to give the impression that power had a popular base and that political decisions were arrived at through public procedures.

The People's Role in Politics

These changes enlarged opportunities for the expression of opinion (including distrust and disagreement), and they gave greater and more explicit meaning to participation. Piazzas and markets were the natural sites for popular political expression, whether spontaneous or planned (radicals believed that the nobles used market days to mobilize their sharecroppers against the republic). As political activity became more familiar and associational networks spread, patriots used shops, cafes, and pharmacies as sites for mobilizing support. Once in power, they would tend to seek more institutional, public settings.

The revolutionary experience widened the political horizon in terms of the issues addressed and the vocabulary used. Following the example from France, the governments established in Italy gave new incentives for certain kinds of activity and associations, provided rules within which civil society could function, and stimulated more focused public activities. Local interests and conflicts became more directly tied to national politics, broadening engagement in political life. As the government reached more deeply and more directly into society, the state became the focus of expectations and resentments that gave politics greater immediacy and significance. The networks, associations, exchanges, and collective action that constitute social capital increased with the stimulus of revolutionary activity, gaining importance as more and more issues and interests became politically charged. These activities expanded further with the opportunities provided by the institutions and policies of the revolutionary regimes, despite the restrictions on political freedom.

Italy in the Wake of Napoléon

By John A. Davis

*John A. Davis is a historian at the University of Connecticut. In this se-
lection, he explores how the defeat of Napoléon Bonaparte effected dramatic change in Italy and the rest of Europe.*

*After the French Revolution turned violent in the early 1790s,
Napoléon gradually seized power and made himself the emperor of
France. To increase his domain, he used his formidable military to force
other nations—including Italy—to become part of his expanding empire.
Eventually, the nations of Europe united to fight Napoléon, hoping to
overthrow him and reorganize Europe on their own terms. Through a
long series of conflicts that came to be called the Napoléonic Wars, the allied forces of Europe finally defeated Napoléon at the Battle of Waterloo
in Belgium in 1815.*

*With Napoléon's removal from power, it was left to the allies to deter-
mine the future for the places that had been swallowed up by the French
empire. For the most part, Italy's status as a disorganized group of territories that had long been under the sway of more powerful nations did
not change. Most of Italy was returned to the Austrians, who had claimed
it just before Napoléon's invasions began.*

*Although Italy underwent no dramatic political change following
Napoléon's defeat, the event did have a significant effect on the people.
The principles of freedom that had led to the French Revolution caused
many Italians—and the people of other European nations as well—to
take the idea of popular rule more seriously than even before. It was an
appealing concept. In fact, as Davis demonstrates, Italy's experience with
popular rule under the French—in theory if not in practice—inspired
several attempted revolutions in the decades after the fall of Napoléon.
Over time, this revolutionary spirit would help launch a broader movement for unification and independence in Italy.*

John A. Davis, "The Age of Risorgimento," *The Oxford History of Italy*, edited by
George Holmes. New York: Oxford University Press, 1997. Copyright © 1997 by
Oxford University Press. Reproduced by permission.

The Revolution in France in 1789 marked the start of a period of foreign occupation, political upheaval and revolution in the Italian states that lasted until a unified and independent Italian monarchy was created in the mid-nineteenth century. The changes precipitated by the Revolution were to play a major part in this process, most obviously because they brought about the rapid collapse of the *ancien régime* [old political order] principalities in Italy: by the time that Napoleon's Empire finally unravelled, every Italian state had been remodelled in some degree along lines originating from the Revolution. When the Italian rulers returned from exile in 1814, they found themselves masters of centralized and autocratic states immeasurably more powerful than the limited *ancien régime* monarchies they had abandoned.

Political Struggles

The old order had been changed, but not effectively replaced. Along with new forms of autocratic government, the Revolution had also given new force to ideas of political democracy and representative government. From this dual legacy came the struggles between autocracy and liberalism that dominated political life in Italy in the decades that followed (Italy was the theatre for major revolutions and insurrections in 1820–1, 1831, 1848–9) and which were only resolved through the process of political unification that resulted in the creation of a single constitutional monarchy in Italy under Victor Emanuel II of Savoy.

In that respect, the political struggles in Italy in these years were part of a more general process of political change in Europe. But in Italy they took a particular form because political change was inseparable from independence. For two decades after the Revolution, the political destinies of the Italian states were governed by France. Then in 1814 the Congress of Vienna made Austria the dominant power on the peninsula. [Austrian statesman] Prince [Klemens] Metternich's famous claim that Italy was "a mere geographical expression" could not disguise the fact that Vienna was the power behind every Italian throne and the unifying force behind the otherwise untidy mosaic of dynastic principalities. Political change was therefore inseparable from independence from Austria, providing Italian reformers of widely different political colours with a common enemy. . . .

The news of the fall of Napoleon's Empire had been received in the Italian states as a death foretold, and the principal concern of the propertied classes was to ensure a peaceful transfer of power and avoid the anarchy of the 1790s. This was also the policy of the Austrian government although it was not shared by all the Italian rulers, most notably Duke Francis IV (1815–46) of Modena who set out to delete every trace of the French occupation, and Victor Emanuel I of Savoy (1802–21) who revoked all French legislation in the subalpine territories of the kingdom of Sardinia and banished those like [Camillo Benso di] Cavour's family who had "rallied" to the French regime. In Rome, Pope Pius VII (1800–23) restored the Jesuits and the Inquisition and abolished toleration for Jews, although Cardinal Consalvi did attempt to maintain the impetus of administrative reform. In the duchy of Parma, on the other hand, the former empress of France, Maria Luisa of Austria (1815–47), retained French institutions, while in Tuscany the younger brother of the Emperor Francis, Archduke Ferdinand III (1790–1824), also looked for continuity. In Naples, Ferdinand IV (1815–25) only regained his throne after Joachim Murat had been defeated at the Battle of Tolentino (3 May 1815). Here, too, Prince Metternich was keen to avoid any repetition of the royalist purges of 1799 in Naples and ensured that extreme reactionaries like the Prince of Canosa were kept out of power. Initially at least, the Neapolitan Bourbons not only held out an olive-branch to the supporters of [Neapolitan Joachim] Murat's government and retained the majority of the French reforms, but through the creation of a new unified monarchy actually extended the reforms to Sicily as well. When in 1816 Ferdinand IV, king of Naples and Sicily, changed his title to Ferdinand I, king of the Two Sicilies, Sicily lost its centuries-old autonomy as a separate kingdom.

Revolution and Insurrection

Neither reconciliation nor reaction brought political peace, however, and in 1820 and 1821 Naples and Turin were both targets of revolution. The Italian revolutions took their cue from Spain, following an attempt early in 1820 to restore the Spanish constitution of 1812. Ominously for the Italian rulers, both revolts began in the armies. In Naples, an insurrection by a group of army officers in July 1820 quickly spread throughout southern Italy and forced Ferdinand I to concede a constitution. In Sicily, the leaders of the revolution in Palermo at once demanded the restoration of the island's autonomy that had been abolished in 1816.

The great landowners were the main force behind the revolution and their separatist demands quickly brought the Sicilian revolutions into conflict with the liberal government in Naples. On the mainland Mezzogiorno too (i.e. Italy south of Rome), the provincial notables also demanded greater autonomy from Naples.

Vienna was considering an appeal for help from Ferdinand of Naples when new insurrections broke out in Piedmont. The initiative again came from a group of army officers, some of whom were in contact with the king's cousin, the prince of Carignano (and later king), Charles Albert (1831–49). In March 1821 an insurrection that started in Alessandria spread to other Piedmontese cities. Victor Emanuel abdicated and his successor Charles Felix (1821–31) fled to Modena. Charles Albert made cryptic statements in support of the rebels, then changed his mind and also fled. But Charles Felix returned at the head of an Austrian army that defeated the liberals led by Santorre Santarosa in a brief engagement near Novara. By mid-April the revolution was over and for two decades Piedmont would be ruled by reaction and repression. Another Austrian army was despatched to Naples, where it brought the revolutions to an end and remained billeted for eight more years at the expense of the Neapolitans. . . .

New Revolutions

The Spanish rising of 1820 had triggered the Italian revolutions of 1820–1, and the July Revolution in Paris in 1830 was the cue for the next wave of insurrections in Italy. While visiting Rome in 1830, Louis-Napoleon (the future Napoleon III) had been in contact with certain members of the secret societies, and in the belief that Louis-Philippe's new government in France would give support, Ciro Menotti and Enrico Misley began planning an insurrection in Modena. In February 1831 the ringleaders, including Menotti, were arrested, though not before insurrections had spread from Modena to Bologna and other parts of central Italy. Pope Gregory XVI requested Austrian intervention, and although French support for the risings did not materialize, on the pretext of deterring a permanent occupation of the Papal States by the Austrians, the French government did send a detachment to Ancona. By the end of March, however, the Austrians had regained control and on 26 May Ciro Menotti and other conspirators joined the growing ranks of martyrs to the cause of independence.

Fears that the insurrections and France's intervention might drag the European powers into war resulted in an international conference. The British government was concerned that France seemed intent on regaining a foothold in Italy, and did not wish to see Austria's control over the region weakened. However, the British representatives also insisted that papal misgovernment was the real cause of political unrest in central Italy, and called on Vienna to use its influence to reform the papal administration.

Giuseppe Mazzini, Early Revolutionary

For Giuseppe Mazzini (1805–72), however, the insurrections in central Italy were further evidence of the need for a revolution that would sweep away the existing Italian rulers. While the revolutions showed the strength of support for Italian independence, Mazzini also blamed their failure on the inability of the secret societies to provide effective leadership. This was precisely what Mazzini wished to offer, and in his *Manifesto of Young Italy* in the previous year he had called on Italian revolutionaries to abandon secrecy and work openly for a single cause: the creation of a single Italian nation. Young Italy was founded in Marseilles on 14 August 1831, and Mazzini at once attempted to put his revolutionary ideas into practice. But his correspondence was intercepted (not for the last time), and in 1833 his associates in Turin, Chambéry, Alessandria, and Genoa were arrested by the Piedmontese police. All were tortured, a number were executed, and Mazzini was sentenced to death *in absentia* [in his absence]. Not deterred, he resumed planning an invasion of Savoy to coincide with a rising in Genoa (1834), which would have involved [revolutionary leader] Giuseppe Garibaldi (1807–82) had it materialized. When this plan too had failed, Mazzini left Switzerland for London in 1837.

After 1833 Mazzini was almost permanently in exile, and returned to Italy only in 1848–9 and in 1860. His followers in Italy were dogged by censorship and police harassment, although insurrections planned or inspired by Mazzini and Young Italy continued through the 1830s and 1840s and into the 1850s. But Mazzini's influence was also divisive. Young Italy had been set up to counter the influence of the secret societies, and in 1834 Mazzini quarrelled with Filippo Buonarroti (1781–1837), the leading champion of the French revolutionary tradition in Italy. . . .

The People Express Resentment

There was no opportunity for political dissent, but criticism of commercial policies did become more open. In Lombardy and Venetia, Vienna's preference for Trieste over Venice and Austrian commercial regulations that restricted access to other Italian states caused resentment, while the refusal of the Neapolitan government to relax its high protectionist tariffs brought it into conflict both with the southern landowners and with its principal trading partner, Great Britain. As a result, the principles of economic liberalism began to find support even amongst groups that had hitherto shown little interest in politics.

Among the professional classes, poor career opportunities were also an important cause of resentment. Opportunities for a career in the military were limited after the revolutions of 1820, while the [Catholic] Church had few attractive openings for educated men. Openings in law, medicine, architecture, civil engineering, accountancy, and agricultural and commercial services were growing, but not fast enough to keep up with demand. But the rulers were eager to limit the expansion of their bureaucracies and to restrict access to the professions. In Lombardy, for example, the Austrian government gave preference to Austrians and Hungarians in public employment and made entry more difficult for Italians by extending the length (and hence cost) of the university courses required for entry into public service. In Naples, university courses were available only in the capital where students were closely watched by the police and the government repeatedly refused requests that additional universities be established in the provinces.

For women, there were as yet no public careers that were considered respectable, and for the women of the emergent Italian middle classes opportunities for any kind of public career were if anything narrower than they had been for their aristocratic predecessors. The small number of women who featured in liberal circles were aristocrats, while amongst the middle classes women's education was generally confined to moral and spiritual training provided by nuns.

Middle-class resentments were less threatening than those of the rural populations, however. Commercial expansion and population growth combined to exacerbate [make worse] the desperate land-hunger of the rural poor, which was compounded by new legislation in the Kingdom of the Two Sicilies, the Kingdom of Sardinia, and Lombardy in the 1830s that extended the privatization of former feudal estates and village commons. The intervention of all these governments to accelerate the processes of privatization and commercialization in the agrarian economy, while still adhering to the anti-modernist ideological principles of the Restoration, revealed all too clearly the contradictions confronting the legitimist regimes. . . .

The Revolutions of 1848–1849

When it did come, the storm broke at the point most distant from Vienna. Rioting that started on 2 January in Palermo [in Sicily] during the processions in honour of the city's patron Santa Rosalia turned into the first of the European revolutions of 1848. On 29 January Ferdinand II granted a constitution in an attempt to prevent further disturbances and the other Italian rulers followed: Leopold of Tuscany on 17 February, Charles Albert on 4 March, and Pius IX on 14 March. In each case, the concessions were designed to buy off the opposition by granting limited voting rights to small groups of property-owners, but the flimsy conservative provisional governments immediately came under attack from more radical elements and from leaders ready to mobilize the discontents of urban workers and peasants.

Pressure for wider political reforms grew after the revolutions in Paris in February and, above all, in Vienna on 13 March. With Austria apparently on its knees and Prince Metternich in flight from the capital, the situation in Italy changed dramatically. In Venice, the Austrians withdrew and a moderate republican government headed by the lawyer Daniele Manin was established on 23 March. In Milan, however, the 81-year-old Austrian military commander Field Marshal Radetzky tried to hold firm and turned his artillery on one of the most densely populated working-class districts of the city. This barbarous attempt to shell Milan into submission provoked a popular rising which after five days of fierce street-fighting (18–22) forced Radetzky's army to withdraw.

The Piedmontese monarchy now entered the lists in an attempt to gain control over the nationalist movement. On 23 March Charles Albert's government declared war on Austria and a Piedmontese army entered Lombardy at the request of the Milanese moderates who feared that the democrats might seize power. Charles Albert's commitment to the struggle against Austria initially won the support of radicals like Carlo Cattaneo and

Mazzini, who had hurried to Milan from England. But when his government insisted on the speedy annexation of Lombardy, fears grew that Charles Albert's real concern was to increase the size of his own kingdom. The Lombard democrats mobilized against fusion with Piedmont, but Charles Albert's position was strengthened by votes in favour of annexation to Piedmont in Piacenza, Parma, Modena, and Reggio in May, followed by Lombardy and the Venetian provinces in June, and finally by Venice in July.

Cattaneo accused Charles Albert of gathering votes while Radetzky was collecting soldiers, and on 24 July the Piedmontese army was decisively defeated at the first Battle of Custoza. Charles Albert withdrew across the Ticino and sued for an armistice, while the Austrians occupied Milan, Modena, and Reggio Emilia. But even before Custoza, the Piedmontese monarchy's attempt to lead a national crusade against Austria had run into severe difficulties. On 29 April Pius IX denounced the war against Austria and shattered the conservative illusion that independence could be achieved in alliance with Rome. On 15 May Ferdinand of Naples staged a counter-revolution, suspended the Neapolitan parliament, and withdrew from the war against Austria.

After Custoza Mazzini proclaimed that the war of the princes would give way to the war of the people, and as the Austrian troops reoccupied Lombardy the radicals began to take power. In October a radical government led by Giuseppe Montanelli came to power in Florence, and in December Vincenzo Gioberti headed a government with radical sympathies in Turin. But most important of all, Pellegrino Rossi, the leader of the conservative provisional government in Rome, was murdered on 15 November; on the twenty-fourth, Pius IX and his cardinals fled to Gaeta and put themselves under the protection of Ferdinand of Naples. This gave the democrats their first real opportunity. Elections were held in January for a Constituent Assembly which met on 5 February and four days later proclaimed the Roman Republic. On the same day Leopold II fled from Tuscany and a provisional government headed by Giuseppe Montanelli and Francesco Domenico Guerrazzi called for the declaration of a republic and alliance with Rome and Venice. In early March Mazzini reached Rome and the Roman Republic voted for unification with Tuscany.

By now the Austrian counter-attack was imminent and Charles Albert made a final bid to regain the political initiative.

But the Piedmontese army was forced to surrender at Novara (23 March 1849), leaving the Austrians in command of northern and central Italy. Charles Albert abdicated and the armistice was signed by his son and successor, Victor Emanuel II (1849–78). But just as the Austrian victory at Custoza had floored the conservatives in 1848, the second Piedmontese defeat at Novara in 1849 now doomed the radicals. In Genoa they tried to reject the armistice, but the rebellion was put down by Piedmontese troops. The revolution collapsed in Tuscany too, and to avoid an Austrian invasion the moderates and conservatives invited Archduke Leopold to resume his throne (28 July). Only Rome and Venice

MAZZINI'S SPEECH ON NATIONALITY

Giuseppe Mazzini was one of Italy's earliest revolutionaries and advocates of unification. He believed it was critical for Italy to establish a democratic government if it were to grow both economically and culturally. In this excerpt from an 1852 speech, Mazzini discusses the role that nationality and revolution should play in the development of Italy and other European nations.

It was not for a material interest that the people of Vienna fought in 1848; in weakening the empire they could only lose power. It was not for an increase of wealth that the people of Lombardy fought in the same year; the Austrian Government had endeavoured in the year preceding to excite the peasants against the landed proprietors, as they had done in Gallicia [in Spain]; but everywhere they had failed. They struggled, they still struggle, as do Poland, Germany, and Hungary, for country and liberty; for a word inscribed upon a banner, proclaiming to the world that they also live, think, love, and labour for the benefit of all. They speak the same language, they bear about them the impress of consanguinity [close relation], they kneel beside the same tombs, they glory in the same tradition; and they demand to associate freely, without obstacles, without foreign domination, in order to elaborate and express their idea; to con-

were left. In Rome, the Republic delegated power to a triumvirate consisting of Giuseppe Mazzini, Carlo Armellini, and Aurelio Saffi, while Giuseppe Garibaldi took charge of the city's defence. Both Naples and France had sent armies to restore the pope, and in June General Oudinot's forces laid siege to Rome. The defence was organized by Garibaldi and lasted until early August, when he led a masterly retreat that enabled some 4,000 defenders to escape. In Venice, Manin also held out until August, even though the city was under constant bombardment, blockaded by the Austrian fleet, and suffering from cholera.

In the south the revolutions had followed a different pattern.

---

tribute their stone also to the great pyramid of history. It is something moral which they are seeking; and this moral something is in fact, even politically speaking, the most important question in the present state of things. It is the organisation of the European task. It is no longer the savage, hostile, quarrelsome nationality of two hundred years ago which is invoked by these peoples. The nationality . . . founded upon the following principle:—*Whichever people, by its superiority of strength, and by its geographical position, can do us an injury, is our natural enemy; whichever cannot do us an injury, but can by the amount of its force and by its position injure our enemy, is our natural ally,*—is the princely nationality of aristocracies or royal races. The nationality of the peoples has not these dangers; it can only be founded by a common effort and a common movement; sympathy and alliance will be its result. In principle, as in the ideas formerly laid down by the men influencing every national party, nationality ought only to be to humanity that which the division of labour is in a workshop—the recognised symbol of association; the assertion of the individuality of a human group called by its geographical position, its traditions, and its language, to fulfil a special function in the European work of civilisation.

Giuseppe Mazzini, "On Nationality, 1852," *Modern History Sourcebook*, http://www.fordham.edu.

After Ferdinand II's coup of 15 May the revolutions swept through the mainland provinces, but by the autumn had been crushed. In September a Neapolitan army disembarked at Messina to end the separatist revolt that had started in Palermo in April, and when Neapolitan forces entered Palermo in May 1849 the revolution in the south from which all the others had started was finally over.

After the Revolutions

In Italy, as in the rest of Europe, the revolutions ended in defeat for liberals and radicals alike, but brought about changes that were to prove irreversible. Hatred of Austria was even more intense and now was sanctified by new symbols of heroism and martyrdom. Most important of all, the struggle for independence had now acquired a new legitimacy through the participation of the Piedmontese monarchy.

Rather than uniting them around a common cause, the events of 1848–9 had also shown how deeply Italians were divided. As well as struggles between moderates and radicals, between urban reformers and rural unrest, the revolutions had also unleashed a spate of violent municipal rivalries. Indeed, it might seem that the struggles for greater municipal autonomy that set Genoa against Turin, the cities of the terra firma against Venice, Livorno against Florence, the Legation cities of Bologna and Ferrara against Rome, the provincial towns of the southern mainland against Naples, and Sicily against Naples were more important than the struggle against Austria. But these reflected more than petty local rivalries, and above all the strength of resentment to the centralization of power that had resulted from the French reforms. The demands for greater provincial and municipal autonomy were an essential element in the reform programme.

The revolutions had proved especially divisive for the radicals. The defeats of 1849 led to recriminations and Mazzini, in particular, came under increasing criticism. To the attacks levelled from the federalist camp by Cattaneo and Ferrari were now added those of the Neapolitan democrat Carlo Pisacane who blamed Mazzini for failing to address the grievances of the peasants, in his view the only revolutionary force in Italy. In place of Mazzini's endless and unsuccessful urban conspiracies (another would end in disaster in Milan in 1853), Pisacane proposed a programme of agrarian reform that would transform the struggle for national independence into a peasant guerrilla war similar to the Spanish War of Independence against Napoleon.

These arguments touched on one of the bitterest experiences of the revolutions for many radicals. In many parts of Italy the peasants had initially rallied to the revolutions, but once it became clear that neither the liberals nor the radicals had any intention of redressing their grievances rural Italy turned against them. In Lombardy, for example, some disillusioned peasants welcomed the returning Austrian armies in 1849, while in the Veneto, Tuscany, the Papal States, and the south rural unrest either shook off all political control or took a counter-revolutionary turn.

If the radicals had proved unprepared for these spontaneous outbursts of rural protest, the resulting violence and disorder caused many landowners in the Veneto, Lombardy, Tuscany, Emilia, Romagna, and Lazio to wait anxiously for the Austrians to restore order. The legitimist governments tried to exploit these fears by playing the card of law and order, and in the Austrian territories military tribunals meted out summary justice to peasants who had taken part in the revolutions in an atmosphere of judicial terror and reprisal. But this was no longer enough. The violence of the repression after 1849 left Italy increasingly out of line with other European states. [British statesman] William Gladstone's ringing denunciation of the appalling conditions in which Ferdinand of Naples had imprisoned the Neapolitan liberals was only one example of the ways in which Italian absolutism now struck European liberals as a perverse anachronism. Within Italy, the violence of the restoration did as much as the turmoil of the revolutions to persuade growing numbers of Italians that without independence there could be no political stability in Italy. But while the revolutions had dispelled the myth that independence could be achieved in alliance with the Papacy and without fighting Austria, they had also shown that the nationalist cause could be channelled towards conservative political ends.

This was why the establishment of a constitutional monarchy in one of the oldest and most conservative principalities in Italy proved to be the most fundamental and decisive change brought about by the revolutions. The endorsement of the nationalist cause by the House of Savoy turned the struggle against Austria from a subversive and revolutionary cause into a conservative but progressive one. After 1849 Piedmont's constitutional monarchy stood as an open affront to every other Italian ruler, making Turin a haven for nationalists, liberals, and democrats from all over Italy. If the revolutions left the radicals divided, they had given the moderate nationalists a new sense of solidarity and purpose. Victor Emanuel II's proclamation of 20 November 1849 from the castle of Moncalieri in which he undertook to preserve the constitution, providing that the new parliament in Turin ratified the armistice with Austria, laid the basis for a programme around which the expansionist ambitions of the House of Savoy and the political aspirations of the Italian liberals could converge.

THE HISTORY OF NATIONS
Chapter 5

From Unification to Fascism

Risorgimento: Italy's Drive for Unification

By Denis Mack Smith

Even though Italy's history stretches back to ancient times, there really was no Italian nation until 1860. Unification under one government came only after a long struggle known as risorgimento, *a word that referred to a rebirth of the Italian spirit, exemplified by a drive for national unity.*

Creating a new Italian nation was a difficult process. Despite common experience and bonds the people shared—cultural movements, religion, and periods of domination by foreign powers—no true sense of nation existed. Italians related best to the people of their own region, and the peninsula was a mixture of different dialects, governments, and traditions. After the Napoleonic wars and the Congress of Vienna in the early nineteenth century, however, some Italians began to envision a united Italy— one that would be strong enough to make life better for all its people and to protect itself from foreign influence.

Among those "revolutionaries" who wanted not to overturn the government but to create one government out of many, was Giuseppe Mazzini, who tried to convince his fellow Italians that unification was not only practical, but was almost a religious duty. Mazzini was generally dismissed as a radical, but he was followed by others who became more successful in pursuing his dream. The most famous—and successful—of the Italian revolutionaries was Giuseppe Garibaldi. With his troops, known as "Red Shirts" for the uniforms they wore, he helped defeat the leaders of the separate Italian territories, paving the way for a new government that would govern all of Italy.

In this selection, historian Denis Mack Smith explores the long history of risorgimento. Highlighting the roles played by the colorful leaders who fought not only royal rulers but each other to achieve their goals, Smith shows how one nation came to be created out of a group of territories that had once been almost foreign lands.

Denis Mack Smith, *Italy: A Modern History*. Ann Arbor: University of Michigan Press, 1969. Copyright © 1959 by The University of Michigan. Reproduced by permission of Yale University Press (London).

Until 1860 the word *Italy* was used not so much for a nation as for a peninsula. . . . It is therefore with geography that Italian history must begin. Too often have poverty and political backwardness been blamed on misrule and foreign exploitation, instead of on climate and the lack of natural resources. We need not go so far as to believe that the destinies of a nation are altogether shaped by its wealth and position: a peninsular situation in the Mediterranean may suggest but does not compel a particular choice of allies, the lack of raw materials can make a country either weak or aggressive (or both), an unkind climate may as easily stimulate as depress, and overpopulation can be a military asset as well as an economic liability. But such characteristics are bound to define the scope of a nation within certain limits. It has always been historically important that the Apennines divide Italy from top to bottom and that the Alps cut her off from the rest of Europe; mountains may not be removed, even by faith.

Italy as a Geographic Unit

Italy was a territorial unit many centuries before she became a national state—unlike The Netherlands, for instance, which had been politically a state before seeming to be either a nation or a geographical entity. The natural frontiers of Italy are more or less clearly defined, three sides bounded by the sea, and the fourth following the long chain of the Alps. There have been certain ambiguities within these limits. Corsica [a French island in the Mediterranean] and Nice [a French port] have sometimes been claimed from France, Canton Ticino from [southeast] Switzerland, Malta [Mediterranean islands] from Great Britain; and southern Tyrol [in the eastern Alps], Trieste [in northeastern Italy], and Fiume [in western Croatia] have been disputed with Austria-Hungary and Yugoslavia. Furthermore, the professors have dutifully justified Italian claims to these disputed provinces on grounds of geology, history, and ethnology. Even a physical barrier so formidable as the Alps by no means coincides with the linguistic frontier, and large cisalpine [located on the south side of the Alps] areas are French, German, and Slav by speech.

Neither the existence of these doubtful frontier provinces nor that of tiny enclaves in San Marino and the Vatican City [small, independent countries within Italy] weakens the compactness of Italy so much as do the differences and sometimes the animosities between its component regions. This parochialism is the product of both geography and history. The various regions still preserve something of their individual customs and literature, their peculiar type of economy and methods of land tenure. . . . Up to 1859 the regions were still politically divided, with different historical traditions of government and law. Weights, measures, and coinage varied everywhere, the ducato of Naples differing from the oncia of Sicily, the papal scudo from the Piedmontese lira. As many as twenty-two different customs barriers existed along the course of the Po [River]—a striking example of that municipalism or *campanilismo* which impeded national unification and the advance of agriculture and industry. . . .

Italy and National Unity

Italy had always been a unit geographically. In religion, too, she had been practically homogeneous since [Pope] Gregory the Great [540–604], and something of a common Italian language and culture had existed from [poet] Dante [1265–1321] onward. Until 1861, however, she had never been a political entity, and hardly was one even then. As the Neapolitan historian Luigi Blanch had said ten years before, "the patriotism of the Italians is like that of the ancient Greeks, and is love of a single town, not of a country; it is the feeling of a tribe, not of a nation. Only by foreign conquest have they ever been united. Leave them to themselves and they split into fragments." Some national consciousness had certainly existed on and off for centuries, but it had been vague and tenuous, something manifested only in the wilder speculations of a Dante or [Renaissance philosopher Niccolò] Machiavelli, and many had argued on the contrary that national unity would be ruinous rather than profitable, as well as morally wrong. Not much national feeling had in fact existed before the nineteenth century, and even an Italian customs union like the German *Zollverein* was impracticable until Piedmont [a region in northwestern Italy] could impose it. North and south Italy had hardly ever been united under the same rule, but government had for centuries been parceled out between autonomous cities and foreign dynasties, all of whom had an interest in resisting every patriotic movement not led by themselves and suppressing any neighbor who became too important.

Yet in time each invader took on the color of his surroundings. . . until by 1861 these many cities and provinces, only excepting Venice and Rome, stood united in a single state. True enough, there were still important internal divisions, and more than one civil war lay ahead. It is true also that unification was achieved by methods which some Italians detested. Nevertheless, many people would have agreed that the five great powers of Europe had by 1861 become six, and in every free country people looked with warm sympathy and admiration at the rebirth of Italy. The how and why of such an achievement provide one of the fascinating themes of modern history.

Renaissance to Risorgimento

Italy of the *risorgimento* [the movement for unification] was a far cry from the divided Italy of the Renaissance. In the later Middle Ages, Italians made their country the center of European religion, art, and literature, and also of the new capitalist, urban civilization developing around the Italian inventions of banking and credit. Yet, while inhabitants of the medieval Italian communes consciously belonged to a wider community, their loyalty was by no means to a nation, but first to the city and then to Christendom. No threat of invasion by Saracens, Normans, or Germans succeeded in unifying them into a state for mutual aid, and some local rulers always sided with every invader for the sake of their own private advantage. Italy must be the most invaded country in the world, and Lombardy one of the world's great battlefields. Even where temporary leagues of cities could be formed in self-defense, they were never lasting, but melted away with the danger that engendered them or with a new danger which required a new alignment. By 1500, however, the eighty city-states scattered through Italy had been hammered into ten provinces by the more successful and unscrupulous of the local tyrants and civic oligarchies.

Italy in 1500 was about to drift into a period of somnolence during which she lost her commercial and cultural primacy. This was due at least in part to her failure to constitute a national state like contemporary France and Spain. Machiavelli might dream of a more united country, but in practice his ideal prince did not succeed in rallying enough of Italy to combine and play the new game of power politics in Europe. Instead, the French invasion of 1494 from the north, countered at once by that of Spain from the south, opened a new era of civil war and foreign subjection, in which Italy became the cat's-paw, the battlefield, even the private perquisite, of one European nation after another. Once again, one party in every local quarrel was always ready to side with the invader in order to curb a rival faction or a neighboring province. Milan tried and failed to become master of northern Italy. Successive papal families attempted by force of arms to win a temporal hegemony, but [Italian ruler] Cesare Borgia [1475–1507] made too many enemies and so failed to succeed by a narrow margin. Then it was the turn of Venice, only to be crushed by France and a confederacy of other jealous provinces. So strong were these internal jealousies that Florence was left alone to resist the Spanish invasion, while her leading family, the Medici, chose to support the Spanish emperor against their own native city. Florence and Rome were both put to the sack and ruined, and the civilization of the Renaissance was shocked to a standstill.

At the same time the Ottoman Turks and the corsairs of Greece and Africa were obstructing the trade routes which Venice and Genoa had used for their prosperous commerce with the Levant [countries on the eastern Mediterranean]. The commercial centers of Europe were shifting away from the inner Mediterranean to the Atlantic seaboard, where ports looked out to a new world largely discovered by Italians. But Italy herself failed to meet the challenge. Although still the richest country in Europe, although Venice had for centuries sent ships into the Atlantic, and though Genoa was not much further from the Spice Islands than was Amsterdam or London, nevertheless politics did not allow the necessary adjustments to be made. The interests of Italy were subordinated to those of her new Spanish overlords, and the inherited splendor of centuries was dissipated in profitless civil war.

In the two centuries before the *risorgimento,* only the several regions had their individual history, and this was often a pale reflection of transalpine Europe. After the death of [Renaissance artist] Michelangelo in 1564, and from the time when [philosopher] Bruno [1548–1600] was burned and [scientist] Galileo [1564–1642] silenced, Italy lived in a backwater. Certain regions managed to retain some political independence, for example, Venice sheltered behind her lagoons and Genoa screened by the Maritime Alps, but only as shadows of what they had once been. . . .

The Invasion of Napoleon

It was with the Napoleonic intrusion into Italy, between 1796 and 1814, that the various regions of the peninsula were forced back into the mainstream of European history. Napoleon even created a prototype kingdom of Italy based on Milan. This was an artificial, puppet state, with a population of only six million out of a possible eighteen. But the Napoleonic armies brought with them the germs of liberalism fostered by the French Revolution of 1789, and introduced a minor industrial revolution sufficient at least to provide some of the war equipment required. Experience of Napoleonic rule convinced some people how much Italy stood to gain from strong centralized government, for the French brought more efficient methods of administration and a far more enlightened code of law. Customs barriers were broken down, and the decimal and metric systems of measurement were introduced. The mercantile classes appreciated this, as they appreciated the better roads, the enlarged market, and the destruction of entails which at last made possible the free transfer of land. Fortunes were made on a scale hitherto impossible, and liquid capital suddenly reappeared and sought an outlet in profitable enterprise.

But neither the novelty nor the permanence of Napoleon's contribution must be exaggerated. Some of these reforms had been anticipated in Italy during the Enlightenment, and the rest, once Napoleon had gone, mostly lapsed. The Kingdom of Italy split up again into its constituent elements, and the emperor's laws were usually repealed. Most Italians were glad to be rid of him, less because he was a "foreigner" than because heavy taxes and conscription were obnoxious, and because they hoped that the milder government of pope or duke would be less interfering and easier to disobey. In one real sense, moreover, his legacy was one of division, in that he brought north Italy still further within the economic ambit of France, and his road over the Simplon pass drew Milan nearer to Paris. This notwithstanding, shortly after Napoleon's final defeat the German scholar [Barthold Georg] Niebuhr could write from Rome that Italy was bound to be united in the course of a generation or two, and [French writer] Stendhal in his diary noted the same trend. That such a revolution was at last conceivable is to be ascribed largely to Napoleon's influence. It is significant that so many leaders of Italian nationalism descended from people who became rich under his regime.

Birth of the Risorgimento

One cannot give wholly satisfactory reasons for the rise and fall of nations. No simple answer will explain why Spain, whose share in defeating Napoleon was infinitely greater than that of Italy, derived thereby no stimulus to a national rebirth like the *risorgimento*, and received no similar inspiration from the new ideas of nationalism, liberalism, and romanticism. In Italy these ideas caused a ferment compounded of bitter criticism and boundless enthusiasm. Politically, the 1814–15 Restoration might be called a disaster: the Viennese emperor returned to Lombardy, the Bourbons to Naples, the Austrian grand duke to Tuscany; Venice was no longer a free republic but a province of Austria, and Genoa had become a dependency of Piedmont; nor was Piedmont yet a wholly cisalpine and Italian power. Everywhere the aristocracy recovered their privileges and power. But on the non-political plane new forces were at work. There was a feeling of *italianità* [idea of Italian nationalism] which thinkers were beginning to rationalize and statesmen to exploit. There was the liberating wind from the French Revolution blowing freely through the world with its message of political deliverance. There was also an expanding commercial and agricultural middle class with new needs generated by an industrial revolution and by the revival of trade routes in the Mediterranean.

The Middle Class

Without these middle classes it is difficult to see how enough backing could have been found for national unification. They found it irksome to have eight separate states in Italy, each with tariff barriers, individual coinage, and measures. Not only the merchants and textile manufacturers of northern Italy, but also some of the landowners who produced grain and wine realized that economic progress presupposed a larger internal market. There was scope for increasing agricultural profits, and some landlords saw the advantages of a centralized government which could build roads and railways, and give them fiscal protection and defend their interests abroad. The commercial classes of Lombardy felt that the Austrian government, for all its relative honesty and enlightenment, exploited their province, and they expected more consideration from a government of Italians.

Economic Changes

Economists such as [Camillo Bensodi] Cavour were at the same time looking forward to a Suez Canal, and calculating that the shortest route from England to India might include the railroad

they wanted to build from Turin [in northwestern Italy] to Brindisi [in southeastern Italy]. The canal was not finished until 1869,
but long before then another obstacle disappeared with the destruction of the Barbary pirates [from northern Africa]. At last it
seemed as if the Mediterranean might recover its importance as
the main highway of world trade. At a time when Turkish power
was declining, it was the more important that a united Italy
should be ready to capitalize these potential advantages, for by
the 1830's both Greece and Serbia had won their autonomy from
Turkey, and Mehemet Ali [an Albanian soldier who served in
Turkey] in Egypt and France in Algeria were altering the
Mediterranean balance of power. As things turned out, the canal
was in fact to bring few positive advantages to Italy; there was no
great influx of trade from the East, and ships did not stop to
bunker in a country which lacked the necessary coal. It was none
the less important that these changes were, in advance, thought
likely to make Italy's fortune if only she were sufficiently united
to exploit them.

Cultural Changes

Quite as impressive as these economic factors, and by and large
affecting different people, was the common Italian culture now
more in evidence, and the currency being given on a literary and
intellectual level to the concept of United Italy. In 1825–27
Alessandro Manzoni published *I promessi sposi,* the most influential novel ever written in Italian. Manzoni was from Lombardy,
but the year after publication he visited Florence, and in the next
edition fifteen years later he had corrected the style to conform
more with the Tuscan dialect. This in the end proved decisive in
confirming Tuscan as the classic prose style for Italian literature.
The purists objected, but like all masterpieces it carried its own
compulsion, and another essential step had been taken toward national consciousness. Meanwhile [writers] Grossi and Guerrazzi
found the educated public avid for tales of medieval Italian he-
roes who once beat the French and the Saracens, and [poet]
Leopardi's patriotic odes had to be confiscated by the Austrian
censorship lest they should incite people to revolt. Literature thus
helped to reassure Italians that they were not so unfit as some of
them imagined for war and politics. . . .

Before this economic and cultural revival could develop into
a political *risorgimento,* someone had to transmute ideals into ac-

tion. Centuries of foreign rule had left Italy not only without a nucleus around which a national movement could gather, but also without experience of free government. Forty years of trial and

GARIBALDI FREES SICILY FROM THE KING OF NAPLES

Giuseppe Garibaldi is probably the best known of Italy's leaders for independence. In May 1860, he led his army of a thousand volunteers, known as the Red Shirts for the uniforms they wore, in a campaign against the king of Naples. Their success that day above the hills of Palermo, Sicily, helped establish the united nation of Italy.

Flames are bursting forth in all directions, and walls are falling with a crash across the narrow thoroughfares, while the shrieks and yells of the wounded, as they are removed to more sheltered positions, combined with the hurrahing of the patriot soldiers, as they drive the troops step by step towards the Royal Palace, realized to the beholder the idea of a dozen Pandemoniums in one. All through the night does the fighting continue uninterruptedly, and there is little or no sleep to be obtained by even a non-combatant, who at any moment may be awakened by a live shell in his bed.

On Tuesday the fighting was harder than ever. An attack was made on the Palace, and one wing was taken from the soldiers and held for a considerable period; this exploit was performed by young [Guissepe] Garibaldi, at the head of fifteen men, and had he not been recalled I believe he would have established himself firmly. When it is considered that Garibaldi entered the city with only a thousand of his own people whom he could depend upon, the result achieved is surprising.

Frank Vizetelly, "Garibaldi Liberates Sicily," *Illustrated London News*, June 1860.

error were therefore necessary after the Napoleonic period in order to test the various methods and parties which gradually became engaged in the crusade for independence. At one extreme there was the orthodox means of open war and diplomacy; at the other, plotting, piracy, and assassination. Besides conservative monarchists, there were professional anarchists, republican agitators, starving peasants, discontented soldiers and students, all with different aims and methods, but all helping, often unintentionally, to create a united Italy. Of these it was the revolutionary republicans who first persuaded people that unification might be feasible, and who then, by many isolated acts of revolt, forced the conservatives and the lukewarm to join with them in half-unwilling alliance.

Very soon after the Restoration of 1814–15 [return of monarchy], secret societies became active with the avowed policy of overthrowing the Vienna settlement. In Genoa and Sicily, which had lost their old autonomy to Piedmont and Naples respectively, even conservative aristocrats had an interest in revolt. So had the discharged officers of Napoleon's army and the civil servants who had staffed his government. In 1820–21, therefore, and again in 1831, uprisings took place in several of the larger Italian cities to remedy various local and individual grievances. But they lacked cohesion and co-ordination. Certain towns in Sicily preferred to side with the Bourbons [ruling family] at Naples against the island capital, Palermo, of whose position they were jealous, and in Bologna the "foreign" refugees from Modena were disarmed even though both cities were fighting Austria.

By 1848, the next year of revolutions, some of the malcontents had realized the need for sacrificing local animosities in a common cause. Soldiers from insurgent Naples joined with Tuscans, Romans, and the Piedmontese army in trying to save the gallant insurrection of Milan, and the Sicilians invited a Piedmontese duke to be their king. Once more, however, all ended in mutual recrimination, Milan accusing Piedmont of treachery and selfish aggrandizement, Piedmont replying that the Milanese were clouding the straight issue of independence with a controversy over republicanism upon which patriots were divided. Province was divided against province, class against class. The poor were not interested in political independence, but only in the price of salt and flour; landowners fell back on the old dynasties rather than countenance the occupation of their land by

the peasants in arms; and as for the merchants, they might have
wanted freedom, but not at the price of forced loans and inflation. In 1849, therefore, the old regimes were again restored, and
although some people had tasted liberty and learned to fight on
the barricades, the bitterness of civil war and defeat soured the
cause of patriotism.

It is not possible to say exactly who took part in these insurrections. No doubt it was a small minority, for the wars and risings of the *risorgimento* had little effect on ordinary people. If not
the intellectuals, it was at least the intelligent, in particular the
professional classes, the lawyers, doctors, and shopkeepers who
manned the Palermo barricades in 1848—so observed William
Nassau Senior, the economist. Italian lawyers were not as conservative as English lawyers: they were poor in money and esteem, usually excluded from the judicial bench and high society,
full of abstract ideas, and hence ready to accept change and revolution. Furthermore, they were a numerous body, for most respectable families were ensnared in hereditary lawsuits, and universities were equipped to teach only medicine and the law.
Lawyers were therefore a dangerous element in society.

University students, too, were rebellious by nature. They were
the first to join [revolutionary Giussepe] Garibaldi's volunteers,
and no university could or would be bold enough to refuse them
a degree if some successful patriotic escapade made them miss
their examinations. Patriotism offered a glorious relief from the
crabbed, patriarchal system which kept them, even after marriage,
cooped up in ancestral *palazzi* with generations of relatives.
When ruled by austere, authoritarian parents like those of the
poet Leopardi, the young were bound to be in revolt. Little travel
was possible for them before the age of railroads, and there was
no sport except the very necessary art of fencing. In their drab
lives a town riot was a tonic and an intoxicant, and in between
riots they could show their national enthusiasm by refusing to
buy taxed tobacco, by cheering certain arias of [composer
Giuseppe] Verdi, or by wearing the conical Calabrian hat after its
prohibition by the Austrians as a patriotic symbol. The student
population of Italy, as of many other countries later, was an ideal
revolutionary force. While students had less to lose than men
with responsibilities, their education fitted them to understand
what they were fighting for, or at least enough about it to make
it seem thoroughly glamorous. Besides being persecuted by gov-

ernments as a source of seditious infection, many of them had
small hope of profitable employment in existing society, and all
wished to build a brave new world where brains were as important as birth, and where the white-collared man was king.

Giuseppe Mazzini, Early Revolutionary

The teacher and inspiration of rebellious youth was Giuseppe
Mazzini, a republican, a nationalist, and by far the greatest prophet
of the *risorgimento*. Mazzini was born at Genoa in 1805, and lived
as a revolutionary agitator, sacrificing personal comfort, the company of his family, and the lives of his friends. Exiled from Genoa
and Piedmont in 1831, he was then expelled from Switzerland and
France, and spent most of his remaining years planning the resur-
rection of Italy amid the fogs of London. He launched numerous
societies and newspapers to convince people that Italy could and
must be unified through the exertions of ordinary people. No
trust should be placed in princes or in political alliances, he maintained, nor in any appeal to mere self-interest, for the problem was
moral more than political, and ordinary citizens must learn that
they alone by their own sacrifices could redeem themselves. A nation should be something spiritual; not like America which "is the
embodiment, if compared to our own ideal, of the philosophy of
mere *rights:* the collective thought is forgotten: the *educational* mission of the state overlooked. It is the negative, individualistic, ma-
terialistic school." Mazzini, on the contrary, made national unification a religious duty, and convinced his disciples that it was part
of God's providence, in which belief they discovered a quite in-
valuable sense of inevitability and self-confidence.

Mazzini's practical application of nationalism was by means of
continual insurrections, thereby making people conscious of their
power and of how to use it in executing God's purpose. He used
to visit Piedmont surreptitiously, defying a sentence of death, and
frequent uprisings testified to the valor of his lieutenants and to
his own fascination. There exists today an edition of his writings
in over a hundred volumes, ranging from a manual on guerrilla
warfare to the thousands of incendiary letters which kept conspiracy alive. Personally one of the mildest of men, sad, lonely,
and affectionate, he thus became one of the most feared and
hated personalities in Europe.

It is easy to say with his detractors that Mazzini was a failure.
Not only were many of his disciples killed in insurrections which

seemed hopeless from the start, but his enemy Cavour was to oust him from the revolutionary leadership, and in 1872 Mazzini died an unhappy and disillusioned fugitive. . . .

Garibaldi Continues the Fight for Unity

Italians found their greatest general of modern times in Giuseppe Garibaldi, the inspired leader of guerrillas. Garibaldi was rough and untutored, with little grasp of long-term strategy, but with remarkable flair for irregular warfare. His success with his men, who loved him and believed him invincible, was above all one of character, for he lacked calculation and guile, was unambitious for himself, and devoid of cheap ostentation. He was an honest man with the reputation of being one, whereas Cavour and Mazzini never freed themselves from the suspicion of double-dealing and unscrupulousness. No one could meet Garibaldi without recognizing his single-minded and disinterested love of Italy, and no one failed to be charmed by his courtesy and simplicity of manner, or to be bewitched by his voice. He was temperate even to parsimony, and when his headquarters in 1860 was at the magnificent Palace of Caserta [in southern Italy] he would still wash his own shirt and sleep on hay with his saddle for a pillow. There was no need in his army for routine discipline, and as he himself was fearless and tireless, so he seemed to turn ordinary men into supermen.

Southern Italians venerated their deliverer as a saint, and in distant countries workmen who had never seen Garibaldi gave up their half-holidays to make arms for him. English dukes begged for his portrait; one of them, himself a cabinet minister, had a son who ran off to join Garibaldi's volunteers; and their wives even raided Caserta to comb out the hairs from his brush for keepsakes. The romancer Dumas followed him around to get copy for novels, and, in return for this privilege, equipped a yacht on which to make red shirts for the revolutionary troops. It was Garibaldi's generous good nature that won over public opinion in Europe to favor the deeds of a buccaneer. From Hungarians to South American Negroes, men of every country joined the bravest of Italian youth in the fantastic army which he could conjure up from nowhere and then as magically disperse again. Chivalrous enthusiasts linked up with charlatans and professional adventurers, for it was not least among Garibaldi's services that, alongside the patriots, he could enroll those social outcasts who are always in the van of any revolution or counterrevolution, the people who thrive on disorder, and who . . . have been among the most combustible and explosive elements in Italian society.

Garibaldi called himself a republican and a socialist. In practice, however, he loyally served the monarchy, and to Mazzini's disgust meekly surrendered to the king the dictatorial powers over the half of Italy which he had conquered in 1860. His confusion of mind helped the process by which most of the republicans and revolutionaries rallied to the throne. . . . Thousands [of his volunteers] were later to become generals in the regular Italian army, although he himself crumpled up the notice of his own appointment and threw it out of the window. Away from the battlefield, his own political beliefs, for all their honesty, were trite and shallow. He distrusted Mazzini and hated Cavour. As he was quite unable to understand the difficulties of Cavour's position, he blasted him as a coward, a traitor, and a fomenter of civil war. Where Cavour believed in parliaments, Garibaldi was all for a dictatorship modeled on [Roman Emperor Julius] Caesar's, and armed with "fasces" [a Roman weapon]. He genuinely believed in what he called liberty, and yet thought that it could and should be forced on people for their own good. Unskilled in public speaking—except from balconies—he had no patience with the talk and the delays of parliamentary government, and so dictatorship was the natural form of government he had chosen for southern Italy in 1860. This would-be republican, anticlerical democrat that he was, had presided from the royal throne during pontifical high mass in the Cathedral of Palermo, claiming the royal rights of apostolic legateship (although a notorious heretic), clad in red shirt and with sword unsheathed as the Gospel was read.

Under all his panache, Garibaldi had neither the ruthlessness nor the ambition and intelligence of Cromwell or Napoleon. He turned up rarely in parliament, sometimes wearing his poncho and red shirt to the dismay of the frock-coated deputies, but he was far happier back on his farm, away from the smart men of politics, awaiting some new call to arms. His real work was finished when Cavour took over the Italian revolution; and like Mazzini he became disillusioned with the Italy which Cavour and the moderates had made. . . .

Italy Unites at Last

For many years he [Cavour] had believed that Italy might in the distant future become an independent nation, but in practice his own immediate plans were for a kingdom of northern Italy, linked by alliance with other Italian states. The fact was that he disliked revolutionary republicanism as much if not more than he loved national unity, and he feared that Mazzini's insurrections would embroil him with France and undermine the predominance of Piedmont which depended on French support. Luckily he was met halfway by some of the more practical revolutionaries who had abandoned Mazzini's utopianism. Futile republican uprisings, for instance those of the Bandiera brothers in 1844 and [Carlo] Pisacane in 1857, convinced radicals like [Daniele] Manin and [Giuseppe] La Farina that a national revolution could succeed only if supported by the Piedmontese army, and accordingly they placed their hopes on convincing Cavour that public opinion was now ready for a unified Italian kingdom. It was Garibaldi's conquest of Sicily in 1860 which finally persuaded him that Manin was right.

Cavour at first did all he dared to stop Garibaldi from sailing on this madcap venture, and even after the landing in Sicily he remained for a while unhelpful and skeptical. But, as always, he was clever enough to let events take their course without implicating himself too far, and, while fully prepared to disown the revolutionaries if necessary, he was equally ready to lend a hand and reassert his influence should they prove victorious. His diplomatic tact had already been shown earlier in 1860, for against much opposition he had sacrificed the two northeastern provinces of Savoy and Nice to France, and so won Louis Napoleon for an accomplice in the acquisition of central Italy as a *quid pro quo*. Plebiscites [elections] had then been held in Tuscany and Emilia to confirm their annexation. And not content with this, Cavour then suggested to Britain that, while France wanted no more than a state of northern Italy as a check upon Austria, it might be a British interest that an even larger Italy should emerge as a counterpoise to France in the Mediterranean. It was at this point that Garibaldi evaded the Piedmontese and Neapolitan fleets and landed in Sicily.

The sudden news of Garibaldi's overwhelming success made Cavour decide that the best chance of controlling the revolutionaries was to outdo them at their own game. While still pretending to treat with the Bourbons, he sent secret agents to try to forestall Garibaldi with a more conservative insurrection at Naples, offering promotion to officers in the Neapolitan army and seducing politicians from their loyalty. When Garibaldi arrived at Naples first, Cavour was still not to be outdone. He quickly engineered popular uprisings in the Papal states as a pretext to invade Umbria [region in central Italy] and the Marches [region on the Adriatic Sea], and annexed most papal territory except the area around Rome. He was then able to advance southward and force Garibaldi by the threat of civil war to yield Naples and Sicily as well.

Legitimists and Catholics everywhere were profoundly disturbed by this invasion of the Papal states, but Cavour gave the ingenious excuse that only thus could the anticlerical Garibaldi be prevented from overthrowing the government of Rome itself. "The aim," he said, "has been holy, and perhaps this will justify any irregularities in the means which we have had to use." Almost before people could see what he was about, Cavour had unified most of Italy and held the usual rigged plebiscites to regularize the fact. When parliament met early in 1861, a new kingdom of twenty-two million people could be officially declared in existence. Only Rome with its French garrison, and Venice under Austrian rule, remained outside.

The Political Struggles of United Italy

By Serge Hughes

After Italy became a unified nation in 1860, many revolutionaries seemed to think their work was done. What some people failed to realize was that the business of governing the new nation would prove far more difficult than that of creating it.

One of the first problems Italy's new government faced was the fact that the people at large were not especially interested in the daily goings-on of politics. They were concerned about the economy, taxes, and other matters that affected their own lives, but they were not willing to give much thought—or support—to the politicians who were struggling to make the new nation stable.

Political parties, which could now be formed with complete freedom, emerged in rapid succession. Each claimed to have the philosophy that would make Italy efficient and prosperous. Almost as quickly as these parties came, they failed and disappeared.

In this selection, Serge Hughes, a professor of Italian from Hunter College who has written widely about Italian politics and history, discusses the confused state in which politicians found themselves in the years after Italy was unified. Hughes shows how even those parties that seemed capable of surviving minor setbacks, such as the Socialists and Liberals, were rarely able to agree even among themselves about the best policy for Italy. As a result, the late 1800s constituted an extremely turbulent time for the Italians as they grappled with the implications of unity.

From the beginnings of the unification of Italy in about 1815 to the culminating entry of Italian troops into Rome on September 20, 1870, the Risorgimento—meaning the Resurgence, or Uprising—for the relatively few who actively

Serge Hughes, *The Fall and Rise of Modern Italy*. New York: The Macmillan Company, 1967. Copyright © 1967 by Serge Hughes. Reproduced by permission.

participated in the movement, appeared as a cause that would not experience anticlimax. In 1859, Count Camillo di Cavour set the firm foundation of the new state with the annexation of Lombardy, Emilia and Tuscany to the Piedmontese kingdom of the house of Savoy (the kings of Sardinia). A year later, 1860, [Giuseppe] Garibaldi with his *Mille,* his one thousand followers, conquered the South and virtually doubled the territories of the emerging nation. In the same year, troops of Victor Emmanuel II took over the Papal States of Umbria and the Marches in central Italy. In 1866, Venice and a part of Venetia came under Italian dominion. The occupation of Rome seemed the last upward thrust of a movement that gave no sign of arching.

How to Govern a United Italy

But after some twenty years of post-Risorgimento rule, even the most ardent patriot admitted to faded illusions. The business of governing with authority and justice was harder than the expulsion of the Austrians from northern Italy and the occupation of papal Rome. In the 1870's, the cry of Risorgimento leaders, "Now that we have made Italy, we must make Italians," had the ring of exuberant self-assurance; a generation later it was heard less frequently, and then more with bitter irony than with confidence. By 1890, it sounded like an empty slogan or adolescent braggadocio. Italians were not united, and the numbers of the indifferent had not lessened perceptibly. If there was any recognizable change, it lay in the fact that their wait-and-see attitude had become more hostile, less passive.

The indifferent—the largest class in Italy, and one that cut across all economic and cultural divisions including peasants, the middle class, and a substantial segment of the landed aristocracy—had never been won over to Risorgimento ideals. From their beginnings, those ideals had flourished among only a small part of a small middle class, and twenty years later they had not gained wider acceptance. In the prodigiously varied Italian class structure, the new nation remained very old. In 1890, as in preceding centuries, the unity of Italy continued to be largely cultural, that of the few who saw in classical culture and in Italian literature since 1300 a common patrimony. In all other respects, however, there was no bond of interest common to all classes. The Piedmontese aristocracy did not have the same outlook and values as the Tuscan, and neither had much in common with southern aristocrats; it was very much the same with the other classes. The peasant of the North was quite different from his counterpart in the South, and the differences were more decisive than the similarities. Members of the southern middle class had been very active in the Risorgimento, but twenty years of Liberal rule had not brought about a fusion of their interests and values with those of the northern middle class, of which Cavour was the most gifted representative. . . .

The Position of the Catholic Church

In the 1890's the restitution of the city of Rome to the Popes was no longer a real issue, but the Vatican stood firm in its contention that the state had no right to legislate on spiritual matters, that on this principle there was no room for compromise. The papacy remained adamant in particular on its application to the education of the young. Leo XIII took a fresh and active interest in the moral-political problems of the times and the *Rerum novarum* of 1891 was a precedent-shattering encyclical that ultimately opened up new possibilities for Catholic attitudes toward politics within and without Italy. At the time, however, there were no repercussions of the encyclical in the practical political sphere among Catholics in Italy, and none on the official traditional papal policy toward the new Italy.

How many Catholics considered what the Pope had to say politically relevant or acceptable is hard to say. Not all Catholics supinely deferred to pontifical wishes: The 1860 referendum in the Papal States attested to the overwhelming preference of the citizens of those regions for Victor Emmanuel II. Italian Catholics knew how to distinguish between the black-and-white language of pontifical doctrine and the give-and-take necessary in dealings between two strong adversaries. Strengthened with this type of wisdom, a great number of believers holding very divergent political views managed to come to some sort of compromise in which they felt no less Italian than Catholic.

In this respect, twenty years of Liberal rule based on Risorgimento ideals brought about a softening of attitudes in some quarters, but hardly in all quarters: Masons in 1890, as in 1860, regarded themselves as the custodians of freedom, dedicated to the destruction of superstition and clerical obscurantism, or its synonym, Catholicism; nor was there any dearth of Catholics of equal fervor who considered themselves the defenders of God

and Church against the apocalyptic Beast of the atheist Risorgimento state. Fortunately, relations between Catholics and Liberals were not consistently on this level, but even in instances where
they improved perceptibly they did not change drastically. There
were still Catholics who recalled with pride that at the height of
the church-state conflict in the 1870's a Piedmontese bishop refused the last sacraments to a Catholic in Cavour's government
unwilling to retract his support of certain Liberal measures; and
there were Masons who glowed when they reminisced about
how Garibaldi had called the Vatican, *senza peli sulla lingua* (without circumlocution, a square mile of dung).

More serious, though, post-Risorgimento Italy not only failed
to raise perceptibly the level of religious polemics; it also further
complicated the Catholic problem. Catholics were not in out-
right opposition to the new state, but neither did they give it
their wholehearted support; and in this peculiarly indecisive
stance . . . they were the most striking anomaly in a very anom-
alous state. There were Catholics openly willing to work with
Liberals and vice versa, just as there were undercover groups of
Liberals and Catholics working toward official reconciliation between church and state. Each time these groups appeared to be
making some progress, however, they were invariably disavowed
by one or both of the parties.

But compared with the problem of growing division among
the Liberals, the complexities of the Catholic problem appeared
almost picayune [trivial]. Risorgimento Liberals closed ranks and
made a sterling show of unity against the Austrians and the Pope,
but in dealing with the multifaceted domestic problems of unified Italy, they ran into a beehive of difficulties. In a very short
time, divisions that had been discernible even in the heart of the
Risorgimento struggle—conflicts between monarchists and republicans, between the King and Garibaldi, between federalists
and the proponents of a strong central government—now re-
asserted themselves, and in a much sharper form. . . .

The Republicans

The Republican Party in the 1890's was led in its denunciations
of the government by a most articulate spokesman, Giovanni
Bovio, a man of ample nineteenth-century cut and the author of
some bad romantic plays. Together with the older and much more
sedate Agostino Bertani, Bovio carried on an attenuated Mazzin-

ian policy [of representative government]. Since times had changed remarkably since the 1870's, the Republicans' attacks on the Liberals in the 1890's often had the support of former enemies, the Radicals, a group that followed the policies of the aging Garibaldi, the fiery old leader of the *camicie rosse* (red shirts). Before his death in 1882, Garibaldi, who never had much sympathy for the monarchist cause and repeatedly clashed with both [Giuseppe] Mazzini and Victor Emmanuel II, took an unqualified stand against the Liberals and the monarchy. Post-Risorgimento Italy had disillusioned him, as it had many others. Its leaders, Garibaldi charged, did not trust the people; they had no interest in implementing the vision for which he had fought. The gist of the General's indictment was that for them, the central problem of political Italy was the need of a balanced budget, not the urgent needs of education, literacy, land reclamation and agricultural reform, and—not the least of the General's preoccupations—eliminating clericalism and superstition. Compulsory, universal education, universal suffrage, a firm commitment to the humanitarian, egalitarian principles of the French Revolution—these were the principles to which Italy should be dedicated. Instead, they were being trampled on. Thus contended Garibaldi.

This passionate denunciation of a revolution betrayed found its spokesman after Garibaldi's death in the Radical, Felice Cavallotti—like Bovio, a bad playwright and poet but a vigorous, sentimental, swashbuckling rhetorician. With Bovio and his Republicans, Cavallotti and his party constituted what was known as the Extreme Left, a very small group in Parliament (quite naturally so, given the make-up of the electorate). But it was the only alternative to the two amorphous groups—the Liberal Left and the Liberal Right—that made up the ruling party.

The Liberals

From 1870–76, Liberals of the Right, a group of austere political leaders best represented by the inflexible Quintino Sella, followed each other in rapid succession in the office of prime minister. Despite numerous Cabinet reshufflings, they had to their satisfaction saved the country from the threat of national bankruptcy that followed hard upon the Risorgimento conflict. This success, together with a cautious foreign policy oriented toward Germany and Austria-Hungary, was their great accomplishment. Their achievement, however, made Italy the most heavily taxed country in Europe; this helped explain the landslide victory of the Liberal Left candidates at the polls in 1876. The defeat of the Right, however, was not exclusively attributable to its financial policy, nor was the triumph of the Left an unqualified improvement. In general, the leaders of the Liberal Left were not noticeably superior to those of the Right in political skills, and they were certainly several notches below them in political morality. The Left did pass some urgently needed reform measures and they were not as paternalistically high-handed in decreeing political priorities, but in many respects they tended to substitute a peculiar mixture of self-interest and wordy righteous indignation for the excessive austerity of the Right.

With Agostino Depretis, however, the Left had a talented political leader, who for eleven years, from 1876 to 1887, the year of his death, did his best to erase still further the indistinct lines that separated the Liberal Right and the Liberal Left; thus he ruled with a coalition of both groups that virtually obliterated what was left of the old divisions. . . .

The Struggle to Create Unity

Twenty years of post-Risorgimento rule demonstrated that national unity was fragile, even somewhat fictitious, that Risorgimento *élan* [enthusiasm] was not enough to weld Italy into a truly united country, or to govern it well. The new nation desperately needed a unity made up of diversity, a unity that only strong parties could provide, parties that would not simply be variations to the right or left of a nebulous liberalism, parties that would not become the instruments of well-meaning, or not so well-meaning, strong men, but that would give voice to profound differences of opinion within the country and construct the framework for a workable coexistence. Though such parties would of course run into many vexing problems, it was still true that the dissatisfaction and restlessness caused by the preparty web in which Italian political life had been caught from 1860–90 signaled definite moral-political progress. The beginnings were naturally humble ones, and Italy would long continue to suffer in particular from one political question mark: the anomaly of Catholics who neither fully entered into nor quite abstained from political activity. But however humble, it was a beginning; in this sense, the work of the Extreme Left, and even more so that of the newly founded Socialist Party, the great political innovation of the time, marked the disillusioned 1890's as the beginning of a new stage in the political experience of modern Italy.

The Socialists

In Parliament, the Socialists had only insignificant numerical strength, but in the country, it was evident even in 1892, when they first constituted themselves as a party, that they needed only an enlargement of the very narrow electorate to increase their representation rapidly. Although there were a few deputies among the Liberals, like the southerner Giustino Fortunato, who were actively interested in what was then called the "social question," and even more among the Extreme Left, only the Socialist Party made the exploitation of the poor and the privileges of the rich its well-nigh exclusive concern. This gave the Socialists one of the essentials of a party: a loyal and increasing following. The Socialist Party was the natural spokesman—indeed, the only one—for the inarticulate, the destitute, the poor, with a thousand and one justified grievances; and the condition of the peasants and artisans was indeed deplorable. Workers in the Lombard rice fields and those in Sicilian sulphur mines labored at least twelve hours a day; the exploitation of child labor was commonplace; and until the mid-1880's all workers' strikes were illegal. Needless to say, such embryonic labor unions as existed were powerless, and they certainly had no say in fixing wages or hours.

Like the Extreme Left, the Socialist Party had the very real disadvantages of having no real party apparatus, discipline or unity. They did, however (and this was very important), have a firm, definite outlook on life and politics—a Marxist outlook—and they were adamant in their denunciations of *trasformismo* [the art of winning over opponents by toning down existing differences].

The Anarchists

Marxism was many things in many lands, but in post-Risorgimento Italy, the Marxism of the Socialist Party was principally a means of marking off Socialists from the bourgeoisie and the Liberals, the party in power—a marking off that was proper to a legal, law-abiding party. To this end, in 1892, the Socialists broke completely with the Anarchists, who until then had fought off all attempts to distinguish them from Socialists. Of course in an Italy where real parties did not yet exist, the Anarchists were not so very different from other groups fighting the government.

All opposition parties had more or less anarchical [antigovernment] tendencies, and if the Anarchists stood out, it was perhaps because they theorized their very lack of unified theory. The Anarchists—a striking assortment of discontented and indignant members of many classes, despairing idealists of all ages, frugal artisans, authors of unpublished manuscripts, the bored and the frustrated—were proud of their claim to represent the most vehement expression of the prevailing disillusionment. Moreover, since they had a good number of clandestine and semiclandestine publications, they made their boasts and their laments heard. Some who considered themselves authentically anarchistic proclaimed that the only effective action against the tyrant state was armed insurrection. Others sharing the same conviction but less fond of violence, emigrated to Brazil, where they established an uncorrupt, peace-loving Anarchist colony. Still others, with little faith in terrorism or rebellion, boldly hoped—and their vision was considered a kind of madness—that they might yet see an Italy with an eight-hour day, universal suffrage, and like blessings. . . .

In the decades following, revolutionary ambitions continued to dwindle in Italy. In March 1882, to the stunned amazement of his followers, Carlo Cafiero, after Malatesta the most publicized of Italian Anarchist leaders, called for anarchists to run for Parliament instead of blowing it up. In that same year, outraged Anarchists were fond of pointing out, Cafiero literally did go mad. In contrast, Italian Anarchists were busy abroad. Santo Casino's assassination of the French president, Sadi Carnot, in 1894, and Michele Angiolillo's murder three years later of the Spanish prime minister, Antonio Canovas, showed that terrorism was more than a speculative persuasion among Italian Anarchists. But within Italy in the 1890's, anarchist violence was generally no threat.

Nevertheless, considering the swollen reputation rather than the real accomplishments of Anarchists in Italy, Italian Socialists had much to gain in making a clean break with them. But the new party did more than break with the Anarchists; it also did its utmost from its very beginnings to show that where it was strongest it was also peaceful and law-abiding. In Emilia-Romagna, the rich farmland area of central Italy where there was a centuries-old tradition of bloody conflict between peasants and landowners, Socialists were the voice of moderation. Their most respected leader, Andrea Costa, founder of the first Socialist newspaper, the famous *Avanti!*, so named in honor of the German *Vorwärts*, was an ex-Anarchist from that region, and as the first Socialist to be elected to Parliament he, far more than the great landowners, stood for restraint and reasonableness. Camillo Prampolini, another prominent Socialist from the same region, was another pillar of moderation. He dedicated himself with dubious success and admirable fervor to Socialist evangelization, to the preaching of a socialism that was peace-loving, lawful and morally superior to the Catholicism of the peasants of Romagna.

The Socialists' break with the Anarchists and their decision to be unequivocally lawful brought the party not only within the law but also close to the Extreme Left. Undoubtedly, the Socialists would have moved closer yet, and the entire history of modern Italy would have been quite different, had Italian socialism not been Marxist, with all the intransigence that that implied toward enemies, and even toward friends. But Italian Socialists had to be particularly on guard against doctrinal compromise. They were aware that doctrinal vagueness had ruined the Liberals; it had led them logically to a trasformismo that had contributed to a political pragmatism concerned only with the party's continuance in power. Doctrinal Marxism conceivably would be of some help in warding off any danger of assimilation into trasformismo—remote as that possibility seemed in the 1890's. . . .

The Need for Political Unity

In the nineties, however, neither the Liberals with their theoretical vagueness nor the Catholics with their official policy of non-participation in national politics and their *vorrei e non vorrei* stance, were in a position to smile at the difficulties faced by the Socialists. The Italian political structure of that decade was a large glass house. It ill behooved any group in it to look condescendingly on the efforts of others to work out a firm theoretical basis for a party. The construction of a strong party was a work to which sooner or later all rival parties would have to apply themselves. To ignore that requirement was simply to ensure a future of a bankrupt trasformismo. For it was already clear by the mid-1890's, even to those very much in the rear of the avant-garde, that trasformismo was rapidly exhausting its possibilities. At the turn of the century the need for solid theoretical foundations of political parties was not to be denied. That need was imparting a new shape to old politics.

Italy Enters
World War I

By James Rennell Rodd

World War I broke out in 1914 after the assassination of the heir to the throne of Austria-Hungary. Because the nations of Europe were involved in an intricate system of alliances, virtually every nation on the continent (as well as others around the world) eventually took part in the war.

Italy, still striving to keep its government and economy stable, at first declared neutrality, despite its own alliances. To induce Italy to maintain that neutrality, the Triple Alliance offered to cede certain regions to Italy, such as Trentino and Trieste. Through the long process of deciding what course Italy should take in the war, both the people and the politicians went through major shifts in mood. Eventually, political pressures from within and without led to Italy's joining the war on the side of the Allies, against Germany and Austria-Hungary.

Author James Rennell Rodd was a British diplomat who served in Italy in the years leading up to World War I. Because of his position, he had a close-up view of Italian leaders as they struggled with the difficult decision of whether or not to enter the war. As a British official, Rodd wanted Italy to join the fight on the Allied side, which included Great Britain. When the government did, in fact, declare war, Rodd, like most Italians, supported the decision heartily.

I t was made clear to the right people that Germany would endeavour to obtain as the price of Italy's neutrality the surrender of the Trentino [region in northern Italy] and a rectification of frontier on the Isonzo [river in western Slovenia and northeastern Italy], concessions no doubt of great importance, but wholly inadequate, as it proved, to stem the growing tide in favour of intervention. In regard to Trieste [an inlet at the head of the Adriatic Sea], Germany was just as little inclined as Austria was to consider its cession to Italy. To secure the acceptance

James Rennell Rodd, *Social and Diplomatic Memories, 1902–1919*. London: E. Arnold & Co., 1925.

of any such offer it would be necessary to gain the suffrages of a majority in the Chamber [legislature]. This entailed making sure of at least the tacit support of [Italian prime minister Giovanni] Giolitti, whose mysterious influence over individual deputies and groups seldom failed, when he elected to exercise it, to rally some three-fifths of their number to his side. Many rumours were circulated at this time regarding visits exchanged between [German ambassador Bernard] Bülow and Giolitti. In his memoirs Signor Giolitti has categorically stated that he only paid one visit to the Prince in December 1914, on which occasion discussion of all delicate questions was avoided. He was away from home when the visit was returned. They did not meet again till 1922. The legends therefore which grew up regarding their personal intercourse must be rejected.

Some colour was however not unnaturally given to the presumption that Giolitti was familiar with Bülow's proposals by a letter which the former wrote to his friend and quondam *chef de cabinet*, Signor Peano, on the 24th of January, 1915, with a view to its publication. In this letter he repudiated the reports of his relations with the special German Ambassador [Bülow], and also described his alleged policy of neutrality at all costs as a fable. But this significant phrase occurred: "Given the actual conditions in Europe, it is my belief that *much* may be obtained without going to war, but only those who are in the Government are fully qualified to judge of this matter." The popular instinct immediately seized upon the word *parecchio,* translated by *much* in the English version of the memoirs, though it might be more justly rendered by *a certain amount.* The unsentimental suggestion implied in the *parecchio di Giolitti,* that Italy's policy should be to obtain something for nothing, was unsparingly used by his antagonists to discredit the veteran statesman, who has since frankly admitted and given his reasons for his opposition to Italy entering the war. I fully accept his disclaimer of the reported interviews in Rome. But I have always presumed that Giolitti, in view of the influence he could exercise and of his consistent advocacy of neutrality, was, vicariously at any rate, kept fully informed throughout of Bülow's activities and proposals.

Negotiations for Neutrality

Later, in March, when the Catholic deputy, [German statesman Matthias] Erzberger, some of whose fierce tirades against Great

Britain in the *Germania* and the *Tag* I had seen translated in the Italian Press, was for the second time in Rome, and reported to be endeavouring to persuade the Vatican to exercise pressure on [Austrian Emperor] Francis Joseph to cede the Trentino, I had myself the opportunity of having an hour's conversation with Giolitti. It would not have been opportune that our meeting should have become public property, and with the exception of those who arranged the interview no one, so far as I am aware, ever knew that it had taken place. I felt, however, that it would be unwise in these critical times not to make contact with a statesman of his authority and position. Giolitti on that occasion insisted on the paramount importance which the obligations of loyalty had always had for him. After a good deal of perfectly amicable fencing without coming to close quarters on a direct issue, I received the definite impression that he was then as firmly as ever wedded to neutrality.

The heavy losses of battleships in the attack on the Dardanelles on the 18th of March, which the presence of a moderate landing party would have converted into a most successful action, had an unfortunate moral effect on the hesitating Balkan States and indeed on the weak-kneed everywhere. But there were compensations, such as the destruction of the *Dresden* after her successful career of commerce-destroying. And now an important step forward was taken towards the end on which all my thoughts were concentrated. For, while the efforts of the special Ambassador, of Erzberger and of the peace party to preserve Italian neutrality were being daily intensified, negotiations were secretly initiated with the Italian Government for an agreement which would take immediate effect in the event of Italy ranging herself in line with the Allies. It is curious after the event to read in Erzberger's record of his experiences during the struggle that a deputy with whom he was intimate informed him that the Italian Government did not wish for war, . . . and that [foreign minister Sidney] Sonnino was more reluctant than ever. Simultaneously I became aware of certain unostentatious preparations for future contingencies, such as the replacement of married by unmarried railway officials in the Venetian area and a large extension of hospital accommodation in the big cities. For reasons into which I need not enter the negotiations which led to the Pact of London were known to the fewest possible individuals, and the bases of agreement were drafted in London. I at any rate had now no doubt as to Sonnino's intentions, nor had I any that he would carry the Ministry with him. But there remained the graver question of whether they would have the support of Parliament and of the people. To ensure the latter—and ... it is the people who have the last word in Italy—it then seemed essential that the future security of a country which had lived under the intolerable menace of the Austrian guns, whether on the northern frontier or in the Adriatic, should be absolutely guaranteed. No half-measures or inadequate assurances would command the national adhesion.

Sonnino was in my opinion at that stage genuinely anxious that no counter-irredentism [movement against non-Italian territories becoming part of Italy] should be created by the incorporation of an undue number of non-Italians in the kingdom. But he had a very definite problem to face. The continuous chain of islands forming a natural barrier along the eastern shore of the Adriatic, behind which destroyers and submarines could move and assemble undetected, had constituted a standing menace to the opposite defenceless coasts of the Italian peninsula which possessed no ports worthy of the name between Venice and Brindisi. Vallona in Albania could not be made available for naval purposes without an expenditure of many millions, and were it to be permanently held this would only be as a precautionary measure to prevent it from falling into other hands. Slavism had always been regarded as a potential danger, and if Italy was to enter into a combination in which peoples having rival interests were already engaged, it would be necessary for her to assure herself that she was not going to fight for a settlement which might prove to her own ultimate disadvantage.

Terms for a Possible Partnership

It was then still an accepted doctrine that Russia would some day become a naval factor in the Mediterranean, and, though she might not be suspected of any design to absorb the southern Slavs, the obligations of racial affinity had already been practically demonstrated. Italian statesmen were therefore bound to consider the possibility of the establishment of naval bases independent of their control which might at a future time become a danger to their country. The opinion of naval experts was unanimous in regarding the Cursolan Islands as offering an ideal naval base and therefore a danger to Italy if left in any other hands. It was imperative to satisfy Italian exigencies in respect of a position which was claimed to be a key of the Adriatic. This was therefore one of the issues on which depended the mobilization of a million and a half of men, which might moreover, as it seemed then, carry with it the decision of Roumania, possibly also that of other Balkan States. The Russian Government, which had on its own initiative suggested the transfer of Dalmatia [region on the western Balkan peninsula] to Italy, made difficulties about the islands, on grounds which were apparently sentimental, as it seemed hardly probable that her statesmen were contemplating the remote possibility of reserving them as a naval base. The attitude of Russia in regard to the co-operation of Italy gave me at one time considerable anxiety. For Great Britain and France the future of the islands had little direct interest. Dalmatia, however, was a thorny question, because while the coastal towns were Italian in culture and tradition, the hinterland was wholly Slavonic, and at the same time there was force in the contention that the two were neither logically nor economically separable. The unity of Dalmatia was moreover being warmly advocated at home by a number of travellers and publicists. But at such a moment sentimental considerations were not very likely to prevail against practical ones. . . . As regards the islands, however, he [Sonnino] was rigidly immovable.

Some other questions besides territorial rectifications were included in the Pact, which was to be completed by a military convention. Its terms have now long been known and amply discussed. If I have referred here to one or two particular issues which presented difficulty at a critical moment, and which must have given my friend Imperiali [the Italian diplomat in London] some sleepless nights in London, it has been rather to emphasize a belief which I have always entertained, that considerations of security and not imperialist ambition inspired the Italian statesmen who conducted negotiations.

A suspicion of Imperialism was, I think, too readily entertained outside Italy by those who did not understand the depth of a sentiment which claimed the reunion of certain areas, not strictly comprehended within the geographical limits of the peninsula, but always regarded as essential outposts; which owed all the civilization and prosperity they possessed to Italian tradition, enterprise, and settlement. It is true there had never been a united Italy after the downfall of the Western Empire until the nineteenth century. But the municipal institutions which had been the strength of that Empire, reviving after the Dark Ages in small states and city republics, had maintained a sort of common Italian ambience over an even wider area, and later the links re-established by Venice with the eastern Adriatic shore had engendered a spirit of kinship rather than of dominion. A century of Austrian domination in the Narrow Seas had on the other hand humiliatingly reminded a reunited Italy of an insecurity of tenure which every patriot ardently desired to see eliminated.

By the beginning of April a stage was reached at which there was little left to divide us if Russian sentiment did not raise further obstacles. Meanwhile Germany was urging on a very reluctant Austria that certain territorial concessions must be made to Italy forthwith and that it would be fatal to insist on deferring the surrender of the Trentino until after an eventual peace. I could not be blind to the fact that Bülow had the support of a very strong combination which made no secret of their preference for the *parecchio,* if it could be secured at once, to the alternative of War. There was reason to believe that . . . strong influence could be brought to bear on senators and deputies connected with the many industrial enterprises which it controlled. Giolitti had been absent from the capital for some weeks; but the Giolittian groups began to consolidate themselves. . . .

The Pact of London

On the 26th of April I entered in my diary the two words *Nunc dimittis* [now you may dismiss me]. I had received the anxiously awaited telegram announcing the signature of the Pact of London. Its terms, the practical execution of which would obviously have to depend on the situation existing after the termination of hostilities, have since been much criticized. . . . But no one who reviews without prejudice the position of the Allies in the early months of 1915, and not least that of Serbia herself, is entitled to criticize their acceptance by the British Government. Nor could Italian statesmen have decided to bring a hesitating and divided nation into a war of such magnitude and danger without having first obtained assurances believed by them necessary to safeguard the future of their country, which would be called upon to make immense sacrifices. There remained certain formulae to be completed when the opportune moment came, but I felt that we were now practically in alliance with Italy. . . .

It now seemed quite justifiable to assume that only a brief interval of time would suffice to bring to their inevitable conclusion the discussions [over Italy's neutrality] with Austria-Hungary which the Minister for Foreign Affairs had been conducting in an evidently unyielding spirit regarding the compensations claimed in virtue of the terms of the Triple Alliance as a consequence of the modification of *status quo* in the Balkans. And yet the gravest crisis in the long battle had still to be affronted.

In this last phase the Italian Government had of course to act alone, and the enemy's manoeuvres to gain for neutrality the support of a chamber which was not really representative of the country seemed about to be crowned with success. The Austro-Hungarian Government, on the strength of reports received from Rome, continued up to the last to believe that Italy was only "bluffing," and would never go to war. So confident were they in this opinion that relatively few troops were concentrated on the Italian frontier. Erzberger, who had been once more summoned to Rome in the first days of May, complains of the delusions and inactivity of Baron Macchio, the Austro-Hungarian Ambassador. Suddenly at the eleventh hour the gravity of the situation was brought home to them, and when it was too late they decided to make larger concessions. But on the 4th of May the Italian Government notified Vienna that they withdrew any proposals they had put forward for agreement, denounced the Treaty of Alliance, and resumed entire liberty of action. Their intention had been to maintain the strictest secrecy regarding the action then taken until the meeting of Parliament. I did not myself learn the formal denunciation of the Triple Alliance until several days later, when circumstances made it desirable to take the public into confidence. The enemy missions, having now realized that it was too late to deflect [leading statesman Antonio] Salandra and Sonnino from the course on which they had resolved, rested their hopes on displacing the Government in office by intriguing with the opposition. But the people became cognizant of this intrigue, and then the strength of the popular voice, the *ultima ratio* in Italian national life, was revealed.

The People Respond

A majority among the masses had in my opinion been with us throughout. It was not only nor perhaps chiefly that the outbreak of the world's war made Trieste and the Trentino appear no longer an unrealizable dream. People had long ago made up their minds as to who was responsible [for the war], and they had followed closely and with growing indignation the unscrupulous methods of warfare by which the will of Germany was to be enforced on the world. Public sentiment, always quick to respond to the appeal of elemental justice and instinctively intolerant of prepotency, had been profoundly stirred by that treatment of Belgium, which even Count Moltke admitted to have been "certainly brutal." [In a letter addressed to General Conrad von Hoetzendorff and published by the latter in his astonishingly candid memories.] The opening phase of the submarine campaign against merchant vessels, sunk without warning in defiance of the accepted rules of naval warfare, had been responsible for the death of innocent Italian emigrants. The politician and the business world might be intimidated, but the simple man, who discussed these outrages with his fellow, was growing dangerously angry. Humble friends of mine among the working-classes said to me again and again, "We mean to have war." Then, as if to reaffirm the truth of the ancient saying, "Those whom the gods have doomed they first afflict with madness," just at this critical stage came the crime of the *Lusitania* [a passenger ship sunk by Germany], and the outraged feelings of an emotional people only needed a voice to give expression to their resentment. Eloquence is never wanting in Italy, where the word springs ready to the lips. But the occasion demanded not only eloquence but that imagination and inspiration which moves men to possess their souls. Perhaps in no other country in the world could it have happened that at such a moment a poet should indicate the course and take the helm. At the rock of Quarto, where Garibaldi had embarked with his thousand for the Sicilian expedition, [Italian author and soldier Gabriele] d'Annunzio began his apostolate with a speech to the Ligurians [people from Liguria, in northwestern Italy], which went to the heart of the country. A second and a third speech followed, and an enthusiastic crowd assembled to welcome the orator to Rome. . . .

The meeting of Parliament which would have to decide the great issue and confer extraordinary powers on the Government drew near. On the 7th of May Giolitti came to Rome after an absence of several weeks. His personal attitude had remained enigmatic. There is reason to believe that his original intention had been not to oppose Salandra, for whose succession in 1914 he had prepared the way. But there had been subsequent misunderstandings, and considerable bitterness had grown up between the statesmen, with the result that in this critical period Giolitti had been left entirely in the background, which he no doubt resented. Various rumours reached me which, though their source seemed worthy of credit, I had no means of testing. Public opinion in any case charged him with having at a critical hour abandoned a passive attitude for a militant advocacy of neutralism. There had been demonstrations of hostility during his passage through Turin. . . . Nevertheless, upwards of three hundred deputies left cards or letters of welcome at his house on his arrival. What may be described as his tied voters had seldom failed him when he claimed their support to secure him an adequate majority. Giolitti has stated in his memoirs that already before the 9th of May Bertolini, a former colleague in his Ministry who, during his absence, acted as leader of his group in Rome, had informed him of the offers which Austria was making.

It was not, however, till the 11th that the responsible Ministers Salandra and Sonnino received a simultaneous communication drafted in haste, and dispatched during the night, containing the ultimate concessions which Austria-Hungary, under German pressure, was prepared to grant to Italy. . . . The German Empire undertook to guarantee the loyal execution of the arrangement to be concluded to give them effect. It was now proposed that Trieste should become a free city with municipal autonomy endowed with an Italian university. But the time had gone by for negotiations with the Government in office, which had already crossed the Rubicon [a metaphor from an action by Julius Caesar that came to mean *there is no turning back*].

Disruption in the Government

And now it was ascertained by those means which are available to Parliamentary experts that the neutralists intended to defeat the Ministry by some 300 votes out of an approximate total of 500. Giolitti himself, I was given to understand, would take no direct part in the proceedings in the Chamber, but would leave it to his followers to upset the Government. Without a vote of confidence and the indispensable credits Salandra's administration would be paralysed. On the night of the 13th of May it was announced that they had resigned. It was one of the grimmest moments I have ever experienced. Bülow and his allies were chanting victory. If not Giolitti himself, one of his nominees would, they assumed, form a more or less neutralist Cabinet, and all danger of Italy entering the war would be eliminated. But such self-congratulations were premature. They had left the people out of their reckoning.

Already on the 13th certain prominent members of the Giolittian party had been roughly handled in the streets. On the morning of the 14th a crowd shouting "Down with Giolitti!" made an irruption into the precincts of the Chamber, and did considerable damage there. The Ministers who had tendered their resignation were not in a position to make any public statement. But there were discreet indiscretions. The *Corriere della Sera,* in its issue of the 14th, divulged that the Triple Alliance had been denounced, and that an agreement with the *Entente* Powers [France, Great Britain, and Russia] had been signed. Gabriele d'Annunzio made a similar statement at a mass meeting at the Costanzi Theatre, where he stigmatized Giolitti as a traitor. The public became aware that it was only after the Triple Alliance had actually been denounced that Austria-Hungary had definitely formulated concessions, and they realized with growing anger that these conditions had been made known to Opposition politicians before they were actually submitted to the Government. There was a storm of protest against the attempt of a foreign State to intervene in the internal affairs of the country. [In corroboration of what I have here written, the speech made by Signor Salandra on the Capitol on the 2nd of June may be quoted. While giving Prince Bülow credit for entertaining a sincere sympathy for Italy he said, "But how many and how grave were the errors he made in translating these good intentions into action. He supposed that Italy could be deflected from her course by a certain number of millions ill-bestowed, by the influence of a limited number of individuals who had lost the sense of the national spirit, by attempting, though I hope without success, the seduction of Italian politicians." The authority of "the best judge of the situation in Italy" was invoked by the German Chancellor on the day following her declaration of war in order to convince his audience that at the beginning of May 1915 four-fifths of the Senate and two-thirds of the Chamber, including the most serious and influential statesmen, were still against the war; but the mob, supported by the chief Ministers in a Cabinet gorged with the gold of the Triple *Entente,* led by unscrupulous agitators, had threatened the

King with revolution, and the Moderates with assassination, if war were not declared. If the Chancellor meant to include Salandra and Sonnino in his general charge of corruption, he must have assumed extraordinary credulity in his audience.] There were violent demonstrations before Giolitti's house. Cavalry and infantry were detailed to protect the residence of the special Ambassador. From Milan was heard an ominous murmur, "War or the republic!" Trieste and the Trentino were hardly referred to now, and Austria, the traditional enemy, seemed relegated to the second plane. The universal cry was *"Fuori i Barbari!"* ("Out with the Barbarians!") All through Saturday, the 15th, there were popular demonstrations in every part of Italy. The situation was tense. And now the next word was with the King.

Since August 1914 I had seen the King from time to time on various occasions. His Majesty was far too scrupulously observant of his obligations as a constitutional monarch ever consciously to commit himself to any expressions inconsistent with the neutrality of his country. But there had been little indications of friendship in his manner, guarded warnings suggesting prudence in certain courses, and especially a look of comradeship in the eyes, which left me in no doubt as to what his own feelings were. And was he not the grandson of Victor Emmanuel, the Liberator King, and the head of the great fighting House of Savoy? But whatever the King's own personal sentiments might be, he was now faced with a grave constitutional responsibility. His decision, because of the consequences which it must entail, would be the most serious a monarch can be called upon to take. The Government of Signor Salandra, on the eve of a declaration of war, had resigned because they had realized that they would not be supported by Parliament. The King, always the best-informed man in the country, disregarding actuarial forecasts of the Parliamentary vote, took his deliberate stand on what he believed to be the will of the people, so openly manifested in the last two days. On the 16th he confirmed the Salandra Government in office. The nation responded by acclamation. The people had come down into the piazza, and no Chamber could ignore their verdict. And so the great conspiracy failed.

Two hundred thousand citizens of Rome were reported to have gathered that afternoon in the Piazza del Popolo. The estimate seems almost fantastic. But it was on a Sunday when all were out and about. That evening, a golden evening of the Roman May, thousands and thousands of them marched up to the Embassy at Porta Pia. They were not of the type which ordinarily furnishes demonstrations, but an orderly and disciplined throng which seemed to include the best of the bourgeoisie, officials, tradesmen and craftsmen. My wife threw down armfuls of flowers from the balcony. There was a call for the flag, and then a hush fell upon the multitude, expecting a speech. But I had to repress my emotions, and could only say that my duty was still to be silent. It would be for the Government to speak.

Italy Enters the War

I have never witnessed a more remarkable phenomenon than this uprising of the people. There had been nothing like it in Italy since 1859. The few witnesses surviving from that epoch pronounced the enthusiasm of 1915 to be greater. I do not believe the Government themselves had expected such unanimity. After the hectic days, which were referred to as passion week, it was evident that the die was cast. Party pledges and combinations, the insincerities and compromises of political life would have to disappear before a manifestation of the popular will which had cleared the air. Except for that of the irreconcilable Socialists, Parliamentary opposition might now be regarded as silenced. It was, however, dormant rather than dead, a condition which accounts for subsequent developments which it might otherwise be difficult to explain. . . .

Parliament assembled on the 20th of May for the most memorable meeting at which I ever assisted. The galleries were packed beyond their capacity. The President of the Council asked the Chamber to give the Government the extraordinary powers which would be necessary in the event of war. As Signor Salandra made his brief but pregnant statement of the reasons which had made this demand inevitable, members rose time after time to their feet to applaud. Only five rows of Socialists on the extreme left remained seated and grimly silent. The Bill was referred to a Committee which was directed to report forthwith. Meanwhile, Ministers went on in a body to the Senate. By the time they returned the report of the Committee was ready. As the Socialist leader, Turati, who had been appointed to the Committee, had excused himself from attendance, its report in favour of the Bill was unanimous. The reporter, the veteran patriot Boselli, made a touching and impressive address. He was followed by Barzilai, a protagonist of irredentism and one of the orators of the House. Turati then explained the dissent of a group of Socialists who believed that Italy should remain neutral, being heard with impatience. He was answered by Cicotti, as the spokesman of the other group who regarded intervention as an ideal duty. The ballot was taken at 6.50 P.M. There were 483 deputies present, two of whom abstained from voting. The Bill was carried by 407 to 74. Then the Assembly, hitherto restrained, as befitted the solemnity of the occasion, went mad with enthusiasm, and the public in the galleries joined in the patriotic manifestations. As friends pressed round to clasp Sonnino's hand, there was the shadow of a smile upon the handsome ascetic face. . . .

Instructions had been sent to the Italian Ambassador in Vienna on the 22nd of May to announce the declaration of war. The message appears to have been stopped upon the road, as he telegraphed that he had not received the communication which he had been warned to expect. The declaration of war as from the 24th was therefore handed to the Austro-Hungarian Ambassador in Rome on the 23rd. At daybreak on the 24th an Austrian flotilla bombarded Ancona. The Counsellor of the German Embassy then proceeded to the Foreign Office to announce that if the Italians attacked the Austrians they would find German troops with them. This would entail the existence of a state of war with Germany also. . . .

On the following day, the first Sunday of Italy's war, there were organized demonstrations by processions to the Allied embassies. This time we were better prepared to receive them. On the balcony over the entrance in Via XX Settembre [a road in Genoa] the British and Italian flags waved side by side, and flowers and ribbons had been collected. At the head of the procession marched a small pathetic group of old Garibaldians in their red shirts. The veterans of fifty-nine and sixty were bidding Godspeed to the young armies of 1915. There was no longer any need for reticence, and I went down to the front door and from the steps said what it was in my heart to say—a few such simple words as the emotion of the moment inspired. When I had finished I was conscious of arms round my shoulders and rough faces against my cheek.

Benito Mussolini
and Italian Fascism

By Jasper Ridley

After World War I ended in 1918, the Italian government was weak and disorganized. Several political parties struggled among themselves for dominance, each hoping to shape Italy's government in the coming years. By the 1920s, one party had emerged as the leading power in Italian politics—the Fascists.

Benito Mussolini, who came to be called Il Duce *(the leader), worked throughout the 1920s and 1930s to build the strength of his party and to change the Italian government to suit his purposes. Today, the word* fascism *is usually viewed in a negative light, primarily because of the acts committed by Fascists in both Italy and Germany during World War II. Through the use of persistent propaganda and the ruthless elimination of political opponents, Mussolini established a strong regime that had both positive and negative qualities.*

Acclaimed biographer Jasper Ridley, author of more than 300 books, has written about many powerful people from various periods in world history. In this selection, Ridley argues that in many ways Italian fascism differed greatly from the totalitarian governments of Nazi Germany and the Communist Soviet Union after World War II. Although the Italian people certainly gave up some of their rights under the Italian Fascist regime, they also received certain economic and social benefits that, to some, seemed to be as valuable as their civil liberties.

In recent times, many political commentators have pointed out that while Fascist Italy, with its plebiscites, its one-party state, its censored press and the imprisonment without trial of political oppositionists, was certainly a dictatorship, it was not a totalitarian state like Nazi Germany or the Soviet Union under [Joseph] Stalin. There is an irony here, for it was [Benito] Mussolini and his Fascist ideologists who first invented the word 'totalitarian' in 1923 to describe the state in Fascist Italy: unlike the state in the democracies and all previous regimes, the Fascist state was totalitarian because it demanded the total commitment and devotion of all its citizens. But in a number of ways it was milder than Nazi Germany and Stalinist Russia or the royal despotisms of the sixteenth and seventeenth centuries. . . .

The Press and Propaganda

In the first years of the Fascist era, the press was the chief means of propaganda. The first Italian radio stations began broadcasting in 1924, but by 1930 there were only 100,000 radio sets among the forty million Italians. The radio became increasingly important throughout the 1930s, reaching many millions of people in their homes and through the loudspeakers in the public squares. By 1922 cinemas were showing silent films all over Italy, and several private Italian film companies were producing excellent films which competed very successfully with the American films produced in Hollywood and the German UFA productions. The Fascist government produced propaganda newsreels about current events with suitable captions written by official commentators. A law of 3 April 1926 made it compulsory for every cinema to show the official government newsreels, which became much more effective as propaganda after the introduction of talking pictures in 1928.

The Fascist government controlled the press in three ways. The Fascist Party bought shares which gave them a controlling interest in several of the leading national and local newspapers; by 1930 nearly 66 per cent of all newspapers were controlled by the Fascists. Secondly, the newspapers received instructions every day as to the political line that they were expected to adopt, from the government press office, which was at first under the control of Cesare Rossi who gave the order for the murder of [Giacomo] Matteotti [leader of the movement against Mussolini].

Thirdly, there were the powers given to the prefects [government officials] under the decree of 8 July 1924. . . . The prefect could issue a warning to any newspaper editor who had 'damaged the credit of the nation at home or abroad' or who published false news. An editor who received two warnings within one year could be dismissed by the prefect, who could then refuse to consent to the appointment of a new editor to succeed him. The prefect could not exercise these powers without the consent of a committee consisting of the prefect, a magistrate and a journalist; but he could order the seizure and confiscation of any issue of a newspaper without consulting the committee, and prefects used this power of confiscation more often than they issued warnings. A stricter control was imposed by the law of 31 December 1925, which set up the Order of Journalists and prohibited anyone from being a journalist unless he was a member of the order.

Subject to these restrictions, independent newspapers could be published, and an editor could express his individual views, and even criticize some aspect of government policy, if he combined this with general support for the government and for Fascism, and especially with lavish praise of the Duce [Mussolini]. The newspapers of Farinacci, Giovanni Preziosi and Telesio Interlandi, and various Catholic ultramontane journals, denounced the Jews many years before this became Mussolini's official policy. The *Giornale Italiano*, which was owned by Mussolini's Jewish minister, Finzi, and *Israel*, the official organ of the Italian Jews, replied to this anti-Semitic propaganda. . . .

Fascism and Art

These differences of opinion and journalistic polemics were particularly marked on questions of art, literature and science. Already, before the First World War, the Futurist movement in art had supported the revolutionary nationalist ideas that afterwards expressed themselves in the interventionist campaign of 1914–15 and the Fascist movement after the war. They claimed that their modern art was revolutionary and Fascist as opposed to the stodgy, conventional art of the old conservative bourgeois [middle-class] parties and classes. But the ideas of the Futurists were opposed, often with great vehemence, by other more conservative elements in the artistic establishment. The Fascist leadership did not give a ruling as to which side was right, or proclaim an official 'Fascist art' which must be adopted by all artists, as a 'Socialist art' was prescribed in the Soviet Union. Both sides were left free to denounce each other year after year, with tactful praise of the Duce intermingled with their criticism of their rivals.

The arguments were particularly bitter among the architects. Did modernistic buildings best express the new revolutionary spirit of the Fascist era? Or was the classical architecture, based on the buildings of ancient Rome, a better expression of the incomparable genius of Mussolini? There were similar arguments among scientists, geneticists, biologists and anthropologists as to the significance of racial as opposed to environmental factors in producing the glories of Fascist Italy.

This freedom of discussion, which was so different from Nazi Germany and Soviet Russia, showed both the strength and the weakness of Mussolini's regime. It was his strength that he was tolerant enough to allow these differences of opinion. The draw-back was that his toleration extended to allowing his Fascists from time to time to riot, burn and murder. He might urge them not to do so, but they knew that they could flout his wishes with rel-ative impunity.

Mussolini never exterminated the radical left-wing of the Fas-cist Party, as Hitler exterminated Ernst Roehm's SA on the 'night of the long knives' on 30 June 1934; still less did he put to death—before 1943—nearly every other member of the gov-ernment and party leadership as Stalin did. He played the various local Fascist bosses against each other, and sometimes ordered the OVRA [Organization to Watch and Repress Anti-Fascism] to trail them. [Fascist leader Italo] Balbo once discovered that the OVRA were tapping his telephone. He telephoned Mussolini in a rage, and protested. Mussolini said that of course the OVRA were tapping his telephone; it was an elementary security pre-caution. What else did Balbo expect? Balbo realized that there was no answer to this rhetorical question, and that was the end of the incident.

Education in the Fascist State

The greatest importance was placed on education, and the in-doctrination of youth. This was particularly important in a coun-try where every child was indoctrinated in Catholic Christianity from the very earliest age. Mussolini's first Minister of Education was the philosopher Professor [Giovanni] Gentile; and although Gentile resigned from the government in protest after the mur-der of Matteotti, he was persuaded to rejoin the Fascist hierar-chy, although not as a minister, when the repercussions of the murder had died down. He was put in charge of drafting the syl-labus and laying down the guidelines of elementary, secondary and university education, and of publishing the *Enciclopedia Ital-iana*, which was to rival the *Encyclopædia Britannica* and the French *Grand Larousse* in completeness and scholarship.

Gentile's educational theories were very different from those of the Socialists who had exercised great influence in the years before the First World War. The aim of the Socialists had been to spread literacy among the people. Gentile wished to produce excellence, and provide a suitable education for the élite, the meritocracy, the hierarchy, the *gerarchia*. He explained that education was of secondary importance as long as Mussolini was alive, when everything could be left to his infallible wisdom and brilliant leadership. At present, it was only necessary to train children who would obey and follow him without question; but Fascism would survive him, and when he was no longer among them they would have to produce a generation who would be able to fend for themselves.

Along with the state schools, there were many private schools in Fascist Italy, particularly the Church and convent fee-paying schools where many children of the upper classes were educated. They were allowed to run themselves, but were obliged to follow Gentile's national curriculum, just as religious teaching was made compulsory in all state schools. . . .

But in educational policy, as in other matters, free discussion was tolerated in the press and elsewhere. Scholars were free to criticize Gentile's decision that the schools should teach more about ancient Rome and less about ancient Greece; more about the Risorgimento and less about the history of modern Europe; more about Garibaldi and less about Cavour. The most eminent of these critics was the classical historian Gaetano De Sanctis, who had always opposed the Fascists; he continued to argue that the free governments of ancient Greece were more worthy of study than the military regimentation of ancient Rome. But Gentile appointed him to be the editor of the classical section of the *Enciclopedia Italiana*.

Teaching Children to Be Fascists

Gentile's successors as Minister of Education, Pietro Fedele and Giuseppe Belluzzo, carried through a purge of teachers and of textbooks after 1925, to eliminate all traces of anti-Fascism in schools and to comply with Mussolini's directive of December 1925: 'The government demands that the schools should be inspired by the ideals of Fascism', and should not be hostile 'or agnostic' about Fascism. In all schools, including the private and convent schools, an hour was devoted every week to physical

training. The physical training instructor was a Fascist—a Donna
Fascista in the girls' convent schools—who combined the physical instruction with uplifting talk about the role of Fascism and
the Duce in elevating the physical and moral health of the Italian people.

The six-year-olds in the schools learned to read and write
from the primer that had been made compulsory in all state and
private schools; they copied, slowly and laboriously, the sentences
in the printed book on to the ruled lines of their copybooks.
'Long live the King! Long live Italy! Long live the army! Long
live our Chief Benito Mussolini! Down with Russia! Long live
Africa! Long live our soldiers! Long live our King and may he always be victorious! Long live our DUCE, our Chief, and the
founder of Fascism! Long live Italian Rome!'

By the age of seven they had moved on to their second exercise book. 'Children love Benito Mussolini. Benito Mussolini has
worked and will always work for the good of our country and
of the Italian people. You have often heard your Daddy say it,
you have heard Mummy say it, you have heard the teachers say
it. If Italy is today stronger than before, we owe it to him. Let us
salute him altogether *A noi!*' ('Come on!', the Fascist slogan).

At nine they could take more advanced dictation. 'The immediate post-war years were a dark period for Italy. The revolutionary idea came as propaganda from Russia to our country. Industry, commerce and transport were at a standstill. Our country
was threatened with utter ruin by the continual strikes and the
occupation of the factories by the Communists, when Heaven
sent us a man who uplifted our destiny—Benito Mussolini. On
28 October 1922 the Blackshirts entered Rome, and our King
confided the government to Benito Mussolini, who immediately
restored order all over Italy. During his years in government He
has conferred incomparable and great benefits which have made
Italy ever more beautiful and ever more powerful.' In the Italian
language, capital letters are used less than in English; but references to the Duce were always in capitals, and usually the whole
word 'DUCE' was written in capitals.

Propaganda for Adults

More subtle forms of propaganda were sometimes adopted with
adults, though here too much of the propaganda was crude. A
very popular and best-selling calendar, with a page for every

month, was published every year for housewives to hang up in their kitchens. Each page contained a recipe for some dish, and the housewife could consult the calendar for instructions while she was cooking the dish. In the middle of each page there was a photograph of Mussolini and a quotation from his speeches. Most housewives did not look at the photograph or read the quotations, but studied only the recipe; but they were nevertheless aware, at least unconsciously, that the Duce and his words of wisdom were in their kitchen.

In the cities, towns and villages of Italy, the slogans issued by the Duce and the party were displayed on the hoardings and painted on the walls in the streets: '*Credere, obbedire, combattere*' (believe, obey, fight); 'if I advance, follow me; if I stand still, drive me forward; if I retreat, shoot me'; and '*Noi tireremo diritto*', which English commentators have wrongly translated as 'shoot straight', but in fact meant 'Carry straight on regardless'. Another slogan, the most popular of all, was displayed everywhere, and constantly quoted: '*Mussolini ha sempre ragione*' (Mussolini is always right).

The intellectuals beat all the others in their eulogies of Mussolini. The philosopher Ottavio Dinale wrote in *Gerarchia* in July 1930 that all the qualities and virtues of Alexander the Great and Caesar, of Socrates and Plato, of Virgil and Lucretius, of Horace and Tacitus, of Kant and Nietzsche, of Marx and Sorel, of Machiavelli and Napoleon, and of Garibaldi and the Unknown Warrior [all great historical and cultural figures], had been reproduced in one man—Benito Mussolini.

No wonder that Mussolini, glorified on all sides every day, was not particularly impressed when the King twice offered to make him a duke, the first time after he had induced Yugoslavia to cede Fiume to Italy, and the second after the signature of the Lateran Treaty with the Vatican. It was enough to be '*Capo del governo, Duce del fascismo*'; as head of the government and leader of Fascism, he felt that he did not need a dukedom, and that if he accepted it he would look rather ridiculous. . . .

The Demands of the Regime

In view of the fact that the Fascist regime interfered comparatively little with academic and intellectual freedom, nearly all the intellectuals were prepared to subscribe to Fascism and then continue as before in their intellectual and creative work. In 1931 a new law required all university professors to take an oath of loyalty to Fascism. This was the most direct interference with academic freedom which had so far taken place; but only eleven out of 1,200 professors in the whole of Italy refused to take the oath and lost their positions. Mussolini's old colleague, [conductor] Arturo Toscanini, was one of the few who refused to compromise. In the general election of 1919 he had stood, together with Mussolini, as a Fascist candidate in Milan; but when the violence, arson and murders began, he turned against Fascism. He always refused to play the Fascist hymn *Giovinezza* at the beginning or end of his concerts and operatic performances. In 1930 he made a successful foreign tour, and received a great ovation when he conducted at the Albert Hall on his first appearance in London. But the Fascists did not forgive him for refusing to play *Giovinezza*.

In May 1931 a Fascist congress was held in Bologna. During the congress, Toscanini conducted at the Giuseppe Martucci memorial concert. The Fascists stormed into the concert hall and demanded that he play *Giovinezza*. He refused. They assaulted him, punching him and his wife, and beating them with canes. Neither he nor his wife was seriously injured, but he was ordered by the prefect to stay in his house for his own protection and to surrender his passport to the authorities. The case attracted much attention in the international press. After a month his passport was returned to him, and he was allowed to travel on foreign tours. Next year, when Mussolini talked to [German biographer] Emil Ludwig, and they discussed music, Mussolini went out of his way to say that Toscanini was the greatest conductor in the world. Toscanini eventually settled in the United States.

The Effects of Fascism on Everyday Life

As far as the majority of the population was concerned, Fascism did not greatly interfere with their ordinary lives. Young men were liable to be called up for compulsory military service in peacetime, but this applied in most countries of Europe, though not in Britain, which, except during the First World War, had always relied on a small volunteer army, or in Germany, where conscription had been forbidden by the victorious Allies in the Treaty of Versailles. The ladies and gentlemen of Roman society continued to go to balls, night-clubs and theatrical first nights, to expensive hotels in the mountains for winter sports and summer holidays, and to the fashionable golf clubs. The lower middle class and factory workers found that food and minor luxuries could be bought at reasonable prices in the shops and markets, and that they could occasionally take the family to lunch and dine at popular restaurants and to an evening at the cinema.

They all appreciated the fact that Mussolini had made the trains run on time, as was often pointed out by his British admirers. This aroused much ridicule among the left-wing intellectuals: Mussolini was suppressing the fundamental freedoms of the Italian people, and was being praised for so trivial an achievement as making the trains run on time. In Britain in the 1920s trains nearly always ran on time, and Englishmen did not appreciate, as their grandchildren would do and their Italian contemporaries did, the inconvenience of having trains that do not run on time; nor did they realize that if Mussolini had made the trains run on time, it was because he had stopped strikes and other disruptive practices by the railway trade unions. The intellectuals were reluctant to admit that many Italians, like many people in other countries, attached more importance to making trains run on time and causing other things to run efficiently in their humdrum lives than to preserving freedom of speech for opposition politicians, journalists and writers.

The Benefits of Fascism

The Fascist regime brought some real benefits to the people. For the ordinary Italian, whether he was an industrial worker, a peasant, or a lower-middle-class bank clerk, the Fascist organization, the Dopolavoro (after work), provided recreational and sporting activities and opportunities that most of them had never had before. A month's summer holiday was given, free of charge, to all children in the Fascist youth movement. A doctor examined every child and decided whether a holiday in the clean air of the mountains, or one at the seaside, would be better for his health. The child would then be sent to a holiday centre in some hotel that had been acquired for the purpose. The holiday centre was run chiefly by women in the Donne Fasciste organization who had volunteered to do the work. It was a happy month for the children, who still remember[ed] it nostalgically sixty and seventy years later. Nothing like this had been done for the children in the days before Mussolini, and the holiday camps did not survive his downfall and death. No one provides them for the children in post-war Italy.

There were other advantages in belonging to the Fascist Party and its youth movement. Children who were bullied at school, or ill-treated by unkind schoolmasters, appealed for help to the leader of the local Balilla, who spoke to the schoolmaster and the parents of the bully. A law provided that wounded ex-servicemen must be offered work if they asked for it, and in the Trentino the law applied to those inhabitants who had been conscripted into the Austrian Army in the First World War as well as to those who fought in the Italian Army. When Fortunato Pancrazi, a wounded ex-serviceman who had fought for Austria, went to an employer and asked for a job, the employer refused to employ him; he said that he sympathized, but it would not be profitable for him to employ a man whose incapacity made him a less productive worker than other employees; and that in any case the law did not apply in favour of soldiers who had fought on the Austrian side. Pancrazi went to the local branch of the Fascist Party. They told him that the law did apply to ex-servicemen who had served in the Austrian Army, and they visited the employer, who made no further difficulties about employing Pancrazi.

It was certainly a way of enforcing a worker's rights without being impeded by bureaucratic red tape. No intervention by government inspectors, no delay, no form-filling, no hearings before industrial tribunals, no appeals and prolonged litigation in the courts. Instead, the local Fascist Party secretary called on the employer and made it clear that if he did not play fair by his employee, some Fascists would come and beat him with cudgels, or burn down his house. The warning was nearly always effective.

Fascism and Italy's Role in World War II

By Paul Corner

After World War I, when Italy received few benefits in exchange for the many lives and funds lost in the fighting, some Italians—particularly the Fascists—formed a deep resentment toward the other nations of Europe. By 1939, when Adolf Hitler, the leader of Nazi Germany, started World War II with his invasion of Poland, he found a ready ally in Italy's Fascist leader, Benito Mussolini.

During the years that led up to the war, as Mussolini and his Fascist Party consolidated their hold on the government, they had worked to create an environment that equaled Hitler's Nazi Germany in totalitarianism. An agreement to fight on the side of the Nazis seemed to be a way for the Fascists to spread their policies abroad. When the war came, though, things did not go as Mussolini had hoped. Hitler alone ran the war, allowing Mussolini little or no input. Italy became almost a satellite state to Nazi Germany. As a result, Mussolini came to doubt his decision to become Hitler's ally, as did most of the Italian people.

As author Paul Corner, a history professor at the University of Siena, explains in this selection, Italian resistance to Hitler and his war goals helped bring about Mussolini's overthrow. Eventually, after a fierce invasion by the Allies, Italy changed sides and joined the Allied forces to fight Germany. With its old alliance with the Nazis broken and with Germany in defeat, the Fascist Party that had led Italy into the disastrous war virtually disappeared.

The memory of the First World War and the 'mutilated victory' was never very far from Fascist consciousness; the pursuit of international recognition and Great Power status was a direct consequence. Themes which stressed the unjust

Paul Corner, "Italy 1915–1945: Politics and Society," *The Oxford History of Italy*, edited by George Holmes. New York: Oxford University Press, 1997. Copyright © 1997 by Oxford University Press. Reproduced by permission.

treatment of 'proletarian' [working-class] Italy at the hands of plutocratic [wealthy] and imperialist nations proved particularly effective in mobilizing Fascist public opinion and clearly struck a chord in the country at large. The rhetoric of war which Fascism adopted (the battles for wheat, etc), the militarization of society through numerous uniformed groups, the quest for national self-sufficiency in food and other products—all built on this sense of resentment and conformed to a vision of society in which the dynamically aggressive 'new' Italian would eventually triumph in the battle for the national rights which had been denied him. War was built into Fascism (or a part of Fascism) from the outset; indeed, the pursuit of patriotic and nationalist objectives provided the legitimation for violence and for authoritarian government. ... The logic was unassailable: opposition to Fascism meant opposition to the nation, and was therefore tantamount to treason.

Italy Strives for More Territory

Diplomacy, belonging to the real world, was of course another matter, as the 1920s had shown. Then, circumstances had dictated caution, even if some kind of revisionism manifestly remained the basis of policy. Italy had ambitions in the areas of the Danube [in Germany], the Balkans, and the Adriatic, which influenced her attitudes to both France and Germany, and in North Africa, where France and Britain were called into question. [German dictator Adolf] Hitler's election in 1933 and the failure of [Benito] Mussolini's proposed four-power agreement (a kind of extended Locarno [region in Switzerland]) effectively dashed Italian hopes of expansion in Europe, turning Mussolini's attention exclusively towards Africa. The decision to invade Ethiopia seems to have been taken as a consequence of increasing international tensions, which suggested that the favourable moment might not recur, and from a desire to galvanize a Fascist movement which, with the crisis, had fallen distinctly into the doldrums.

The campaign itself was longer and far more costly than had been expected. It was fought with a savagery (poison gas, massacres of civilians) about which, even today, little is known in Italy. But politically it was a great, if rather ephemeral [short], success for Mussolini. League of Nations sanctions against Italy played into his hands and his announcement in May 1936 of the acquisition of empire seemed to confirm that Fascism had defeated not only Ethiopia but also those who wished to perpetuate international injustice. Italy cheered; domination of the Mediterranean—*mare nostrum* [Latin for 'our sea', as the Romans had referred to the Mediterranean]—was clearly just round the corner.

Setting the Stage for World War II

Victory in Ethiopia was probably the high point of the regime. It produced a short-lived general consensus and it seemed to justify Fascism in its persistent militaristic emphasis in civilian life. But the longer-term consequences of the war were disastrous, both in foreign policy and in internal affairs. Italy's relative isolation during sanctions had pushed her further into the arms of Nazi Germany, making her more than ever dependent on Germany for raw materials and fuel. As a result, Mussolini made concessions to Hitler over the status of Austria, thus giving up the one good card he had to play against Nazi expansionism. Success in Ethiopia also persuaded him to send 'volunteers' and military equipment to support [the Fascist leader of Spain Francisco] Franco, a commitment to the Fascistization of Europe which an impoverished Italy could hardly afford.

At home, the war carried Fascism into what has been termed the 'totalitarian phase', a phase which saw the attempt to increase the Fascist presence in the daily life of Italians in an effort to produce a truly Fascist nation. This period was dominated by war and expectation of war and the greater organization and regimentation of both population and economy corresponded to the need to form a nation capable of withstanding the pressures of a European war when it came. . . .

Hand in hand with recasting the Italian character went the streamlining of the economy. The cost of the Ethiopian war had been enormous ('pacification' continued throughout 1937 and 1938) and the effect on Italy's gold and foreign currency reserves dramatic. This required the government to take an even firmer hold on economic affairs. The lira [Italian currency at that time] was finally devalued in 1936, opening the way to rising inflation; autarky [national economic self-sufficiency] became official formal policy in the same year, with all expenditure of foreign exchange for imports controlled by government licences; efforts were made to find substitutes for essential raw materials like rubber and petrol; and the government even sponsored exploration for gold in the river-beds of the pre-Alpine hills. Increasingly, the political requirements of production came to the fore; scarce resources had to be controlled very carefully, and only the State was able to do this. The much-vaunted corporations, formed over a decade before 1935, which were supposed to bring employers, party officials, and workers together in collaboration according to areas of production, were far too complex and inefficient organisms to carry out the task. New bodies had to be set up. The result was an incredible multiplication of State agencies and of parallel bureaucracies which worked in a disjointed and uncoordinated manner in an effort to produce an efficient war economy. Predictably, the effects were limited. By 1938–9 there was a clear awareness that essential industrial expansion required large injections of capital and that this could only be provided through further compression of consumption, price and wage controls, and control and direction of investment. Before the outbreak of the war the Fascists managed only to limit consumption effectively. Indeed, the paradox of the late 1930s was that, as the political element in the organization of the economy became ever more marked, the economic results became less and less satisfactory.

Ultimately the Ethiopian war and the totalitarian phase of Fascism had destabilizing consequences for the regime. Inflation took its toll. The 1940 annual report of the Bank of Italy acknowledged that 'there has been a certain reduction in real wages' of industrial workers, while white-collar workers, suffering from rising prices, from increased taxes, and from the various forced loans and special levies of these years, also saw their economic advantages greatly reduced. As serious for the regime was the distance which many industrialists and large landowners began to take from Fascism. Divisions arose between industrialists as a result of the heavy State intervention in the organization of trade and investment, favouring a few to the detriment of many. Landowners in general were aware that, despite 'ruralism', the political weight of agriculture had declined under Fascism and that their returns reflected this fact. Even the backbone of rural Fascism, the sharecroppers, began to resent the requisitioning of crops at low official prices by the State authorities.

Murmurs of discontent, even if fairly loud, did not really threaten Fascist survival, however. By the late 1930s it was evident that the regime was facing serious difficulties and that the mechanisms it had invented to overcome them had had little effect. But there seems little question that, without the war, Fascism would have continued for some time. Certainly, there were problems with the institutional framework (Mussolini's irritation with the monarchy was becoming ever more obvious) and there were

FIGHTING FOR HITLER AND PROTECTING THE JEWS: ITALY'S DUAL ROLE IN WORLD WAR II

When Adolf Hitler, the leader of Nazi Germany, started World War II with his 1939 invasion of Poland, Italy's Fascist leader, Benito Mussolini, joined the war as Hitler's ally. Part of Hitler's plan was to murder the Jews of Europe, whom he considered inferior to his own Germanic people. Although Italy was formally on Hitler's side, few Italian people supported his goals and many worked actively to save Jews.

Italy's humane attitude toward Jews extended beyond its own people and beyond its national borders. Wherever the Italian army was the occupying power, as in parts of Yugoslavia and France, the Jews were protected from serious harm. Yugoslav Jews report that they were taken almost from the hands of the approaching Germans onto Italian army trains, dressed in Italian military uniforms, and brought to Italy, where they were concealed.

Over the centuries Jews had become well-integrated into Italian society. Even during the period when they were forced to live in ghettos, Jews continued to participate in business and other relationships with Gentiles. . . .

Thousands of stories are documented about efforts to save Jews from the Holocaust. People do have a choice between good and evil; a caring individual can make a difference; resistance is both possible and effective. It is ironic that while the nation of Italy was serving Hitler, many Italians were protecting Jews and other refugees.

Margherita Marchione, *Yours Is a Precious Witness*, New York: Paulist Press, 1997.

doubts about the future; the succession to Mussolini remained an unanswered question and the second generation which had grown up under Fascism was showing increasing signs of disaffection from an ageing and ossified hierarchy. The Racial Laws [aimed to discriminate against Jews], introduced in 1938 in an attempt to flatter Hitler, were generally unpopular, as was the burgeoning alliance with Nazi Germany. But discontent and disaffection were very different from open and active opposition; compliance, even if more and more grudging, remained the most common attitude.

Italy Enters World War II

The possibilities of Italy not becoming involved in the war were, of course, very few indeed. Mussolini's vainglorious personal diplomacy with Hitler made Italy virtually a hostage to Germany by 1939 (there are even suggestions that he did not read the Pact of Steel [between Italy and Germany] before signing it). Any trace of the 'deciding weight' policies of the mid-1930s, by which Italy sought to avoid commitment in order to sell herself to the highest bidder when the decisive moment came, had disappeared. But, irresponsible diplomacy apart, the ideological imperatives of Fascism made the choice of neutrality almost impossible. Fascism had been organized from the start along militaristic lines and had always expressed itself through the rhetoric of war; it had been an attempt to carry the nationalist values of the First World War—discipline, aggression, heroism, hierarchy, patriotism—into peacetime and to regiment and unify a notoriously divided society under those values. The ultimate test of this venture was obviously war itself. To have refused the challenge would have represented a betrayal of all that Fascism had tried to construct.

After a period of non-belligerency (but not neutrality) determined by lack of economic and military preparation, Mussolini entered the Second World War in June 1940. Italy was still unprepared, as all the chiefs of staff were aware, but a rapid and total Nazi victory seemed assured and Mussolini needed, to use his own cynical phrase, 'a thousand Italian dead at the conference table'. Public opinion, always in doubt about the Axis alliance [with Nazi Germany], temporarily suspended disbelief and rallied to the cause, although there were none of the celebrations seen in the 'radiant May' of 1915 [when Italy entered World War

I]. Very much aware that he risked being swallowed whole by a much more powerful Germany, Mussolini first attempted to pursue a parallel war which would keep the Italian position distinct from the German, but the attempt proved futile. In both Greece and North Africa the Italian campaigns faced disaster and had to be rescued by the intervention of the *Wehrmacht* [German army]. The war at sea went equally badly, the navy finding itself without essential air-cover at vital moments. Mussolini's insistence on sending Italian troops to the Russian front in 1941 was a desperate attempt to maintain some political control over the course of a conflict which was getting totally out of hand, but even this attempt failed miserably. Most of the Italian soldiers died as they attempted, after [the battle of] Stalingrad, to walk home through the Russian winter of 1942; Hitler twice refused to listen to Mussolini's counsels for a separate Russian peace.

Problems for the Fascists

The Duce [Mussolini] found himself with responsibility but no power—a bad position for a dictator. It was ironic that a regime which had consistently preached the virtues of war should have been found so wanting in the event. The lack of preparation and appalling conduct of the war were, in fact, signal indications of the weaknesses of the regime. These lay less in objective factors—shortage of raw materials and food, which autarky had been unable to remedy—than in the complete inadequacy of the decision-making structure of Fascism. Mussolini had always deliberately ensured the fragmentation of the Fascist élite around him, just as he had encouraged the rivalry between the armed forces in order to be better able to divide and rule. With the concentration of power, decisions became haphazard, uncoordinated, and often contradictory, frequently made on the spot and without reflection in order to satisfy an immediate request. Indeed, it might be said that one of Mussolini's weaknesses was an inability to choose; faced with an alternative he would either put off a decision or try to have it both ways. These defects were reproduced throughout the entire Fascist construction: coherent and monolithic on the exterior, fragile and fissured within. Certain parts of the Fascist edifice might, in fact, work very well; it was the whole which did not hold together. The tensions of war revealed the cracks in the structure; as Mussolini himself was well aware, Fascism had failed the ultimate test it had set for itself.

Resistance Movements

Under the impact of military disaster, food shortages, and Allied bombing, opinion in Italy turned rapidly against Fascism. By early 1943 those conservative forces which had sustained Mussolini throughout the *ventennio* were beginning to look for a way out in the hope of saving what they could. Their minds were further concentrated when in March popular discontent became obvious as workers went on strike in the factories of Turin—the first major strikes for nearly twenty years. Covert anti-Fascist organizations, mainly Communist, emerged to lead the protest which, if it started as a strike against appalling work conditions, soon became openly political in content. Facing the threat of radical popular participation in the evolution of events, conservatives and moderates began to look towards the king and the Vatican to help in ending Italian involvement in the war. Mussolini's defenestration [being thrown out the window] by the Fascist Grand Council in July was, at least on paper, a premiss [something assumed beforehand] to the continuation of a new, more moderate Fascism. In fact, with the subsequent arrest of Mussolini, Fascism collapsed almost overnight and power returned to the king.

The German Invasion and the Resistance

Hopes of containing popular feeling ended when Germany invaded Italy following the armistice of 8 September [in which Italy surrendered to the Allies]. While the king fled rather ignominiously from Rome to Brindisi, German forces took over northern and central Italy and those parts of the south not already controlled by the advancing Allies. Mussolini, rescued from his mountain prison by German gliders, returned to Italy as the head of a puppet Fascist State: the Italian Social Republic (RSI) or Republic of Salò. Strong anti-Fascist sentiment now took concrete form; Communists, Socialists, and Catholics took up arms to fight Nazism and Fascism in what became both a war for national liberation and a civil war. The partisan war was effective, if often tragic. It was marked by numerous episodes of savage reprisal against unarmed civilians by both Nazis and Fascists, which had the effect of uniting a large part of the population in either active or passive resistance to Fascism. Mussolini's republic tried to recapture support by a pathetic attempt to return to the radical and socialistic ideas of the Fascism of 1919 and 1920. More in evidence was the brutal violence of that first Fascism as the 'black brigades' of the RSI distinguished themselves for their cruelty to their fellow Italians.

Dominated by the Communists, the Resistance movement represented a new phase in popular participation in Italian politics, often explicitly identified as a continuation of the lapsed struggles of 1919–22. For the young, who could not remember those struggles but who were faced with possible enforced conscription to the RSI, it was a time of choice; in fact, many former Fascists chose the partisan bands rather than the black brigades, who were seen as German stooges. The bands formed a school of politics for those who fought in them and it was under their influence (and that of the Vatican) that party politics developed once again in Italy. The Communist leader, Palmiro Togliatti, aided this process by shelving all revolutionary pretensions (which Moscow would never have supported) in the name of the greater priority of national liberation. Although treated with a certain diffidence by the anti-Communist Allies (particularly the British), the Resistance represented a great advance on the social conflicts of the first post-war period; at its end it was no longer possible to question the right of workers and peasants to their place within the political framework.

The end came in April 1945. With the liberation of Milan, Mussolini fled from Como, apparently in an attempt to reach Austria. He was stopped by partisans, recognized, and shot. The next day his body was taken to Milan and hung upside down for public execration [denunciation, cursing] in Piazzale Loreto, the piazza where, a few days before, the bodies of murdered partisans had been similarly exposed as a macabre warning to the restless population.

The Fascist Legacy

Ironically, Mussolini had succeeded in uniting Italians briefly—but against Fascism rather than for it. None the less the legacy of Fascism was to be far-reaching. Quite apart from a disastrous war fought on Italian territory, Fascism bequeathed poverty, inefficiency, a mediocre cultural provincialism born of intellectual isolation, and a political practice which had erected clientelism to system, generalized petty corruption, and made the use of public office for private gain the norm. The economic reorganization of Italy which had taken place under Fascism demonstrated all the imbalances determined by the social priorities of the regime—imbalances which had certainly served to retard rather than accelerate development. But it was at the political level that Fascism witnessed its real defeat. The attempt to form a nation, to give Italians a single identity in the Italian State, had proved a total failure. This was perhaps inevitable in an authoritarian populism which attempted to achieve mobilization through myths of past greatness and illusions of future conquest—illusions pursued at the cost of material well-being. In the end, the benefits of Fascism became less and less evident, even to its supporters, the deficiencies ever more apparent. Fascist pretensions were ultimately far beyond the means available to the regime. Many had known this all along; the tragedy was that it took a world war to burst the bubble and make it obvious to everyone.

Italy's Modern Challenges

Corruption, Crime, and the Mafia

By Letizia Paoli

Ever since Italy first united in the 1860s, the nation has struggled to create a stable government and society. Through the late twentieth century and the early twenty-first century, among the most troubling issues have been the influence of the Mafia and the prevalence of corrupt government officials.

Author Letizia Paoli is an expert on criminology who studied at the Max Planck Institute for Foreign and International Criminal Law in Freiburg, Germany. In this selection, Paoli argues that the Mafia and corruption in politics are traditions that date back perhaps to the time even before Italy became a unified nation. As a result, it has been extremely difficult to curb these criminal activities.

In the early 1990s, a series of political purges began in Italy. Several powerful government leaders were arrested and tried on corruption charges. By the end of the decade, many Italians were hopeful that the removal of this large group of politicians would at last clean up Italian politics and make the government more efficient and trustworthy. The reforms enacted at that time did, in fact, have a big impact, but the purges were only the beginning of what will be a long process of removing crime from Italian society.

I llegality and crime are frequently assumed to be intertwined with the history of Italy to a greater extent than in any other Western country. They are often presented as key variables in understanding Italy's past and present. Are these assumptions correct? If so, why? How do crime and illegality manifest themselves in Italy? What are the historical roots of these phenomena? What is their impact on the economic, political, and social life of the country? What has been done to control contra legem [illegal] activities in Italy? This essay will give an answer to these questions....

Letizia Paoli, "Crime, Italian Style," *Daedalus*, vol. 130, Summer 2001, p. 157. Copyright © 2001 by the American Academy of Arts and Sciences. Reproduced by permission of Daedalus: Journal of the American Academy of Arts and Sciences.

The Mafia

Contrary to what most scholars maintained up to the early 1980s, judicial inquiries carried out since then have proved that formalized mafia groups do exist. Cosa Nostra in Sicily and the 'Ndrangheta in Calabria [the heel of the Italian peninsula] are the largest and most stable coalitions and are each composed of about a hundred mafia groups. Their members are estimated at about three thousand and five thousand males respectively.

Though it is not possible to establish clear lines of continuity, antecedents of the contemporary mafia associations existed in the 1880s, if not before. The discovery of new documents in archives and a more objective analysis of the already known papers has demonstrated the presence of mafia groups in Sicily and Calabria since the mid-nineteenth century. . . .

As secret brotherhoods using violence, Southern Italian mafia associations have remarkable similarities to associations such as the Chinese Triads and the Japanese Yakuza. With their centuries-old histories, articulated structures, and sophisticated ritual and symbolic apparatuses, all these associations—and the American descendant of the Sicilian Cosa Nostra—have few parallels in the world of organized crime. None of the other groups that systematically traffic in illegal commodities have the same degree of complexity and longevity.

Cosa Nostra and the 'Ndrangheta share another important peculiarity with the Chinese Triads and the Japanese Yakuza.

Unlike other contemporary organized crime groups, they do not content themselves with producing and selling illegal goods and services. Though these activities have acquired an increasing relevance over the past thirty years, neither the trade in illegal commodities nor the maximization of profits has ever been the primary goal of these associations. As a matter of fact, it is hardly possible to identify a single goal. Southern Italian mafia coalitions are multifunctional organizations. In the past hundred years, their members have exploited the strength of mafia bonds to pursue various endeavors and to accomplish the most disparate tasks. Already in 1876 the Tuscan aristocrat Leopoldo Franchetti pointed out the "extraordinary elasticity" of the associations of malfattori (evildoers): "the goals multiply, the field of action widens, without the need to multiply the statutes; the association divides for certain goals, remains united for others."

Among these tasks the exercise of political domination has always been preeminent. The ruling bodies of Cosa Nostra and the 'Ndrangheta claim, above all, an absolute power over their members. They control every aspect of their members' lives, and they aim to exercise a similar power over the communities where their members reside. For a long time, their power had a higher degree of effectiveness and legitimacy than that exercised by the state. In Western Sicily and in Southern Calabria mafia associations successfully policed the general population, settling conflicts, recovering stolen goods, and enforcing property rights. Even today, although most of these rules are no longer systematically enforced, mafia families exercise a certain "sovereignty" through a generalized system of extortion. As a state would do, they tax the main productive activities carried out within their territory. . . .

Its [the mafia's] history as well as its cultural and normative apparatus . . . today constitute a constraint as much as a resource. By building a strong collective identity, shared cultural codes and norms enhance group cohesion and create trustful relationships among mafia members. The reliance on status and fraternization contracts, which are nonspecific and long-term, produces a high degree of flexibility and makes the multifunctionality of mafia groups possible. The same shared cultural codes and norms also represent, however, a powerful brake on entrepreneurial initiative.

Especially constraining is one of the preconditions for recruitment: only men born either in Sicily or in Calabria or descending from mafia families can be admitted as members. This rule has long prevented Cosa Nostra and 'Ndrangheta families from adding new members with the experience necessary to compete in the black markets for arms, money, and gold. Rigid recruitment criteria have also hampered the geographical expansion of mafia power. Cosa Nostra, for example, prohibits settling families outside of Sicily. This self-imposed rule has limited its involvement in the international narcotics trade—currently the largest of the illegal markets. 'Ndrangheta families, thanks to their extensive branches in Northern Italy and abroad, played a larger role in narcotics trafficking in the 1990s, importing large quantities of cocaine and hashish from Latin America and North Africa; today, however, the 'Ndrangheta faces new competition from foreign and Italian traffickers with more direct connections to drug-producing and transit countries.

The "will to power" of the mafia associations also negatively

affects security and business decisions, as a Palermitan prosecutor
pointed out in 1992:

> The true goal is power. The obscure evil of organiza-
> tion chiefs is not the thirst for money, but the thirst for
> power. The most important fugitives could enjoy a lux-
> urious life abroad until the end of their days. Instead
> they remain in Palermo, hunted, in danger of being
> caught or being killed by internal dissidents, in order to
> prevent the loss of their territorial control and not run
> the risk of being deposed. Marino Mannoia [a former
> mafia member now cooperating with law enforcement
> authorities] once told me: "Many believe that you en-
> ter into Cosa Nostra for money. This is only part of the
> truth. Do you know why I entered Cosa Nostra? Be-
> cause before in Palermo I was Mr. Nobody. Afterwards,
> wherever I went, heads lowered. And to me this is
> priceless.". . .

Corruption and Scandal

Unlike the mafia, which has its roots in Southern Italy, corruption
is a nationwide phenomenon. The so-called Clean Hands investigations revealed for the first time the full extent of corrupt exchanges in Italy. The investigations were initiated in Milan, by the
prosecutor's office there. Starting in February of 1992 with the arrest of the obscure manager of a Milan public institution, the inquiries of the local prosecutors quickly expanded, bringing to light
a wide network of illegality and corruption: the so-called Tan-
gentopoli ("Bribesville," initially an allusion to Milan). The spectacular success of the Milan team spurred judges elsewhere. One
after another, politicians who had dominated national politics during the previous decade came under investigation. In November
of 1993, parliamentary immunity was temporarily abolished. By
then, prosecutors in numerous Italian cities had filed 851 requests
for authorization to investigate 447 deputies—more than half of
the members of the Italian Parliament. . . .

Vertical Integration of Corruption

Up until the late 1960s, corruption—meant as an exchange of
money for political favors—was by and large confined to the
country's ruling elite. Only large corporations and leading poli-

ticians took part in these exchanges, which rarely involved the civil service or local government. Corruption was not yet a regular and accepted practice, and there was not a widespread network of people accustomed to paying and receiving bribes.

Starting in the late 1960s, however, a progressive change took place. Corruption lost its elite character. It became a common and socially accepted behavior, spread across all social strata and involving an even larger number of low- and middle-level politicians and bureaucrats. First, kickbacks were paid by the suppliers of goods and services to the government. The "Clean Hands" investigations revealed that companies paid off officials at different stages of the bidding process in order to be included in the list of qualified bidders, to be selected as the winning contractor, to get an inflated price for the job, or to be able to cut corners on quality. In some cases, long-term agreements were reached between companies and the representatives of political parties to manipulate bids and keep potential competitors from winning access to the market. . . .

The Underground Economy

The underground economy is a by-product of the state's efforts to regulate, tax, and supervise the economic activity carried out within its territory. . . . As such, though in differing degrees and forms, the underground economy is a normal, unavoidable component of all modern societies. . . .

The informal sector [of the underground economy] as a whole includes all those economic activities that are unrecorded in national statistical accounts and/or fail to meet such government requirements as registration, payment of taxes, payment of social security for employees, enforcement of health and safety rules, etc. Examples range from undeclared second jobs done during off-duty time to completely "off the book" employment in small businesses and households. Self-employed individuals, whether working full- or part-time, also produce much that is not properly recorded in national economic statistics. Occasionally there are also entire "ghost firms" or even industries that are completely unknown to tax and labor officers, such as the glove industry in Naples, a "ghost" industrial system that in the late 1980s produced two to three million pairs of gloves a year. . . .

Apart from the informal sector of the underground economy, there is a criminal sector. The latter includes the production and sale of commodities that are outlawed by most states and international bodies. Only two goods fully fit this criterion: some drugs, and all human beings. As a consequence of state and international bans, all exchanges of these "commodities" are bound to take place on the "wrong side of the law," and illegal markets have therefore developed.

Following international trends, a national illegal market in cannabis developed in Italy in the late 1960s. In the following decades heroin, cocaine, and, more recently, ecstasy have also been

A Movement to Fight the Mafia

For decades, if not centuries, the Mafia has exercised a good deal of control over Italy, mainly because of its ability to frighten and intimidate anyone who might oppose it. In the late 1980s, however, in Palermo, Sicily—one of the places most heavily plagued by Mafia violence—a group of brave people started a movement to speak out against the Mafia and to try to take back control of their city's affairs.

[In the late 1980s]. . . although Palermo, [Sicily], had an elected city government, the real power resided with the Mafia bosses who controlled public services and city contracts and most business that went on in the city. The Mafia had penetrated the police force, the courts, and almost all the institutions of civil democratic society, making them little more than vehicles for criminal activity and profits.

Through brute force and murder, the Mafia took Palermo's lifeblood. Tax dollars meant for schools, housing, and the restoration of public monuments were diverted to the pockets of the Mafia. Ancient churches, museums, and public buildings were left to rot. The beautiful old opera house was closed; housing built for poor families crumbled. The very water people drank came from wells drilled by taxpayers' money but owned by the Mafia. The economy—which depended on the right of free expression and free association to operate efficiently—stagnated. When it came to civic af-

consumed and traded on a large scale. The traffic in human beings became a flourishing business in the early 1990s. Italy's closeness to the former Yugoslavia and other impoverished East European nations has made it a convenient landing place for thousands of migrants smuggled into the EU from the former Second and Third World. Some of these migrants are then forced into prostitution or otherwise exploited in both the criminal and informal sectors of the economy.

Additionally, many other goods and services—ranging from

---

fairs, most citizens lived in fear behind their curtains and closed doors.

But some brave souls—dissidents of a sort, including a handful of remarkable prosecutors, magistrates, and policemen—fought on. Two magistrates in particular, Giovanni Falcone and Paolo Borsellino, heroically pursued the Mafia and eventually became martyrs in the cause of freedom. Civic society had already begun slowly to reassert itself, but with the murders of Falcone and Borsellino, the citizens of Palermo were galvanized and took to the streets. Women hung bed sheets out the windows with the word Basta! (Enough!) written on them. United in their anger and revulsion, the people of Palermo began to be a community again. They formed groups and associations, and with great courage, began to take their city back....

Today, Palermo is once again safe and beautiful and a source of pride. The restored Massimo opera house is a wonder to behold. The economy is improving.

In a real sense, the citizens of Palermo were engaged in a war against totalitarianism and terror. Their story can and should be an inspiration to everyone who believes in the basic right of men and women to organize and associate freely. Corruption and organized crime are grave, pernicious threats to democracy. But with determination, leadership, and a citizenry prepared to fight for the values of a free society, democracy can overcome.

Sandra Feldman, "Lessons in Courage," *National Journal,* November 13, 1999.

arms and nuclear weapons to toxic waste, jewels, and counter-feited merchandise, from prostitution to gambling to money laun-dering—are marketed daily in violation of specific trade regula-tions and restrictions. Still others are exchanged without paying excise taxes: for example, tobacco has been smuggled on a large scale into Italy ever since the 1960s. . . .

The anomaly of Italy's underground economy thus lies not so much in the profits of the criminal sector as in the truly stag-gering size of the informal sector. The abnormal extension of the latter blurs the boundaries between the legal and the illegal, fosters corruption, and facilitates mafia penetration of the legal economy.

Reasons for Crime in Italy

Complex social phenomena such as those described . . . cannot be explained with reference to a single factor. No monocausal in-terpretation of events is possible. Contemporary mafia associa-tions as well as the penchant shown by present-day Italians for corruption and underground economic activities can be traced back at least to the nineteenth century and have been influenced throughout their long history by a variety of social, cultural, eco-nomic, and political factors.

That said, some key agents can be pointed out. In particular, there is one factor that, more than any other single catalyst, seems to have favored the rise and consolidation of mafia associations, corruption, and the underground economy: the relative weakness and unpopularity of the Italian state ever since the country's uni-fication in 1861. Even today, Italy is the only EU [European Union] country where less than half of the population approves of its own state institutions. . . .

The Influence of the Mafia

Above all, the rise and consolidation of mafia associations must be related to the inability of the Bourbon [royal] government and then, for a long time, the Italian state to exert a legitimate monopoly on the use of physical force in the Mezzogiorno [the south of Italy]. The mafia is not the residue of a lawless past; "it is an outgrowth of the particular form that the process of state formation took in Italy." The mafia developed because national systems of power expanded without fully subordinating local systems of power. Indeed, the central state had to rely on local

landlords and mafia coalitions if it wanted to govern some areas
at all. . . .

The Anticorruption Campaign of the 1990s

It is true, then, that some forms of illegality are more prevalent
in Italy than in other European countries. But it is also true that
Italy has shown a remarkable commitment to fighting crime and
corruption. In the last two decades of the twentieth century, Italy
stood out because of its judicial campaigns against the mafia and
corruption and the support these campaigns received from large
sections of the civil society.

In recent years, a new generation of judges and prosecutors in
Southern as well as in Northern Italy has tried to reassert the independence of the judiciary, which is formally guaranteed by the
1948 Italian Constitution. Starting in 1992, a group of Italian
magistrates attacked corruption in Italy as never before. Their initiative received broad popular support, and this support prevented
ruling politicians from stopping judicial investigations as they had
routinely done in the past. In the course of one year, 1993, the
five ruling parties of the postwar period—including the Christian Democrats—were wiped off the political map. At the same
time, an unprecedented judicial campaign against the mafia also
received broad popular support, even in Sicily.

Antimafia Movements

Whereas people's anticorruption stance was new in the early
1990s, the antimafia movement has a longer history, with roots
in the rural protest movements of the 1890s and the late 1940s.
Throughout the nineteenth and twentieth centuries, furthermore,
there were enlightened minorities who denounced the mafia's
power and its shadowy influence on Sicilian politics and the Sicilian economy. But a truly mass, interclass social movement
against the mafia emerged only in 1982. In September of that
year, General Carlo Alberto Dalla Chiesa, who had been sent to
Palermo in June as a high commissioner to combat the mafia,
was killed, together with his wife and driver. The public reacted
with outrage. Two weeks after the Dalla Chiesa murder, which
followed the assassination of fifteen other state officials and politicians over the previous three years, the La Torre Act was passed.
The new bill, named after the Sicilian Communist leader who

had been killed by the mafia in April of 1982, introduced the crime of delinquent association of the mafia type . . . and authorized the seizure and forfeiture of illegally acquired property of those indicted under this article. Between 1982 and 1986 nearly 15,000 men were arrested throughout Italy for criminal association of the mafia type; 706 were brought to trial . . .

State institutions also reacted to mafia violence with a strong counterattack, which produced the highest peak of antimafia activities in the last fifty years. A new antimafia act was passed in the summer of 1992. Seven thousand soldiers were sent to Sicily to help civil police forces, and antimafia investigations were beefed up. Since then, virtually all of the leading mafia bosses, some of them on the run for decades, have been captured and sent to special high-security prisons. Thanks to the creation of a "Witness Protection Program," more than a thousand mafiosi and gangsters have left their crime groups and have begun sharing their experiences with law enforcement officials. As a result of the antimafia inquiries, Italians now know more than ever before about mafia organizations themselves and the collusion between mafia members and politicians. . . .

The Need for More Changes to Fight Crime

But the campaign against crime and corruption has not been accompanied by a similarly aggressive restructuring of the political system. Notwithstanding the enthusiasm of a new generation of local politicians in Sicily, neither the Southern regions nor the central government were able to launch a coordinated reform to stimulate the social, cultural, and economic development of the Mezzogiorno. On the contrary: with the aim of entering the European Monetary Union, in the early 1990s the extraordinary public intervention in the South came to a brusque halt, and only after several years of delay was it partially supplemented by ordinary funding. In recent years, Parliament passed several new measures to protect the rights of defendants and curb the "excesses" of the early 1990s, which made the magistrates' work objectively more difficult. At the same time, the legislative and executive branches failed to enact reforms that would have made the Italian justice system more efficient. As a result, many of the corruption cases initiated by the investigating judges in Milan and other cities will become statute-barred.

With the partial exception of Sicily, moreover, public support of the magistrates' action did not translate into a cultural revolution. Especially in the North, the judiciary and public opinion did not forge an active alliance against corruption similar to the one that characterized the revolt against mafia power. . . .

By the end of the 1990s, attempts to absorb the innovations and exorcise the consequent traumas of 1992–1994 multiplied, and continuities with past political practices increasingly emerged. In Milan, as in Palermo, the prosecutors and judges who investigated corruption and the mafia are now often criticized. Public opinion has tired of the seemingly endless judicial investigations. Despite convictions on corruption charges, several politicians of the so-called First Republic are again active in the Italian political scene. Others, like Giulio Andreotti, have been acquitted of all charges for want of evidence. Notwithstanding three convictions and several pending investigations on corruption charges, Silvio Berlusconi, the media tycoon-turned-politician who controls almost half of the Italian television and advertisement market, became prime minister in the general election in the spring of 2001.

The window of opportunity, which was opened in the early 1990s to curb the political and economic power of the mafia, tackle corruption, and reduce the underground economy, seems to be closing again.

Italy: A Land of Immigrants

By Jeff Israely

*Jeff Israely is a reporter who has covered international topics that range
from religious and social issues in Europe to the Middle Eastern world of
Islam. In this article, Israely explores the ongoing challenge that the issue
of immigration has presented Italy in recent years.*

*Over the last ten years or more, Italy has experienced a dramatic in-
flux of new immigrants, many of them from the Middle East or Asia,
hoping to find political asylum in Europe. Many immigrants use the
proper methods to enter the country, but frequently, political refugees attempt to enter illegally. If they manage to avoid detection by Italian authorities, they often continue on to other places in Europe.*

*Many immigrants choose Italy as their entryway to Europe because
Italian officials rarely try to stop rafts loaded with new immigrants for
fear of endangering those aboard. Italy's deportation laws are also not as
strong as some politicians would like. As a result, a heated debate is under way to decide whether laws can be changed to help stop the problems
caused by excessive immigration.*

The Adriatic Sea is a glassy calm as the first hint of dawn
turns the horizon a deep, dark blue. Another day is break-
ing across Italy's heel, and nothing more than the faint
lights of a fishing boat is visible from the coast. But after a short
walk along this beach near Otranto, a policeman's flashlight re-
veals scattered shirts and jeans, several pairs of warmup pants, one
kid-sized sneaker, shoes, underwear, a gym bag. Shed like the skin
of a former self, the week-old, waterlogged belongings of perhaps six to eight people are all that remain of the latest wave of
the human tide that crashes on Western Europe's far southeastern shores.

Where They Come From

Over the past decade, a harrowing 96-km motorized raft trip across the Adriatic from Vlore, Albania has become one of the main routes for would-be immigrants seeking work and a better life inside the European Union. Many spend four or five months traveling over land and across other waterways before paying Albanian smugglers 500[euro] to 1,500[euro] to ferry them to Italy. They are usually forced to abandon ship well short of the shoreline, and then wade in to look for a safe place to change into dry clothes.

The immigrants, most of them economic migrants but some seeking political asylum, arrive from all points east and south—China, India and Pakistan, Iraq, Iran and Turkey, the Balkans and North Africa. But if they receive legal resident status, or manage to evade the authorities, they almost all wind up farther north—not just in Rome and Milan, but in Frankfurt, Calais, Dover and London too. Authorities estimate that 20,000 immigrants land illegally each year on the Italian coast. In addition to the Puglia region, they also touch down in Sicily and Reggio Calabria. And police estimate that at least half of all illegal immigrants simply disappear into the landscape.

Legal Attempts at Immigration

Some, however, seek legitimate entry. Leaving behind poverty and a family of six in eastern Turkey, Mustafa Celik made a two-month journey by land across Bulgaria, the former Yugoslavia and Macedonia before begging Albanian smugglers to let him on board a raft for just 300[euro]. "It was all I had," the 38-year-old says, pulling at his shirt to indicate that he arrived in Italy with just the clothes on his back. After a choppy ride across the Adriatic, the smugglers motioned for the 40 or so passengers to jump into the water. Celik, soaking wet, was picked up by police and brought to a nearby church-run holding facility north of Otranto to await a month of processing by Italian immigration authorities. Even if his request for political asylum is denied, Celik will simply be given a written expulsion order requiring him to report to Rome's Fiumicino Airport within 15 days. But with no ticket—and often no desire—to go home, most people in Celik's situation simply start the long journey north.

Celik says he was grateful at first to have made it safely to Europe, which he believes offers his family's only chance of escaping poverty. "Where I come from there is nothing," he said. Paris, where his brother works in construction, is his probable destination. But, he adds as his eyes moisten, the last week has given him time to ponder what he left behind: "I think about my family always."

Government Responses to the Immigration Challenge

Until now, E.U. [European Union] leaders have left places like southern Puglia largely on their own to both prevent and protect new arrivals. When the raft traffic first began in the early 1990s in response to political and economic upheaval in Albania, Otranto residents responded with their own blankets and hot meals for the shivering travelers. Four years ago the city converted one of its buildings into an arrival center that provides basic necessities through national funds. In 1999, a border police unit was established, equipped with the same fast and agile rafts that smugglers use. Still, with a lack of top equipment and adequate staffing, at least some officers are frustrated. "This is the border of Europe and we don't have a proper radar," one says. "At least when they arrive, we should know they're here."

The anxiety extends to the ordinary citizens of Otranto, though virtually none of the arrivals ever settles in the area and the national government has begun picking up the bill for their immediate care. "We hosted them, fed them, clothed them—and then they began to steal," says an elderly man buying fish in the port. "Once [the immigrants] come, they never leave."

Italians never challenge a raft with immigrants aboard because of the risk to the passengers. Otranto border police chief Carmine Ingrosso says the open sea requires extra care: "Yes, there are laws that must be respected. But in those very first moments we are concerned solely with the safety of the immigrants." Occasionally, disaster strikes. In the predawn hours of June 8, for example, smugglers forced 43 Kurdish refugees into the water at knife point a kilometer from the coast just south of Otranto. Four drowned.

Such incidents form a tragic backdrop to the wider debate in Italy over immigration. In 1990, the number of new legal immigrants into the country was 24,200; in 2000, it was 181,300, a mere fraction of the 2.2 million already in Italy. The Lower House of Parliament this month approved a bill to make deportation easier and require all immigrants to be fingerprinted. Prime Minister Silvio Berlusconi has been swaying between right-wing allies who want a strict limit on arrivals and industry executives who value them as a ready source of labor. Otranto Mayor Franco Bruni says that the European Union must establish a common immigration policy to coordinate controls and challenge the non-E.U. states that are the source of unchecked arrivals. "Maybe with Iraq it's difficult," Bruni says. "But if Turkey wants to join the E.U., it can't play a clever man's game on this issue."

After working a 10-hour night shift, fisherman Mauro Trotto is back in the port of Otranto at dawn untangling the scorpion fish and mullet from his giant yellow net. The 50-year-old father of five didn't see any immigrants heading inland last night. But over the years he's seen more than his share of over-crowded rafts filled with desperate people. "Most see Europe like we saw America," he says, "a place where you can live well and live free." But with the tide of political opinion turning against immigration, those dreams of a better life may shatter on Europe's shores.

Art Appreciation in Italy

SASKIA REILLY

As the land that spawned the Renaissance, Italy has long been associated with great works of art. Over the centuries, however, many of Italy's art treasures have fallen victim to the ravages of time or the damage of natural disasters or pollution. Recognizing the value of those treasures—paintings, sculpture, and architecture—to the nation's culture and heritage, Italians undertook an ambitious plan to restore and better protect those irreplaceable works of art. Author Saskia Reilly was an intern for Europe *magazine when she wrote this article. In it, Reilly argues that Italy's renewed passion for art will be long-lived. She believes the drive to restore old masterpieces and to protect others from future destruction represents a "new Renaissance" in which the public is intimately involved with its priceless legacy of old masterpieces and the production of new ones.*

Entrepreneur and art historian Luca Ales is convinced that Italy is in the midst of a new Renaissance. In 1991, he and a handful of partners in Rome founded Arcimbuldo, an organization dedicated to heightening public awareness of Italy's artistic heritage. This summer [1999], he spent his weekends showing Romans around the Domus Aurea, Emperor Nero's recently restored 500-room villa, which opened to the public last June.

At the heart of this rebirth is a trend of increased public appreciation for Italy's artistic and cultural patrimony. Ales's organization alone has seen membership jump from forty-five people at its inception in 1991 to more than 900 this year. In Rome as well as in Italy's other major "art cities", from Florence and Assisi to Milan, Verona, and Naples, nearly fifty enterprising organizations like Arcimbuldo have capitalized on the trend. Says Ales, "These days, people are increasingly interested in visiting muse-

Saskia Reilly, "The New Renaissance," *Europe*, October 1999, p. 34. Copyright © 1999 by European Commission Delegation. Reproduced by permission.

226

ums and historic sites, and more often than not, they are willing to spend extra money in order to have a knowledgeable guide explain what they are looking at."

A New Appreciation for Italy's Treasured Art

Increased individual appreciation of art has evolved thanks to a sea change in the attitude toward Italy's art and culture and the public's desire to bring the country's museums and cultural infrastructure into the twenty-first century. Spurring this change in attitude was the pressure to renovate and restore many of the country's treasures in time for the Holy Jubilee, celebrating 2,000 years of Christianity and due to start in December 1999.

Italians have long been conscious that their art cities constitute some of their most valuable assets—both enhancing Italy's standing in the world and bringing in vital tourist revenue. Yet until recently, they have done little to facilitate tourist access to these treasures or to encourage Italians to discover their own artistic heritage.

Hundreds of museums and monuments were closed or remained under indefinite restoration, and those sites that were open to the public were often controlled by powerful unions that limited opening hours and restricted access to many of the galleries. Up until 1994, the Uffizi Gallery in Florence and many other state-run museums closed for the day at 1 P.M.

Making Art Available to the People

This all began to change when Walter Veltroni became culture minister in 1995. Under Veltroni, museums were renovated, streamlined, injected with funds from private enterprise, and forced to extend opening hours to suit the public rather than state employees. In 1997, the minister ordered some major museums to stay open to 11:30 P.M. on summer weekends. In 1998, the number was doubled to nearly seventy. Some thirty museums (including the Uffizi) now stay open until 10 P.M. every working day from April to October.

Veltroni has accused the Italians of neglecting the treasures that were all around them and called for a new attitude toward Italy's cultural heritage. In response, Italy has been working on speeding up the renovation of its 769 state museums and monuments and has recognized the importance of contemporary forms of merchandising. Most newly [re]opened museums, including the Uffizi, the Borghese Museum, and National Gallery of Contemporary Art, now have bookshops, coat rooms, elegant cafes, multimedia information centers, and electronic ticketing services.

Funding and Improving Art Areas

Veltroni also cleared the way for the establishment of a state-run lottery to fund major works of cultural significance. The total costs of restoring the Uffizi, following the 1993 bombing, came to $15 million. A full third of the funding came from the national lottery.

Not just the major art cities have benefited from this injection of energy and resources. In 1998, Italy unveiled plans to build a new Mario Botta-designed Museum of Contemporary and Modern Art in Trento, a city in northeastern Italy. The $55 million structure, set to open in 2001, will be paid for by a combination of government and private funding and will contain major works by twentieth century Italian artists.

Veltroni's successor, Giovanna Melandri, has had the opportunity to preside over the Culture Ministry in the final months of preparation leading up to the millennium. A protege of Veltroni, the thirty-seven-year-old Roman has run a tight ship, overseeing the removal of the scaffolding from newly restored sites.

Art restorer Maria-Christina Ghezzi has seen firsthand how scaffolding became part of the Italian landscape. This year, she spent four months of her summer in Assisi, at the Basilica of St. Francis. After spending a month as a volunteer in 1997 following the earthquake that sent frescos by Renaissance masters Giotto and Cimabue crashing to the ground, Ghezzi was invited to participate in the restoration of the historic Basilica. Twelve companies and fifty restorers participated in the restoration of the frescos. Together with three colleagues, Ghezzi spent her days pressed up against a Giotto fresco that depicted the confirmation of St. Francis' stigmatas. She says it was a labor of love.

Restoring Italy's Cultural Heritage

According to Ghezzi, Italy is paying more attention to the restoration of its cultural heritage. "However," says Ghezzi, "restoration will always be a luxury of the spirit. There will always be a shortage of money. There will be moments where art is in fashion, and other times where the belt is tightened."

At the turn of the millennium, it appears that art is in fashion. In Rome and its outskirts alone, the Culture Ministry has financed more than 200 restoration projects with more than $315 million. Last May in Milan, Melandri unveiled Leonardo da Vinci's newly restored *Last Supper*. Though its unveiling sparked controversy over whether the restoration was true to the artist's original conception or whether the artwork had been diminished in the removal of old layers of paint, the completion of the twenty-two-year-long restoration was a triumph for Italians. Only one hundred visitors are now allowed to view the painting at one time. At the time of its unveiling, viewing times were booked all the way through to the fall, proving that despite criticism from abroad, Italians know they are on their way to a second Renaissance.

CHRONOLOGY

509 B.C.
According to Italian tradition, the last of the Etruscan kings is expelled from power and the Roman Republic is established.

44 B.C.
Julius Caesar is assassinated on March 15.

27 B.C.–A.D. 14
Augustus Caesar reigns as the leader of the Roman Empire.

A.D. 79
Mount Vesuvius erupts in August.

307–337
Constantine reigns over the Roman Empire; during his time in power, Constantine converts to Christianity then begins to encourage—and in some cases force—the people of the empire to become Christians, too.

410
Visigoths led by King Alaric seize the city of Rome.

476
The last of the Roman emperors, Romulus Augustulus, is overthrown and replaced by a so-called "barbarian king."

489–493
Ostrogoths under Theodoric attack and take over Italy.

535
An army from Byzantium, the eastern portion of the Roman Empire, attacks the Ostrogoths in Italy.

568
The Lombards come to Italy and capture about half of the peninsula.

751
The Lombards take over Ravenna; after this, the Lombards control all of northern Italy and are in a position to threaten Rome.

773–774
Pope Hadrian I invites the leader of the Franks, Charlemagne, to come to Italy to conquer the Lombards.

800
Charlemagne is crowned emperor of Rome, which marks the beginning of the Holy Roman Empire.

820s
Muslims from North Africa take over Sicily.

962
King Otto II of Germany conquers Italy and is crowned emperor in Rome.

982
Arabs defeat Otto II when he tries to take over southern Italy.

1072
Normans in southern Italy take over Palermo, Sicily.

1130
Roger II is crowned king of Sicily, Calabria, and Apulia.

1176
The Lombard League, made up of cities from northern Italy, defeats Holy Roman emperor Frederick Barbarossa at the Battle of Legano.

1194
German emperor Henry VI takes over southern Italy and Sicily.

1282
The kingdom of Sicily is divided.

1347
A severe epidemic of plague, called the Black Death, comes to Italy.

1378–1415

A split over key religious issues takes place in the church; in this
  event, called the Great Schism, two separate churches are
  formed—the Western Church, centered in Rome, and the
  Eastern Church, centered in Constantinople (what is now Is-
  tanbul, Turkey).

1381

The War of Chioggia between Venice and Genoa comes to an
  end.

1442

Alfonso V becomes king of Naples.

1454

Several Italian city-states sign the Peace of Lodi, a treaty meant
  to bring peace to the entire peninsula.

1494

French king Charles VIII invades Italy; the Medici family, which
  has ruled Florence for generations, is thrown out of the city-
  state.

1499

Ludovico Sforza, the ruler of Milan, is forced from power by
  French king Louis XII.

1500

Under the Treaty of Granada, France and Spain agree to parti-
  tion Naples.

1511

Pope Pius II sets up the Holy League in an attempt to keep foreign invaders out of Italy.

1512

The Battle of Ravenna between the Holy League and the
  French takes place; after the league's troops return, Pope Pius
  II sends them to force Florence to take back the Medicis.

1513

Niccolò Machiavelli writes *The Prince*.

1527

Holy Roman emperor and Spanish king Charles V attacks and captures Rome.

1530

The Florentine republic comes to an end; Charles V is crowned at Bologna.

1532

Pope Clement VII and Holy Roman emperor Charles V grant Alessandro de' Medici the title of duke of Florence.

1556

Charles V gives up his throne; his son, King Philip II of Spain, becomes the ruler of Naples and Milan.

1563

The Council of Trent, set up to define Roman Catholic principles and to show how they differ from the Protestant ideas of the Reformation, comes to an end.

1569

Cosimo I de' Medici is made grand duke of Tuscany.

1571

In the Battle of Lepanto, King Philip II of Spain and his combined Spanish, Venetian, and papal forces defeat the Turks.

1606

The pope imposes an interdict on Venice.

1618

The Thirty Years' War, which would be fought mainly in Germany, begins.

1623–1628

A constitutional crisis takes place in Venice.

1647

Revolts take place in Palermo and Naples.

1648

The Treaty of Westphalia ends the Thirty Years' War and reorganizes Europe.

1655

Queen Christina of Sweden takes power in Rome.

1668

A barons' revolt takes place in Sardinia.

1706–1708

Milan, Naples, and Sardinia are occupied by the Hapsburgs of Austria.

1713

Under the Treaty of Utrecht, the Hapsburgs of Austria succeed the Spanish Hapsburgs in Italy; the kingdom of Sicily is granted to Victor Amadeus II of Savoy.

1720

Victor Amadeus II is forced to trade Sicily for Sardinia.

1730

Victor Amadeus II abdicates.

1734

A new sovereign court is set up at Naples.

1735

Austria gives Naples and Sicily to the Infante Charles of Spain.

1748

The Treaty of Aix-la-Chapelle is signed, ending the War of Austrian Succession; under the treaty Don Philip, the younger brother of King Philip V of Spain, receives Parma.

1759

Charles VII leaves the throne of Naples to become King Charles III of Spain.

1761–1762

Another constitutional crisis takes place in Venice.

1765

Joseph II of Austria becomes Holy Roman emperor.

1780

Maria Theresa, coleader of Austria, dies, leaving her son, Joseph II, as the sole ruler of all Hapsburg lands.

1796–1799
The French invade Italy beginning the era of the Italian republics.

1797
Under the Treaty of Campoformio Austria gives up the Po Valley to France.

1800
Napoléon Bonaparte of France defeats the Austrians at the Battle of Marengo.

1802
Napoléon is named president of the Italian Republic.

1805
Napoléon is crowned king of Italy.

1806
Joseph Bonaparte, brother of Napoléon, is made king of Naples.

1807
French forces occupy Rome; Joachim Murat replaces Joseph Bonaparte as king of Naples.

1809
The Papal States are annexed to France.

1813
Napoléon is defeated at Leipzig; Joachim Murat defects.

1814
Lombardy and Venetia are annexed to the Hapsburg Empire; King Victor Emmanuel I is restored to power in Sardinia; Grand Duke Ferdinand returns to power in Tuscany; Duke Francis IV takes power in Modena; the Congress of Vienna takes place with the goal of reorganizing Europe in the wake of Napoléon's defeat.

1815
Joachim Murat makes his "Appeal to the Italians"; Ferdinand IV wins back power in Naples; Napoléon, who has returned to try to win back his power, is defeated at Waterloo in Belgium.

1816

The restored Italian states are reorganized; the Kingdom of the
Two Sicilies is created.

1820

A revolution begins in Naples; Ferdinand I of Naples swears an
oath to the constitution; Palermo revolts against Naples and
declares independence.

1821

Austria intervenes in the Naples revolution.

1831

An uprising led by Ciro Menotti takes place in Modena; Austrian
armed forces enter Parma, Modena, and the Papal States;
Giuseppe Mazzini starts his Young Italy political organization.

1834

Mazzini leads a failed rebellion in Piedmont; Mazzini starts Young
Europe.

1845

Another Mazzinian revolt takes place in Rimini in September.

1848

Uprisings take place in Livorno and Palermo; the rulers of several Italian states, including Naples, Sardinia, and Tuscany, allow constitutions; the Republic of Venice is proclaimed;
Austria reoccupies Lombard, Modena, and Reggio Emilia.

1849

A new popularly elected government, called the Roman Republic, is established in February; Piedmont starts a new war
with Austria; French troops come to Italy to put the pope
back into power; Rome surrenders in July.

1852

Camillo Benso di Cavour becomes prime minister in Piedmont.

1853

A Mazzinian uprising takes place in Milan.

1854

Cavour resigns.

1856

In the Paris Peace Conference, Great Britain and France cut off diplomatic ties with the Kingdom of the Two Sicilies.

1858

Mazzini starts a new political movement called *Pensiero ed Azione.*

1859

Victor Emmanuel II of Sardinia signs a secret treaty with Napoléon III of France; Austria invades Piedmont; Leopold II of Tuscany flees.

1860

Cavour returns to office; Giuseppe Garibaldi leads an expedition against royal forces in Italy; he and his forces enter Naples in September; Italy wins independence from foreign powers and begins the process of unification; Jacob Burckhardt publishes *The Civilization of Renaissance Italy.*

1861

The first elections for a new Italian parliament are held; Victor Emmanuel of Savoy receives the title of king of Italy.

1865

Capital of Italy moves from Turin to Florence.

1866

Italy secretly allies with Prussia against Austria; Prussia and then Italy declare war on Austria; Prussia defeats Austria in July; Austria cedes Venetia to Napoléon III, who then gives it to Italy.

1867

Garibaldi's forces invade the Papal States at Mentana.

1870

Napoléon III is defeated at the Battle of Sedan; Italian forces enter Rome.

1871

The capital of Italy is moved to Rome.

1882

The electoral system is reformed; Italy joins the Triple Alliance with Germany and Austria-Hungary.

1892

The Italian Socialist Party is founded.

1895

Abyssinian forces defeat the Italian army at Adowa, Ethiopia, as part of their fight for independence from Italian rule; under the Treaty of Addis Adaba, Italy grants Ethiopia independence and restricts its own African holdings to Eritrea.

1904

A general workers' strike takes place in September.

1911

Italy declares war on Turkey and attacks Libya.

1912

A peace treaty with Turkey ends the Libyan War.

1915

Italy enters World War I when it declares war on Austria-Hungary.

1917

The Italian army is defeated at Caporetto in October.

1918

Italy's forces win a battle at Vittorio Veneto; World War I ends.

1921

The Italian Fascist Party is founded.

1922

The Fascists take power in the March on Rome.

1925

Benito Mussolini becomes the dictator of Italy.

1934

Mussolini meets for the first time with German dictator Adolf Hitler.

1935

Italian forces invade Ethiopia: the League of Nations puts sanctions in place against Italy.

1936
Italy conquers Ethiopia; the Italian Empire is declared; Italy establishes a formal alliance with Germany.

1939
Italy declares that it will not fight in World War II.

1940
Italy declares war on France and Great Britain.

1944
Rome and Florence are liberated by the Allies.

1945
Mussolini is captured and executed.

1949
Italy becomes part of the North Atlantic Treaty Organization (NATO).

1957
The Italian Socialist Party splits with the Communists and begins to form a coalition with the Christian Democratic Party.

1958
Italy becomes a founding member of the European Economic Community.

1962
A coalition of center-left political parties is established.

1964
The first major postwar economic recession takes place in June and July, causing problems among the political parties.

1968
Political protesters, many of them college students, take over university facilities and some secondary schools.

1969
A nationwide strike of engineering workers in September begins a period of labor unrest called the Hot Autumn.

1975

Law reforms are passed; control of certain parts of the media is given to the Commission of Vigilance rather than the government.

1976

Court verdicts pave the way for private ownership of radio and television.

1979

Italy joins the European monetary system.

1980

Silvio Berlusconi makes the first broadcast on his private television network, Canale 5.

1981

Criminal investigations of the P-2 Masonic Lodge begin, launching a battle over political corruption.

1983

In a general election, Bettino Craxi, the first Socialist prime minister in Italy's history, takes office.

1984

Berlusconi's business group takes over the *Retequattro* network, which gives Berlusconi control over all three of the main private television networks.

1990

The Mammi Law puts a system of mixed private and public media networks into place.

1992

The "Clean Hands" movement against government corruption begins; the old party system collapses in a general election; the lira (Italian currency) is expelled from the European exchange rate system.

1994

In a general election, Berlusconi's *Forza Italia* becomes the largest political party.

2001

Silvio Berlusconi is elected president.

FOR FURTHER RESEARCH

General Histories

Luigi Barzini and Michael Ledeen, *From Caesar to the Mafia: Persons, Places and Problems in Italian Life*. Somerset, NJ: Transaction, 2002.

John A. Crow, *Italy: A Journey Through Time*. New York: Harper & Row, 1965.

Peter D'Epiro and Mary Desmond Pinkowish, *Sprezzatura: 50 Ways Italian Genius Shaped the World*. New York: Anchor Books, 2001.

Christopher Duggan, *A Concise History of Italy*. New York: Cambridge University Press, 1994.

Francesco Guicciardini, *The History of Italy*, ed. Sidney Alexander. Princeton, NJ: Princeton University Press, 1984.

Harry Hearder, *Italy: A Short History*. New York: Cambridge University Press, 2001.

George Holmes, ed., *The Oxford History of Italy*. New York: Oxford University Press, 1997.

Serge Hughes, *The Fall and Rise of Modern Italy*. New York: Macmillan, 1967.

Giuliano Procacci, *History of the Italian People*. New York: Harper & Row, 1968.

Denis Mack Smith, *Modern Italy: A Political History*. Ann Arbor: University of Michigan Press, 1997.

Frederic Spotts and Theodor Weiser, *Italy: A Different Democracy: A Survey of Italian Politics*. New York: Cambridge University Press, 1986.

Histories of Periods

Ruth Ben-Ghiat, *Fascist Modernities: Italy, 1922–1945*. Berkeley: University of California Press, 2001.

Martin Boycott-Brown, *The Road to Rivoli*. Rochester, NY: Silver Pixel Press, 2001.

Vittorio Buffachi and Simon Burgess, *Italy Since 1989: Events and Interpretations*. New York: Palgrave Macmillan, 2001.

T.J. Cornell, *The Beginnings of Rome: Italy and Rome from the Bronze Age to the Punic Wars*. New York: Routledge, 1995.

Renzo De Felice, Robert L. Miller, and Michael Arthur Ledeen, *The Jews in Fascist Italy: A History*. New York: Enigma Books, 2001.

Spencer M. Di Scala, *Italy: From Revolution to Republic: 1700 to the Present*. Boulder, CO: Westview Press, 1995.

Will Durant, *Caesar and Christ: A History of Roman Civilization and Christianity from Their Beginnings to A.D. 325*. New York: MJF Books, 1971.

Desmond Gregory, *Napoleon's Italy*. Rutherford, NJ: Fairleigh Dickinson University Press, 2001.

Frederick Hartt, *History of Italian Renaissance Art: Painting, Sculpture, Architecture*. Ed. David G. Wilkins. New York: Harry N. Abrams, 1994.

Richard Lamb, *War in Italy, 1943–1945: A Brutal Story*. Cambridge, MA: Da Capo Press, 1996.

Patrick McCarthy, *The Crisis of the Italian State: From the Origins of the Cold War to the Fall of Berlusconi and Beyond*. New York: Palgrave Macmillan, 1997.

Mario B. Mignone, *Italy Today: A Country in Transition*. New York: Peter Lang, 1995.

Dorothy Mills, *The Book of the Ancient Romans*. New York: G.P. Putnam's Sons, 1927.

Polybius, *The Rise of the Roman Empire*. Trans. Ian Scott-Kilvert. New York: Penguin USA, 1980.

George MacAulay Trevelyan, *Garibaldi and the Making of Italy.* London: Phoenix Press, 2002.

Evelyn S. Welch, *Art and Society in Italy, 1300–1500.* New York: Oxford University Press, 1997.

C.M. Wells, *The Roman Empire.* Cambridge, MA: Harvard University Press, 1995.

Histories of Events or Topics

Graeme Barker and Tom Rasmussen, *The Etruscans.* Lake Oswego, OR: Blackwell, 2000.

Serge Bramley, *Leonardo: The Artist and the Man.* Trans. Sian Reynolds. New York: Penguin USA, 1995.

James Carroll, *Constantine's Sword: The Church and the Jews.* Boston: Houghton Mifflin, 2001.

Michael Grant, *The Twelve Caesars.* New York: Barnes & Noble Books, 1996.

Luigi Guicciardini, *The Sack of Rome.* Trans. James H. MacGregor. New York: Italica Press, 1993.

Henner Hess, *Mafia & Mafiosi: Origin, Power and Myth.* New York: New York University Press, 1998.

MacGregor Knox, *Hitler's Italian Allies: Royal Armed Forces, Fascist Regime, and the War of 1940–1943.* New York: Cambridge University Press, 2000.

Joseph Lapalombara, *Democracy Italian Style.* New Haven, CT: Yale University Press, 1989.

Roger D. Master, *Fortune Is a River: Leonardo da Vinci and Niccolò Machiavelli's Magnificent Dream to Change the Course of Florentine History.* New York: Plume, 1999.

Thomas F.X. Noble, *The Republic of St. Peter: The Birth of the Papal State, 680–825.* Philadelphia: University of Pennsylvania Press, 1986.

Leoluca Orlando, *Fighting the Mafia and Renewing Sicilian Culture.* San Francisco: Encounter Books, 2001.

D.S. Potter and D.J. Mattingly, eds., *Life, Death, and Entertainment in the Roman Empire.* Ann Arbor: University of Michigan Press, 1999.

John Prevas, *Hannibal Crosses the Alps: The Invasion of Italy and the Second Punic War.* Cambridge, MA: Da Capo Press, 2001.

Jasper Ridley, *Garibaldi.* London: Phoenix Press, 2001.

Denis Mack Smith, *Cavour and Garibaldi, 1860: A Study in Political Conflict.* New York: Cambridge University Press, 1985.

Alexander Stille, *Excellent Cadavers: The Mafia and the Death of the First Italian Republic.* Ed. Sarah Burnes. New York: Vintage Books, 1996.

Geoffrey Wauro, *The Austro-Prussian War: Austria's War with Prussia and Italy in 1866.* New York: Cambridge University Press, 1997.

INDEX